Kooth 27t'

TO: Gonita and Floyd

God Bless

CLOSING THE SHOW

The story of the amazing 1969-70 East Highland High School Indians

Michael Catfish Smith

AuthorHouse™
1663 Liberty Drive
Bloomington, IN 47403
www.authorhouse.com
Phone: 1-800-839-8640

© *2009 Michael Catfish Smith. All rights reserved.*

No part of this book may be reproduced, stored in a retrieval system, or transmitted by any means without the written permission of the author.

First published by AuthorHouse 10/22/2009

ISBN: 978-1-4490-0453-8 (e)
ISBN: 978-1-4490-0452-1 (sc)

Library of Congress Control Number: 2009906850

Printed in the United States of America
Bloomington, Indiana

This book is printed on acid-free paper.

This book is dedicated to the late great East Highland High School coach and mentor Haywood Scissum and my son Tayon who would have been a great Indian football player. Special dedication goes to my cousin Valerie Rena (Benson) Lanier who loved everybody. (known as Baba to nieces and nephews)

Special accolades to the staff of the B.B. Comer Library who without their help this book would not be possible.

Dr. Shirley Spears
Mrs. Elizabeth
Mrs. Nelda Vogel
Mrs. Ceclia Dean
Mrs. Leonard

Special recognition to the Indian beat writers-

Lawrence Hale
Jerome O'Neal
Jerry Green
Dan Rutledge
A one man and a typewriter
Production

Contents

	1st Show Football	**xiii**
1.	Introduction xvii
2.	The East Highland High School football team roster for 1969 . 1
3.	The players closing the show in football in 1969 3
4.	The Best Little Band in the Land 9
5.	Conspiracy Theory 13
6.	Speed Speed and Speed 20
7.	The Hill 24
8.	Prelude To The 1969 Opener 32
9.	Prelude Cobb 1968 35
10.	Fall 1969 Sept: The Final Season 39
11.	Reputation Earned 49
12.	The Footrace 53
13.	The Oliver of Fairfield Game 57
14.	The OS Hill Game Indians Express Roll Merrily Along 62
15.	East Highland and Shelby County in the to 20 65
16.	10 Indians Score as East Highland Stings the Hornets 68 to 6 66
17.	East Highland Stings the Hornets 68 to 6 10 Indians Score ... 67
18.	Friday October 3, 1969 The Daily Home 71

19. Offense vs. Defense Indians to Play Westside Tonight 73
20. October 23, 1969 East Highland Remains Undefeated with a 46 to 0 Trouncing of Westside 74
21. The Daily Home Time out for Sports Dan Rutledge 78
22. Indians Take Sixth Win of Season 80
23. Montgomery - Early Word from Montgomery The Daily Home 83
24. Indians with 7th Game of Season Downs TCTS 52 to 0 84
25. Tiger, Indians and Aggies Advance in AHSAA Rankings 86
26. Mighty Indians Poised October 30, 1969 87
27. Big Game Tonight By Dan Rutledge 89
28. Timeout for Sports By Dan Rutledge 96
29. Childersburg and Aggies Rated 3-4 in State 97
30. Tigers Indians and Aggies Advance in AHSAA Ratings 98
31. Childersburg and Aggies Rated 3 and 4 in State 99
32. East Highland Close Childersburg Sylacauga Keep Playoff Positions 103
33. Final Game, The Calhoun County Game 105
34. Lightning Strikes for the Last Time East Highland end Season with 82 to 0 Blast of CCTS 108
35. East Highland High School Indian Intangibles..................... 112
36. Indian Folklore 114
37. Indian Intangibles 115
38. Sylacaugan Wins Grand Prize in State Social Studies Fair 116
39. Two Indians are Small School Award Winners By Dan Rutledge 118
40. Life with the New York Jets By Cecil Leonard, Former Indian Great 120
41. East Highland High School Indian Intangibles..................... 122

42. From the Talladega Daily Home Friday, May 29, 1970
    By Dan Rutledge 124
43. Another East Highland vs Cobb Rivalry 126
44. East Highland Opponents in the Scissum Era 1952-1969 128
45. Coach Scissum and the Indians slighted Again 130
46. 1969 Scoring Race Almost Over, Indians Threatt
    Unofficial Winner By Dan Rutledge 132
47. Honor Roll 136
48. 1969 Football Season Threatt Regains Scoring Lead in Area . 141
49. September 8, 1966 East Highland Stomps Norris 34 to 0 147
50. 1966 Season Indians fall to Cobb 26 to 7 By Jerome Oneal . 149
51. Indian Mistakes Give Westside 13 to 7 Win By
    Jerome Oneal 152
52. East Highland Drubs Cobb 19 to 6 1963 By Lawrence Hall . 155
53. Indian Flashbacks 1953 157
54. 1967 East Highland High School Football Preview 160
55. Thunder and Lightning Strike Riverside 46 to 0 162
56. The East Highland Phylliss Wheatley Game First
    Meeting 1967 165
57. 1967 East Highland Blast Stubborn Childersburg 37 to 0 167
58. From October 3, 1968 the Sylacauga News Panthers
    Slay the Dragons 170
59. East Highland Indians Score 166 points in 5 games 176
60. East Highland vs Westside 1968 178
61. Indians Compete Season in 1963 with Win By
    Lawrence Hale 181
62. A General Comparison between the Two Dominate
    Schools in Talladega County in Football in the 1960s 183
63. Indians vs. Aggies 185
64. East Highlands 1960s decade under Coach Scissum 193

65.	Merger May Mean Sports Dynasty For Sylacauga..................	200
66.	The Aftermath...	202
67.	Indian Summarize the 1969 Football Season	205

2ND SHOW BASKETBALL   211

68.	The 1969-1970 East Highland High School Basketball Team the Starters and Sixth man	213
69.	1969 Basketball Season	215
70.	East highland Bombs Drew High in Thursday Night Cage Action February 8, 1969..	218
71.	Indians on Warpath Toward State Berth 1969	219
72.	Indians Eliminated by Vincent February 1969	220
73.	Indians Lose to 4A Gadsden Carver Rams in Squeaker January 1970...	223
74.	From the Daily Home Thursday January 15, 1970 By Dan Rutledge...	227
75.	Basketball Season 1970 The Laurel Game............................	229
76.	In State Tourney March 1970...	236
77.	East Highland Indians are Number One!	238
78.	From The Talladega Daily Home Thursday, July 16, 1970 By Dan Rutledge...	240

FINAL ACT TRACK AND FIELD   241

79.	Track and Field...	243
80.	East Highland Indians Track Team, ...	247
81.	Track and Field 1968..	249
82.	1968 Track and Field...	251
83.	1968 East Highland Second in Alabama Relays...................	253
84.	From the Talladega Daily Home...	254
85.	East Highland Runs Away With the County Track Title	256
86.	Final results of the 1969 County Track Meet......................	258

87. East Highland Track Team Members 260
88. From the Talladega Daily Home, Saturday April 18, 1970 ... 262
89. The Meet of All Meets 264
90. From the Talladega Daily Home Wednesday, April 22, 1970 265
91. Indians Capture County Title 267
92. From the Talladega Daily Home Tuesday, April 28, 1970 270
93. Indian Record Setter wing 2A Sectional Crown at Auburn ... 273
94. East Highland High School Indians in State Relays 275
95. East Highland All-sport Banquet a Huge Success 282
96. Final Analysis 286

1st Show
Football

The East Highland High School Indians, a black school located in Sylacauga, Alabama, was founded in the late 1930's to educate the colored children of Sylacauga's population of 12,000 located in southern Talladega County. The city is world famous for the beautiful white marble it produces. Closing the show is the story of the mighty Indians of East Highlands sports team and their hall of fame coach, Haywood Scissum. It details in facts the remarkable prep season they had in 1969-70 the final year before whole-scale integration in the state of Alabama. In this last year the Indians football team competing in class 2A won 9 games lost zero and averaged fifty-five points per game. While allowing only six for the season, the defense did not give up any as they finished with 498 points in 9 games. They were denied a playoff bid in spite of these impressive numbers, finishing two and half points short of the 4th spot in the final ranking, a mid the state of Alabama's controversial points system. During the season, the 2A powerhouse Indians played and destroyed two 4A schools, dominated four 3A schools, humbled two 2A schools and toyed with one 1A school. Cobb Avenue, their biggest rival over the years and a 4A, refused to play them in 1969. The basketball team won the 2A state championship with a white head coach unheard of in those days. The track and field team coached by Scissum, a Tuskegee graduate, won eleven of twelve meets they entered dominating all four classes of state competition in the state of Alabama 1A through 4A. They capped this marvelous season by winning the 2A state championship. It was widely felt that the Indians would have won the football championship had they been allowed to play for it, completing a rare hat trick in the three major prep sports during Coach Scissum's tenure of 18 seasons. The Indians won 135 games, lost 27 and tied 11. In a 7 year period in the 60's from 1963 to 1969, Scissum and his Indians won 64 games lost 4 and tied 2, losing only to 4A powerhouse Cobb of Anniston 3 times and once to 3A Westside of Talladega. All heart breaking close losses for the Indians. The Indians finished out the 60's decade winning 84 games losing 11 and tying 2, this while playing the largest schools in the state because schools their own size wouldn't play or schedule them., which was class 2a. During the Scissum's years the Indians sent numerous players to the college ranks to school like Florida A & M, Xavier University in New Orleans, Alabama A & M, State, Tuskegee Institute and the University of Missouri to name a few. This well kept secret of a little black school powerhouse also sent 4 players under Scissum to the N.F.L. and probably would have had a 5th if Derry Lee Holtzclaw who played for Tuskegee in the late 50's hadn't been killed in a car accident coming home to Sylacauga. Holtzclaw, a rare combination of size and speed at 6 ft 2, 220 pounds was thought to be a can't miss pro in those days in the late 50's. The Indians history has been widely covered up outside of Sylacauga by the state and even their unscored on defense has not been recognized properly. But now is the time, 40 years after the final school year for East Highland for the story to be told in full, it is time for the nation to be exposed to the little black school on the hill in Sylacauga that shinned so brightly during Jim Crow and Segregation in Alabama. Today, the East Highland alumni can boast of doctors, lawyers, college presidents, colleges professors, ministers, engineers, naval flight officers, soldiers that fought in two wars the Korean and Vietnam and other military personnel. This is their story.

INTRODUCTION

It was the morning of March 25, 2008. It was a typical cool spring early morning three o'clock in the morning to be exact. I was sleeping like a new born baby wrapped in a blanket as I was unconscious to what was going on in the world around me. Suddenly, I was awaken by a voice powerful and commanding. Tell the story it said. Tell the story so generations will know. Tell the story? I almost thought that I was dreaming. But I soon realize that this was not a dream because the voice that said tell the story it really spooked me how real it was. So, I began to question the voice that was speaking to me in a conversation the way I would if I was talking to a person that I could physically see. Tell the story so generations will know. It was almost like I was being chosen to solve some mystery or bring to the light an injustice where somebody had been done unjustfully wrong. Tell the story so they will know East Highland was about. But, I kept thinking about all of the people in the world and why was I being troubled out of my sleep about this? I was in elementary school when East Highland was shut down and closed forever as a high school in an act brought on my whole scale integration in 1970. So why was I being chosen to tell the story? It was burning inside of me like a melancholy fire. But there are so many others that are graduates of the school that could have done this but I was chosen. I realized being a Christian that God chooses who he wants to do things regardless of personal stature, and I was certain that it was the voice of God that was speaking to me. I had been carrying this torch for the Indians inside of me since the year that the school shut down. I had been in fact motivated along with former Indian Greg Foots Holtzclaw and Indians graduate and alumnus Michael Brownfield to try to convince former Sylacauga city schools superintendent Dr. Phil Hammonds to honor Coach Scissum when the junior high bearing East Highland name was shut down permanently. Coach Scissum was ultimately honored with an athletic field bearing his name at the new junior high, thus I was satisfied that through the Indians and East Highland's name was gone, Coach Scissum would live as long as the new junior high existed in Sylacauga. So, for the former players and alumni, I was happy and thought that my work was complete but here it was again five years later a voice speaking to me about East Highland like I had some work to do that was unfinished. Some how, I knew that I couldn't ignore the voice that was speaking to me if I did I couldn't rest. I had to be obedient to the voice commanding me to tell this story of the amazing mighty Indians of East Highland High School and their hall of fame Coach Haywood Scissum. I ask God to show me the way to fittingly tell the story of this outstanding coach and his wonderful pipeline of athletes who led to the success story of one of the greatest high school coaches and team that my eyes have ever seen. But, how could I do justice to the many outstanding young men that had donned the blue, white and red of the mighty Indians of East Highland High School during a period in our nations history southern history to be exact called Jim crow the 50's and 60's. A time when most black schools suffered with inferior everything in the separate but equal system that was really separate and unequal the Indians seemed to have first class everything, the school was relatively new having been built in 1953. East Highland band led by the very capable hands of Mr. Larkin was always decked in the best allowed with Indians majorettes. The basketball team and the cheerleaders were always sharp and nobody out dressed the Indian football team. Sporting navy blue jerseys with white numbers trimmed in red around the sleeves and white helmets with numbers on each side with red stripe down the middle with blue stripes on each side. White pants with a red stripe down the middle trimmed with blue stripes on each side, they were a top rate bunch for sure. They kept that way by the efforts of Coach Scissum and Principal Lawson. If there was a area that the Indians was lacking in it might have been that the school didn't offer some of the advanced subjects that were taught at the rival city school, but it didn't seem to bother the Indian students who always enjoyed being taught by dedicated teachers and faculty who really cared about the kids and were greatly concerned about their well being and that they received a good education to better themselves in life. They were committed to every kid willing to be taught. This was an area that a lot of black kids really suffered in after the integration in 1970. They found few teachers that would spend the time to motivate the students that weren't up to part with the schools most gifted students. The East Highland alumni can boast of doctors, lawyers, teachers, principals, college presidents, engineers, military leaders and other who just became home makers and good citizens in. In the 1969-70 school year, the final one for the Indians before the federal courts mandated whole scale integration plan the federal courts mandated whole scale integration plan was carried out. The East Highland High School Indians of tiny

Sylacauga, Alabama population 12,000 had one of the most remarkable seasons in Alabama prep sports history. The football team went undefeated in nine games outscoring opponents 498 to six. They averaged 55 points a game and the defense did not give up a single point all season. The six points scored against them came courtesy of a fumble of Alexander City by the Indians backup quarterback Weechie McKinney, a defensive back scooped it up and ran it in for the six points. The Indians won the game 68 to 6, because of a complicated point system one in which some people felt was racist in its content initiated by the state; the Indians were left out of the 2A football playoffs. The basketball team coached by Dwight Duke, a white man went 25 and 6 and won the 2A state basketball championship. The track team was coached by Haywood Scissum.

Haywood Scissum

Haywood Scissum came to Sylacauga East Highland High School in 1952. When Coach Scissum arrived in Sylacauga to take over the Indian fortunes, rock and roll was an infant and Elvis Pressley was a slick haired side burns wearing unknown kid from Tupelo, Mississippi by way of Memphis waiting to be discovered. After playing and starring in football and track at Carver High School in Gadsden, Alabama, Scissum received a scholarship to Tuskegee Institute; there he excelled in two sports football and track. Scissium started on offense and defense for the golden tiger's football team as an end. In track he ran a 9.9; 100 yard dash super fast in those days as he captained the track team. A section of track is named in his honor at Tuskegee called Scissum Curve. Right after receiving his diploma from Tuskegee fate or destiny landed him in Sylacauga, Alabama, where his ability to motivate and coach combined with the mother lode of talented kids in Sylacauga was about to embark him on a successful journey unparallel and rarely seen in a small town like Sylacauga. Coach Scissum had the charisma in his personality that made kids want to play and do well for him. He could paddle a kid or kick him in the behind and the next minute show the kid some love and they would still respect him. This ability to coach and motivate talent allowed him to after 18 years of high school coaching post a 135 wins, 27 losses and 11 ties record would land him in the Alabama sports hall of fame. Scissum was an offensive genius way ahead of his time. Coach Showers told me that often times at halftime, Coach Scissum would draw up plays right from his head on chalkboards that the Indians had not practiced, and then the kids would go out and execute these plays to perfection; of course, the opposing team's defense had not seen them and could not defend them either. On Sundays, Coach Scissum would demand and take his kids to Sunday school and church where he was very active. They developed an openness playing for him. From his resume would be state champions in football, and the south would be the only thing that would keep him from even getting the chance with some of his greatest teams, the powerful invincible Indians era of Hickey Holtzclaw and Griffin from 1963 to 1965, owners of a 34 game win streak. The Cecil Leonard led teams of the early 60's, and of course the Richard Lighting Threat led final team of 1969 the denied bunch in spite of their excellence on the field, these were all championship caliber teams under

Coach Scissum that there never given the opportunity to play win or go home one loss and done playoff football, but Coach Scissum as brilliant and he was as a coach was much more that that. In the Drew Court community where he lived he was also a father figure. In the community, a large majority of his players were from single parent homes where black women had to be momma and daddy to her kids while the sperm donor fathers were absent. Coach Scissum commanded so much respect that often these single mothers would call for his help when a wayward son got out of control. He was in essence a father figure to many a boy without a dad in the house. He served as swim team coach, taught tennis, started a little league and pony leagues. The man had a powerful presence about himself; his last three track teams dominated track and field in Talladega County and the state in Class 2A. In fact, and the Indians didn't care about class and dominated the 3A and 4A schools they rank against in track also. This after the Alabama High School Athletic Association opened up competition for the black school from the NEIAA the colored only affiliations to compete against the white school, called B.U.S.; they were a private school sort of like Briarwood Christians School of today that is located in Birmingham, Alabama. They had the finest white athletes in Jefferson County, but in 1969 and 1970, the Indians trounced them as well as they did all competition no matter the class winning state championships back to back. This is something people old enough to remember still talk about today. It was said that during spring training week at graduation that Coach Scissum would walk the hall ways looking for new talent. He pointed to kids that he wanted to come out and try football, if for some reason a kid he converted didn't show up for practice that night, Scissum would be sitting in that kids living room talking to his mother, the next day that kid would be drawing football equipment. Coach Scissum molded boys into men who became productive citizens in society and bringing it out of a kid. It was told to me that he made Charles Curry play some football in 1965. Translation meaning he made a player out of him. Curry played with Hickey Holtzclaw and Griffin and was said to be on the lazy side, despite

His size, Scissum's foot or paddle usual worked wonders on motivating a kid not putting out his best effort, of course parents trusted Coach Scissum with their children because they knew he loved them and would not do anything deliberately to hurt them. Unlike some coaches of today who only have their own selfish ambition and often made kids feel as if they are doing them a favor and could care less if they played. The talent pool was always plentiful in Sylacauga and Scissum had this ability to tell what position a kid was best suited for. Once he moved Sammy Louis Johnson a talented quarterback, to fullback and he became an outstanding breakaway threat at the position.

Coach Scissum was a hardnosed taskmaster on the field getting physical with his players. As a young coach, in the late 50s he once got down in the trenches with big Richard Olden the team captain and future Los Angeles Rams player. Possibly, to motivate him as they came up out their stance, Scissum hit big Richard under the chin with a fore arm shiver that drew blood and would have made Deacon Jones proud. The move worked so effectively that Richard begged Scissum to get down and try that move again.

A brilliant move on Scissum's part to fire up his star player, of course Richard dominated in the actual game. Coach Scissum would often discipline his players from making mistakes right on the field. If a kid missed a blocking assignment on the line he might find a foot in his behind once he got down in his stance, sometimes the paddle did the trick.

A perfectionist on the field Scissum would often run a play repeatedly until his players executed the way he wanted. Upset with his player's execution on the field once he denied them a water break on a particularly hot August day. One player standing on the sideline close to one of my cousins asked him to wet a towel and throw it on the ground so that he could suck the water out of it despite all of this, Coach Scissum was a brilliant motivator and always showed the kids love after correcting them. They could not stay mad at him because they knew playing for him they was going to win. Often after practices, his players would gather on his front porch and while talking be served lemonade by his wife. The one thing that I knew for certain watching the Indians practice and play as a young boy, was that they were all winners.

From their walks to their talks, the way they lived and bonded with each other like kidding around in the neighborhood. They liked each other, an important elements in building a successful team and program. They were family.

A fraternity of athletes that I along with my friends and cousins and every kid our age that sit on that hill knew we would never be part of a East Highland High School Indian football player, a Scissum man. I believe that every player that ever dressed out for Coach Scissum loved and respected him. His presence in our community was so powerful that once when I was a 8 years old I along with my cousin Yancey who was 9 at the time was standing around the little league field watching him line off the baseball diamond. There were some was some rocks on the field and he said come here son in a commanding voice and pick up these rocks. We both jumped to the task without hesitation. That was what a winner could do even to little kids, motivated us who greatly admired his accomplishments.

Coach Scissum was not only an offensive genius way ahead of his time but I guess he was a defensive genius too, because 4 of his teams gave up less than 40 points in a season. Three of those teams were the 65 bunch which gave up 19 points all season the 68 bunch gave up 24 points all season and the 69 bunch gave up 6 all season. His theory and motto was, you can't beat me if you can't score, all of this while having only one assistant for many years Coach Bernadean showers; the showers, the shop, and math teacher. Coach Dwight Duke joined him for the last two years in 1968 and 1969 to make his staff of three. Unlike today where a single high school team might.

Have a coaching staff of 12 or more coaches looking like a college staff and still losing.

However, Coach Scissum who had a play book that was two inches thick would run plays from the players to execute this offense. The famous end reverse pass play and the Dallas Cowboys lineman shuffle were trademarks of his teams. Coach Scissum, a handsome muscular man when he came to Sylacauga in 1952, was probably the crush fantasy of many Indian teenage girls. He had many great players over his 18-year tenure at East Highland. Among them Derry Lee Holtzclaw who would have probably been his first pro player handle not been killed in a car accident coming home from Tuskegee. The Carpenter brothers, French James and Samuel along with George the Ohio Flash Dorth, John Thomas Harrison, Harold Looney, Bo Chambliss, Paul Hubbard, Billy The Jet Harrison, Red Foster, Charles Davis and Sonny Oden all were very instrumental in helping Coach Scissum lay the foundation for future Indian success that built East Highland into a football powerhouse.

Coach Scissum early examples came from the likes of Vince Lombardi and Eddie Robinson all men like Scissum who could not only motivate but coach them also his ability to bring out the best in average player was legendary. Able to convince a 135-pound defensive back that he could hit like a 200-pound linebacker or a 250-pound lineman up in the field was his trademark motivating a kid to dominate an opponent that out weighted him by 50 pounds or more. Truly all the great coach has this ability. Ironically, the kids that were born in 1952 the year he arrived in Sylacauga would also be the last ones he coached and said goodbye too.

Haywood Big Train Scissum

This article appeared in the Alabama High School Sports Hall of Fame Induction Ceremony held on April 1991 in Montgomery, Alabama.

Many coaches have had outstanding seasons, but Haywood Scissum belongs to a small group of coaches who had one season that qualifies for consideration as the greatest of all times. His 1969 season at East Highland High School of Sylacauga resulted in a nine and zero record. In winning those nine games, East Highland scored 498 points and gave up only six, a lone touchdown scored on a defensive play. In 18 seasons as head coach at East Highland, Coach Scissum complied a record of 135 wins, 27 losses and 11 ties. In the 1960's he had a 34 game winning streak. There were three undefeated seasons and no losing seasons in his 18 years a head coach in the years before the two state athletic associations merged his East Highland teams won the northeastern interscholastic athletic association district football championship nine times in 18 years. He was the district coach of the year nine times. He also coached track for 3 years finishing second in the state his first year and state champion his last two years. He went from East Highland to his Alma Mata Tuskegee Institute where he had a record of 66 wins 48 losses and one tie. He is second behind legendary coach Cleve Abbott on the schools all-time wins list. In 1983, the governor proclaimed a day in his honor and he was recognized with a special activities event in Sylacauga. A native of Attala, Coach Scissum is a graduate of Carver High School of Gadsden and Tuskegee. One letter of support for Coach Scissum came from district attorney Dwight Duke of Scottsboro. He went to East Highland as a young white head basketball coach in 1968; he wrote of Coach Scissum, a coach is often judged by his win-loss record but if you judge Scissum on that standard he may be unsurpassed conference county a state championships. All-star coaching awards and trophies of all types line his wall. I choose however to judge him by the products he produced, the young men who came up under his guidance. Scissum was more than a coach to these boys many of whom were fatherless. Many were the sole supporters of their family. He instilled in them pride a burning desire to achieve and the determination to overcome any obstacle placed in their path. Among Coach Scissum's former players are a college president, a navel flight officer, two physicians and cumbrous businessman, teachers, principals, ministers and other professionals. Eight of his boys went on to captain football teams at Tuskegee.

The East Highland High School Football Team Roster for 1969

Head Coach-Haywood Scissum
Assistant coach Bernadine Showers
Assistant coach Dwight Duke
Team managers- Jerry, Doc Houser, Dewitt Simmons

Roster
Alphonza Olden 82 sophomore
Greg Holtzclaw 24 Junior
Aaron Moon 52 senior
Gary Oden Senior 66
Sylvester Shealey Senior 72
Lynn foster Senior 44
Jerry Holtzclaw Senior 27
Terry Bledsoe Senior 46
Jay Grimmett Senior 15
Albert Oden Sophomore 35
Neil Hart Junior 95
Lamar Prater Junior 81
Wilber Wilson Sophomore 78
James Odum Senior 62
Robert Williams Senior 94
Billy Smith senior 36
Anthony Walton Junior 25
Richard Lightning Threatt senior 40

Michael Catfish Smith

Gill Weechie McKinney sophomore 17
Jessie Powell Sophomore 47
Thaddeus Darby Junior 88
Nathaniel Williams Junior 55
James Williams Senior 87
Sylvester McKinney Senior 84
Calvin Drake Senior 70
James Player Senior 64
Ruben Parks Senior 33
Anthony Russell Senior 76
PA. Young senior 83
Wayne Harris Sophomore 19
Darnel Williams Sophomore 63
Danny Morris Junior 50

The players closing the show in football in 1969

East Highland's rich talent pool was mostly made up of kids from the Drew Court Projects, but many also came from other neighborhoods in the city of Sylacauga they were West Park, South Highland, Oakland Heights, Sunrise, Coaling Road, Overbrook, Walco, Thomas Hill and the Quarry. One player even traveled the 12 miles distance from Goodwater, Alabama, to play for the Indians and Coach Scissum.

The starting line up for the amazing 1969 team

OFFENSE
Quarterback-Jay Grimmett Senior 15
Halfback-Richard (Lighting) Threatt Senior 40
Fullback-Billy Roebuck Smith senior 36
Flanker-Terry Bledsoe Senior 46
Left End- Sylvester Beattie McKinney Senior 84
Right End- PA Young senior 83
Center- Danny Morris Junior 50
Right Guard-James Fatso Odum Senior 62
Right Tackle-Anthony Cooney Russell Senior 76
Left Tackle- Robert Williams 94 Senior
Left Guard- Gary Oden 66 Senior

DEFENSE
Left End-Sylvester Beattie McKinney Senior 84
Right End- Anthony Cooney Russell 76 Senior

Michael Catfish Smith

Tackle-Robert Williams 94 Senior
Tackle-Neil Hart 95 Junior
Nose Tackle-Danny Morris Junior 50
Line Backer- Aaron Moon Senior 52
Line Backer Lynn Foster Senior 44
Corner-Jerry Chic Holtzclaw Senior 27
Corner-Greg Foots Holtzclaw Junior 24
Safety - Richard (Lightning) Threatt Senior 40
Strong Safety- Anthony Walton Junior 25

Key Reserves-
Sylvester Shealey Senior end 72
Wayne Cowherd Harris GB Sophomore 19
Gill Weechie McKinney GB Sophomore 17
Lamar Prater End Junior 81
Nathaniel Williams End Junior 55
James Williams End Senior 87
Alphonso Olden End Sophomore 82

The East Highland High School Indians starting backfield 1969

Quarterback-Jay Grimmett number 15

Jay the younger brother of Tuskegee Institute starting quarterback Johnny Grimmett, the former Indian QB. Jay might not have been the most athletic of the Indians quarterbacks, but he was smart and nifty. Not the fastest but possessing decent speed. He could hide a football better than any high school quarterback I ever seen. This kid had the smile and charisma of Ervin Magic Johnson. He also had the discipline to run Coach Scissum complicated offense. Jay was the youngest of the outstanding Grimmett family of brothers who started at East highland.

Flanker-Terry Bledsoe number 46

Terry, the younger brother of Indian great Mike Homer. Terry was a little person who played much bigger than his size. He had a big heart, not as gifted as Lightning, but he possessed quick feet and played with an attitude that allowed him to excel for the Indians.

Full back- Billy Roebuck Smith number 36

Roebuck was a stocky naturally strong bulldozing fullback who at 5 ft 9", 165 lbs played like a 225 pound back. Smith the thunder in the dynamic duo that was Smith and Threatt, was said to be the equivalent of Lee Buford the measuring stick fullback in Indian football memory. Buford who was so physical and loved contact so much that once in a game he had broke loose for a twenty-five yard touchdown, untouched, saw a cornerback approaching from the right, changed directions and ran straight at and over him for the TD. Jerome O'Neal, the Indian beat writer said of Smith, if he were a little bigger, he would make everybody forget Buford. Smith ran over would be tacklers like a bowling ball knocking down pins. He had a sort of leaping hop style to his running making him look robotic as he attacked a defense.

Tail back- Richard (Lightning) Threat number 40

The star in the Indians offense in 1969 that averaged 55 points was Lightning. Dubbed Lightning in 1966 after he ran a 9.7 100-yard dash by Coach Scissum. He also made a bet with his little league coach that he could make it to third base on a fly ball before it hit the ground. He did it to. Threatt won the 100 and 220-yard dash in the state in 1970. Threatt was perhaps a favorite of Coach Scissum, but you could hardly say he was petted.

Lightning also doubled as a safety on the strongest high school defense I have ever seen. In East Highland's vaunted 52 defenses that were designed to shut down the run. The corners had to have lock down ability. Lightning along with Anthony Walton and corners Jerry and Greg Holtzclaw and along with P.A. Young did a formidable job. Threatt was very explosive on offense like nitroglycerin shaken up breaking many long runs from scrimmage, and on kickoffs where many teams chose to kick away from him.

Right end- Prince Albert Young number 83

A three-sport star in football basketball and baseball, P.A. as he was called could beat you in any sport he chooses to play, including shooting marbles. He was not the swiftest of the Indians stars but always seemed to get open usually 5 yards behind the opposition. Famous for one-handed circus catches and pinpoint in three games as the Indians won the state 2a basketball championship in 1970.

Left end- Sylvester Beattie McKinney number 84

A very athletic 3-sport Indian star won the discuss event as a member of back-to-back state track champion East Highland. Also, the starting center on the state champion basketball team in 1970. The passer on the famous end reverses pass play.

Michael Catfish Smith

The line

The offensive line-

How can I start talking about the starting offensive line without paying homage to the Indians greats that helped shape these fine players, guys like Robert Poor Rob Gunn, Calvin the Russian, McKinney Roland, Slick Morris, Wally Gator, Fulks Anthony , Boot Pratt, Manuel Big Joe Pope and Robert Sleepy Hollinquest. All these guys helped mould starting center Danny Ace Morris brother of Roland Slick Morris, a mean nasty lineman who once scolded young Danny for allowing a defender to get a clean hit on Indian quarterback Jay Grimmett in practice by jacking him up in the collar and telling him "that's your quarterback and nobody hits our quarterback like that." It never happened again. Starting at right guard was James Fatso Odum a one year starter who was a vocal, leader through small, fatso was very physical and known to laugh at opponents after a big hit. Next to Odum was Anthony Cooney Russell at right tackle. Russell a versatile athlete was very fast and aggressive, a knowledgeable player who knew the game of football. Cooney was so fast, in fact that he ran the anchor leg on the Indians record setting state champion 440 relay team, along with Lightning, Smokey, and Jackboy Jackson. Russell could have played any position on this line and was the only Indian in his class of 1970 to beat Cobb. Oden a converted fullback showed how deep the Indians was that Coach Scissum could convert a fullback to the offensive line and never miss a beat, this after losing two starters at the position the following year. Next to him at left tackle was Robert big on Williams. The biggest of the starting offensive lineman and a two way starter, just as dominating on an offensive as he was on defense. Contributing to this duo was Anthony Walton at tailback. Lyn Project Foster, McKinney, Jerry Chic Holtzclaw and his cousin Greg Foots Holtzclaw also received their share of carries on the explosive Indian offense. The offensive line was the backbone of the offense we all know without good blocking it doesn't matter who your running backs are. You've got to win the battle in the trenches. These guys could block and did so well that often Indian backs didn't get touched until they were 5 and 10 yards up the field. Coach Scissum knew how to build an offensive line.

The defensive 1969

The big bad blue monster defense that didn't let an opponent score nor allow a touchdown in 1968, you heard me right! They didn't let anyone put up a single point against them in nine games in that final year. You had a better chance of finding an oasis in the Sahara Desert than you did scoring against these guys. I hear people say that defense is desire and every kid on the Indians defense desired that nobody score on them. If you can't score you can't beat me, was Coach Scissum's motto. This was a remarkable feat when you consider that Coach Scissum played all his kids emptying the bench in most games. Usually after two quarters of play. I don't know what the Indians players were saying to the youngsters who went into the games to replace them but I can probably imagine that the starters were probably telling them to keep the shutout going. To hold it up which they did. The youngsters desire to please Coach Scissum so they could build trust in him to keep him playing them, which probably explains why Coach Scissum never rebuilt but just reloaded. It takes a community of people working together to be a successful program, and the people in the East Highland community loved and supported Coach Scissum for 18 years, and probably would have continued to do so well into the 70's had the school not been shut down. Starting at defensive tackle was;

Tackle=Robert Williams number 94
Very explosive for a big man he was quick and strong and anchored the middle of the line for the Indians. Often had 8 individual tackles in a game for the Indians, high numbers for a defensive tackle.

Tackle- Neil Hart number 95
Big Neil the biggest Indian at 285 pounds complemented Robert well after Coach Scissum's motivating method worked on him. Steady at the position.

Nose guard-Danny Ace Morris
What can I say about big Danny, a super person with a super work ethic. Went about his job with a Yeoman's attitude.

Left Flank Sylvester Beattie McKinney number 84
A sport star in football, basketball and track. One of the stars of the team while dominating his position on both sides of the ball.

Right Flank- Anthony Cooney Russell number 76
Russell was one of the best athletes to ever wear blue and white of the Indians. He was known for his pin point accuracy on his pointing. He also scored 84 points in the state tournament. Wise beyond his years in the sport he would have made a wonderful coach, the fastest end the Indians probably

ever had. He scored many touchdowns on defense running away from opposition. Used his 4.4 forty speed to dominate offensive tackles.

Linebacker- Aaron Moon number 52

Moon was a headhunter small for the middle linebacker position he played but crunk and highly motivated to do the job. He had a knock for the football recovering fumbles and intercepting the football.

Linebacker- Lyn Project Foster number 44

Lyn was tough and rugged would hit you and didn't make mistakes always seem to be in the right position, just a winner.

Corner- Jerry Chris Holtzclaw number 27

The bowlegged wonder Chris was tough carrying on the famous Holtzclaw legacy at the school fooled many opponents by his size. Chris would knock your jock strap off.

Corner-Greg Foots Holtzclaw number 24

Another Holtzclaw that was a tough good athlete who worked hard to achieve his goals. A hitter on defense who didn't get beat at his position fiercely denying pass completions intercepting balls and hitting like a linebacker on ball carriers.

THE BEST LITTLE BAND IN THE LAND

East Highland's best little band in the land was under the direction of Mr. J.M. Larkins of Birmingham, Alabama. Mr. Larkins came to East Highland in the late 1930's and was one of the pioneers that help establish the legend that would become East Highland High School. Mr. Larkins was an outstanding math teacher. In the classroom he was a musical genius who also played in a jazz band called the Snappy Seven. This man dedicated countless hours to the youth of East Highland often he would march his kids through the streets of Drew Court practicing their marching steps to the delight of the residents of the community. When the best little band in the land marched in a parade downtown Sylacauga it was always quite a show for the citizens of Sylacauga both black and white. The best little band in the land was a perfect compliment to East Highland's football team. The band always knew what numbers to play to supplement the greatness of the football team. The band members

Michael Catfish Smith

and majorettes knew that they were performing for a winner the Indians. One particular Indian supreme drummer, Monkey Wrench Corbin would always lead the football team on the field getting out in front of them with his drums beating the Indian war chant! The band, just like the football, basketball and track teams were picked from the most talented kids no matter what class. Mr. Larkins closed the show in 1969 with the Indians going out in style. It would be the last time he directed a high school band because Sylacauga High School, the school the Indians were joining up with already had an established great leader in Fess Simpkins. In fact, a Simpkins still to this day directs the Aggie Band, his grandson. Mr. Larkins chose to finish his career in the Sylacauga School System taking on the task of Band Director for the junior high school, preparing youngsters to play in the Aggies half million dollar band until he retired. The only disappointment for Mr. Larkins and the band was the fact that they chose not to let the Indians play for the state championship in football. The best little band in the land or the baddest little band in the land Indian fans liked to call them was ready to travel when word came that the Indians were not invited to the four team playoff, thus grounding the band for eternity.

The Best Little Band in the Land
Director - Mr. J. M. Larkins

Ricky Borden	Trumpet
Cecil Woods	Trumpet
Kerry Clisby	Trombone
Roger "Chopper" McElrath	Drums
Monkey Wrench Corbin	Drums
Antere Johnson	Drums
Reba Speer	Clarinet
Darrell "Bo Bo" Harris	Drums
John Hurt	Saxophone
Richard Baker	Trombone
Faye Whetstone	Clarinet
Michael Roy Williams	Bass
Lawrence Ervin	Saxophone
Larry Jackson	Trumpet
Chester Cook	Bass
Lisa Cook	Trumpet
Harriet Williams	Clarinet
Michael Muns	Trumpet
Anthony Jackson	French Horn

Closing the Show

Junior Powell	Bass
Stanley Russell	Drums
Melvin Averette	French Horn
Sandra Smith	French Horn
(Class of 65)	
Bessie Smith	Clarinet
(Class of 63)	

The Best Little Band in the Land
The East Highland Majorettes and Cheerleaders

One of the prettiest majorettes I ever laid eyes on was a girl named Judy Salter. Judy was what black people commonly called a redbone, obviously mixed with black, white and Indian ancestry. Judy's life was tragically ended at the age of 26 by the hands of a jealous boyfriend while she was in the company of another man. She was killed with a 30 alt six high powered rifle, right in front of two Sylacauga policemen at the precinct who were in the process of fueling up their patrol car. Judy screamed out for help from inside the car when in along with others as the madman pulled in behind her chaperoned by another mad man. The two officers waited until the perpetrator shot her before they opened fire on him wounding and disarming him. Her funeral was held in the unusual hour of 7:00 p.m. at night. The church was laced with white candles lit in each window. After her funeral her body was taken on a four hour ride to south Alabama to the town of Bay Minette, Alabama, her hometown of birth where she was laid to rest. I mentioned Judy's name first because she was one of the standard bearers of Indian beauty and excellence that the East Highland majorettes represented that had her life tragically cut short. The Indian majorettes were always chosen from among the smartest and cutest with the prettiest legs. Competition like everything else at East Highland was stiff unlike today where some girls go out and make it because their parents are teachers or something. It was an honor for these girls to be chosen to march out in front of East Highland's best little band in the land. The vast majority of them became college graduates and outstanding women in society as well as mother and wives. The best little band in the land was not a large band and the people that marched in it represented the very best that the school had to offer just like the sports teams it was something to be proud of and they certainly made us the Indian faithful very proud to call ourselves East Highland fans. Here is a list of the other majorette not listed by class. Judy was not the first of the excellent Indian majorettes. Some came before her and some after her.

Michael Catfish Smith

Indian Majorettes and Cheerleaders

Majorettes
Earline Knight
Willie B. Lang
Connie Lang
Emily McLemore
Barbara Ann Harrison
Ann Munn
Faye Cook
Barbara Williams
Gail Swain
Judy Salter
Ann Richards Dubose
Maxine Richards Embery
Shirley Pratt
Jenny Louis Fuller
Pearlie Cousins
Ophelia Johnson
Clemmie Johnson
Mildred Johnson
Lola Knights
Maxine Goodgame (Head Majorette)
Carolyn Pilate
Earnestine Goodgame
Ann Leonard
Shirley Grimmett
Fontella Williams
Jean Cook
Bell Leonard
Marcella McMillian

Drum Majors
Dorothy Bankhead
George Lauderdale
Shorter

Indian Cheerleaders
Diane Pilate
Judy Parks
Blanche Jordan
Veronica Duncan
Carol Jemison
Shirley Pratt

Conspiracy Theory

Was there a conspiracy to keep the East Highland High School Indians out of the 1969 2A football playoffs? Why did Alabama High School Athletic Association Executive Secretary Bubba Scott and those who voted the poll rankings back then not feel as impressive as the Indians were on the gridiron that they were not worthy of the playoffs? Why did the courts make two Indian opponents one of which was long time Indian rival Riverside of Northport and Chilton County of Clanton cancel their games with the Indians? Coach Scissum tried hard as he could to find a 10th opponent to fill his schedule in his final campaign as the Indians head coach. This after Cobb Avenue of Anniston, a long time Indian rival chose not to play the Indians in 1969 for fear a loss to the 2A powerhouse might knock them out of consideration for 4A football playoff consideration. Coach Scissum sent out invitations to all the local schools throughout the 5 county areas, but could not find anyone willing to take on the mighty Indians. Cobb might have been onto something and recognized that the Indians were going to be strong with a senior laden team of 25 seniors in 1969. Consider the two common opponents that they faced, Westside (3A) of Talladega and Calhoun County (3A) of Hobson City. Cobb beat Calhoun 50 to 0 and Westside 28 to 0. Meanwhile, the Indians whipped Westside 46 to 0 and trounced Calhoun 82 to 0. It was not unusual for Coach Scissum to have difficulty filling his schedule. Most schools knew about the little giant from Sylacauga and the big reputation they had for taking on opposition much bigger than themselves in school enrollment and beating them. So, with the state knowing all this history about East Highland, why then did Scott and his counterparts deny the Indians their much coveted prize of a state 2A football playoff berth? Was he punishing them for all the lopsided scores that they posed on opponents much bigger than them while running up big margins of victory or was he simply doing the bidding of some people who knew that East Highland would be extinct in a year and state championship in football that would have cemented their legacy forever? It was a known fact that Coach Scissum rested his starters early in most games and in fact there wasn't a game in 1969 where he had to keep his starters on the field the whole game. The closest anyone came to the Indians in a game was OS Hill of Munford in a 36 point margin of victory for the Indians. They had to know that the Indians would have been a solid favorite to win it all. Is it ironic that Sylacauga High School inner city counter parts to East Highland and the school that Indian underclassmen would be attending and call home next year was let in, this after being jumped all the way into the top 4 teams in state, along with the Childersburg Tigers coming out of nowhere in 1969. The Aggies had lost their home opener to Childersburg 21 to 0. But on the strength of an 8 game winning streak they were let in. Childersburg incidentally would have made it also if they had not lost to county rival Talladega late in the season. Both teams were ranked lower than the Indians to start the season but surprisingly lapped them in the rankings along the way. Are you telling me that Sylacauga's 9 win season was more impressive than East High Highlands 9 win 0 loss season? That Childersburg's 8 -1 -1 season was more impressive than the Indians 9 and 0? Why were the Indians left out and the Aggies let in? After all though they were both city schools in the Sylacauga system they didn't play each other and like I said were in two different classes, Sylacauga 3A to the Indians 2A. In 1969, the Indians were supposed to be strong. Everybody knew it. Coming off a 9 and 1 season in 1968 they boasted a roster which contained 25 seniors, strong numbers for a school the size of East Highland. Heck, they were strong numbers for a school of any size but, for some unknown reason they started the 1969 season ranked number 28 in the state 2a preseason polls. Now, I don't profess to be the greatest mathematician but can somebody explain to me how a team can finish 9 and 1 in 1968 with their only loss coming in a close game to a big 4A rival finish the season ranked number 10 in the state in 2A while returning 25 seniors with 17 of them starters with 9 on offense and 8 on defense and drop out of the top ten? Maybe the thinking was to drop them so low that they would have to fight their way from farther back to reach the top four. Something that clearly makes you want to go hum! Meanwhile, the Aggies couldn't have possibly been thinking about a state playoff bid after being humbled so badly after their 1968 season while going 6 and 4 which is pretty mediocre in comparison when you consider that the Indians didn't even lose 4 games in 4 years dating back to 1966. But, on the strength of an 8 game winning streak to finish the season they got the opportunity to play for the state title. The States 4 game playoff format only allowed the top 4 ranked teams in each class to play for the state championship. This format incidentally favored the Aggies to play both games at home in the friendly confines of Legion Stadium, their home field. This decision must have surely been painful and a bitter pill to swallow for the Indians and their fans having to witness the Aggies who were in the same town playing in the same stadium as East Highland and not being closed down as a high school play for the state title that they felt they so richly deserved in their last year of existence. This very stadium where they had set so many scoring margins of victory and records, it was like the Aggies stole their thunder and glory. The Indians must have felt watching those teams play for the title against Sylacauga like they could have whipped any of them including the Aggies. Not to diminish what the Aggies did and all that year winning the 3A State Football title but the school on the hill didn't lose a game all season as the Aggies did n their game with Childersburg while giving up 21 points in a shutout loss. The Indians did not give up 21 points all season plus the Indians routinely beat up on schools much larger in enrollment than Sylacauga. This was done while shattering what then was a scoring record in the state for 9 games. The Indians lit up Sylacauga's Legion Stadium scoreboard like a pinball machine while allowing no one to score against them. Even the Montgomery Advertiser admitted that the Indians probably would have won the 2A state championship in football had they been allowed to play for it. Yet, they were denied in a shocking and stunning decision by the State, the chance to play for it. This decision surprised and saddened the whole East Highland Community. Did the dominance the 2A powerhouse black school exhibited over opponents create envy and jealously from other schools? Was this a clear slap in the face to Coach Scissum and his program? Deny the black school in town in this final season of segregated football but let the white school in? These are some serious questions not answered considering the times we were living in back then, so, let's consider the times. It was the 1960's, an era that would see the end of the Jim Crow and segregation. It was systematically stomped out by the courts through the efforts of Thurgood Marshall, NAACP Lawyer and future Supreme Court Justice and John and Robert Kennedy along with Dr. Martin Luther King and the foot soldiers. The south was reluctant to change at first and it would be 16 years before all of Alabama would fully integrate her public schools. You know what? I'm glad it did for had it come sooner we would have missed out on some of the best football, basketball and track and field my eyes ever seen. This decision in the 1954: Brown vs. Board case ironically led to the establishment of many of the private schools that still exist in the state today. Many whites chose to send their children there rather than risk sending them to school with the negro children who they felt were inferior to their own children, but the large majority of white parents, Sylacauga chose to leave their kids in public school in the Sylacauga City School System which they felt like was one of the best in the state. This school Sylacauga High had gradually began to accept Negro students a few years back to pave the way for whole scale integration which would come in 1970. Only a few black students had chosen to leave their beloved East Highland High School. A lot of them wanted to graduate from the school system they had been in since elementary school. Racial feelings were very hair trigger and inflammatory back then and if some white people didn't say the word nigger in public you sort of got the feeling that they were thinking it anyway. It was the way they treated us when we shopped in the public stores. Some were probably using the universal hate word in the privacy of their homes while enjoying telling a good racial joke at the local country club. It was a time when most white citizens in Alabama and through out the Deep South flew the confederate battle flag and if you met someone flying it or using the logo you knew that you as a black person were not welcome. You knew that most of them still had a chip on their shoulder possibly still mad about a war fought and lost over a hundred years ago which saw black people freed from slavery. But, since many of them couldn't get back at the Yankees, they chose the closest thing that they could get to which was us. This was a time when the heart of Dixie was displayed on Alabama state tag in bold large letters clearly a message to blacks that this was still a state that longed for days gone by. As a black citizen, you knew that change would not come easy. You also knew that somewhere along the line you would experience racism from an encounter with a bigoted person. In those days most black people who chose to stay in the south in spite of the oppressed conditions had to play the step-n-fetch-it dumb Negro role if they wanted to stay employed on a job or borrow money from a bank or credit union. You couldn't be outspoken or you would risk being labeled an uppity nigger or be called militant. It was a known fact in the Deep South that the white man expected the Negro to know his place and to stay in it. Thus some blacks chose to play the Uncle Tom role selling out other blacks so that they would gain favor with the white bosses to continue to feed their families. If a white boss man thought that you were outspoken on a job, he would trump up something to get you fired making an example out of you so no one else would cause trouble and management would stand behind him. Sylacauga's police force had a white cop nicknamed Monkee Lee, who many black youth feared a run in with. I never had a personal run in with him but I knew to avoid the infamous Mr. Monkee Lee. As a black youth growing up and living in those times you knew that the police was not really going to protect you against racial attacks that you might encounter when you were alone. In these times when the word nigger flowed like a river filled with venom from the cars of many white teenagers ad some grownups that happened to catch us walking alone or through the Ogle Tree Plaza at night. The police who witnessed these incidents of racial harassment would merely look the other way or simply slap them on the wrist and send them on their way saying they were just kids having a little fun with us. The local WT Grants Discount Store located in the plaza had a white cockatoo bird that somebody had taught to say "nigger stealing" anytime a black person walked past its cage down the aisle. How that bird knew what color we were is beyond me. Maybe he was just taught the word "nigger" and called everyone that. I don't know for sure because once he uttered the word to us, we broke camp. It was the best and worst of times for us. Good times in high school sports for the East Highland Community, but not so good economically for our parents. In fact the only jobs available for blacks were the low paying ones. Many black women had to work as domestics cooking and helping raise white children along with their own. These were the jobs readily available for our mother and grandmothers. The black men were denied the good paying jobs like Dixie Color, the steam plant and Kimberly Clark Paper Mill. Only a few were allowed on these jobs and they had to know somebody to pull for them to get these jobs. Sometimes, I think these places just hired enough blacks to keep the government off of their behinds. It was like with affirmative action called a quota for blacks but in reality black women and white women in particular benefited more from this than a black man. United Parcel Service, for an example Avondale Mills and the Marble Quarries along with the foundries like Southern Alloy and the hot-as-hell Shell Plant when the Vietnam War was going on were also places where black men could make a decent living in Sylacauga. But even then some had to endure cruel tongue lashings from racist bosses and some co-workers that were resentful that a black man might be on a job that they felt a white person should have been in. Thus many colored kids as soon as they graduated high school and in some cases quit school and joined the army they high tailed it out of Sylacauga and the south which was still swelling with racial prejudice. But the sports arena the leveling fields in society no body out shined the Indians of East Highland High School of Sylacauga, Alabama, in the 1960's and especially 1969. Not even the ones who received the State Championship Blue Map Trophy. So in this football crazy state where the game means so much to so many people why then were the Indians of East Highland left out of the 1969 football layoffs? With their amazing 55 points a game average on offense and touchdown denying defense that didn't even allow anyone inside of their 10 yard line all season? The answers to these questions may never be known for certain but one thing I do know is that for 4 decades after this decision to leave the Indians out has settled in. It still leaves a bitter taste in the mouth of those who loved, cheered, and supported the mighty Indians. Though they say time heals all wounds, this thing has lingered in the backs of minds of many Indian players and fans wondering why they were denied a chance to win it all in 1969. Never the less after blasting St. Jude of Montgomery the 2A state runner up in 1968 and the crown jewel game of the Indians season in 1969 by the score of 70 to 0 late in the season a game won so convincingly over such a strong opponent the Indians thought surely it would catapult them into the top 4 teams in the state considering the fact that St. Jude came into the game ranked number 2 in the state. After all the local newspaper in town had proclaimed the Indians as top contenders for the reading anywhere in the pre season about Sylacauga being top contenders for the state 2A championship in 1969. Somebody must have known something about the Indians and Coach Scissum and their high expectation in this final year of existence of East Highland. But, after demolishing St. Jude, I somehow feel like somebody or somebody's went out of their way to stop this prediction and make sure the Indians did not get in. It certainly was not any opponent on the field of play where the Indians thoroughly whipped every body brave enough to sign on that year. But, one opponent the Indians could not defeat one not on the field of play but one wielding much greater power a pen and paper with the authority to say who goes to the playoffs and who stays at home, one with the power to deny the Indians their state championship dreams. So in a shocking decision the state closed the door on the mighty Indians for ever prematurely bringing to a close the glorious football history of the East Highland High School Indians forever. Changing the hopes and dreams of many Indian faithful dreaming of playing against the best of the rest in the state for a 2A state championship in football, a playoff where they surely would have been the favorite even in Las Vegas. Perhaps this decision made the Indian haters happy like Shottenfreder, a German word which means people who take joy at the misery of others. It was a sadness that only an East Highland player and fan could understand. Sylacauga getting into the playoffs in 1969 and East Highland being left out was like black people inventing rock and roll and Elvis getting the credit for it. In that magnificent year of football in Sylacauga in 1969, where one school went undefeated in football while going 9 and 0 and was denied while the other city school in town went 9 and 1 and was let in where they won a state 3a football championship after they were allowed to compete for it., But since integration in 1970 a year after winning it all the Aggies have finished as runner ups a year after they won it and haven't come close to duplicating their magical championship season of 1969, is it perhaps an old Indian curse since that magical season that the Indians had in 1969, no one has come close duplicating the feat the Indians accomplished where the defense didn't allow a single point all season. And that 82 point margin of victory over Calhoun County in their last game ever will probably stand as a record in Legion Stadium and probably Alabama forever. Strangely enough a year after East Highland was shut down the state decided to change the playoff format from a 4 team playoff to an 8 team format, perhaps feeling guilty for slighting the Indians. It was a decision that would come so inconveniently late for Coach Scissum and his mighty Indians.

Speed Speed and Speed

You have heard the saying that there is no substitute for speed, speed kills you, and you can't teach speed. You either have it or you don't. Webster's dictionary describes speed as the act or state of moving rapidly or the swiftness of action. Well East Highland had plenty of it. These guys could run but not only run they could flat out play the game of football. I don't know how the Indians always seemed to have so much speed on the team. I guess it was hereditary or something. Let's see if we can examine for a minute how that wonderful gift of speed that the Indians possessed was probably acquired. Back in the days of the 1950's and 1960's, children played outside and weren't allowed to sit around inside the house like today. There were no Nintendo's, Play stations and Xboxes to occupy a child's mind like today. Nor was there any internet to spend countless hours surfing on. Three things you came into the house for was water, food and to use the bathroom and watch TV at night. Obviously you slept there also. When it was raining or extremely cold outside were the exceptions. Every day you repeated the same routines. We played dodge ball growing up and tag which helped develop the elusiveness and baseball using a tennis ball and a broom stick mostly straight base and the all time favorite for boys tackle football. Without the helmets and pads and you usually know how to tackle before you ever drew football equipment for organized ball. In tackle football growing up you had to play against 12 year olds if you were 8 and they didn't take it easy on you. You got hit hard and you learned quickly how to juke people and run fast and outside you also involved running from bullies in the neighborhood when your moms sent you to the store usually Mrs. Argo, in the projects. There was this one bully in particular named "Nappy Lou Hollanquest" that would chase you and chunk large rocks at your head. Usually the bullies would be 4 to 5 years older than you. Also on occasion when you were walking to the store outside of Drew Court, you might encounter a racist or two and end up running for your life. If you were unlucky you knew that God was answering your mother's prayers when you escaped safely one more time. These were the times you put to use those wonderful pair of legs that God blessed you with. And you discovered that you with adrenaline pumping could move pretty fast. You would engage in foot races with other kids your age and older to see how you stacked up against them in the speed department. You either found out that you were pretty quick or just average. Now, I am not saying that every Indian player experienced what I just mentioned but I guarantee you that more than a handful did. Let's analyze for a minute about black people and fast legs. Jimmy the Greek Snyder former CBS sports analyst and commentator and now deceased once said while analyzing black athletes that slave breeding by slave owners had made exceptional athletes out of blacks. This was a statement that got "The Greek" in a lot of hot water and eventually fired in our politically correct society. But the truth be known it was probably some truth to his theory. You know that theory he had about blacks let's examine it along with some other facts about black people in history in this country. Early in this nations history when the slaves that were here in the 1600s, the ones who survived and made it through the middle passage were not only lucky that they didn't die and get tossed over the side, but they also were the cream of the crop for they survived diseases and mental anguish brought on by the inhumane conditions that they were subjected to on slave ships and its crew but they had the mental and physical strength to overcome their bad conditions and didn't jump into the ocean and certain death to avoid slavery. They were captured and chosen from many different tribes. They were proud people who were farmers and warrior hunters who roamed freely in their native homeland. They were captured and brought to work for free helping build up the economy of a country that they had no rights in. While living in Africa amidst the many man eaters and predators they had to be fleet of foot. In America they were forced to work from sun up to sun down throughout the south in cotton fields and other labors that they didn't receive a red penny for. It was not uncommon for the slave master to pick out big strong bucks to breed with big strong robust black women to breed strong children to sell and work the cotton fields. So, genetically for centuries he bred strong black boys and girls who became strong healthy men and women. Their only purpose in life was to serve others by working the cotton fields picking cotton to put in a sack. Some chose to use that wonderful pair of legs that God blessed them with and run. But, it didn't work for there were too many fast horses with riders on them. But my point is this, speed is a gift from God and unlike this steroid era that we live in now where people cheat to get an edge the Indians speed and talent was natural. Most black men and women possess it naturally. Let me prove it. Watch the track and field events and you'll see that usually your fastest sprinters men and women are black. Whether they are African America, Cuban, Jamaican or from Trinidad the all can run fast. But it is not like we have a lock on it though to say that all black people is fast is like saying that all white people have IQ's of 180 or that all oriental people know martial arts or that all people from India can charm a snake. But, a great deal of black people can run fast and the Indians were blessed with plenty of them. These guys could run and they could play some football. They proved it on the practice field and in the games. The lineman could run guys like Willie Holtzclaw, Robert Gunn, Joe Hickey, Sylvester Shealy and Cooney Russell. Cooney Russell, in fact anchored the state championship winning 440 relay team for the Indians. It featured Richard "Lightning" Threatt the 100 and 200 yard dash champion. Coach Scissum loved kids that could run fast and in Sylacauga he found plenty of them. If you could run and showed mental toughness you were halfway there with him. I remember Robert Poor Rob Gunn's brother of Joe Nathan Hickey Indian legend once trapping Phylliss Wheatley all word player Larry McKenzie in the end zone for a safety on a play that was designed for McKenzie to use his 4.5 forty yard speed but Gunn using his speed busted up the play by running him down and getting the safety. Gunn had exceptional speed for a lineman. Cooney Russell was perhaps the fastest Indian lineman ever in the history of the school. He once out ran one of Sylacauga High's fastest sprinters, a kid who played running back on the Aggies football team in the 220 yard dash. Russell's speed allowed him to dominate on offense and defense at his tackle and end positions. He once picked off a lateral in mid air and took it to the house 80 yards for a touchdown pulling away from defenders that were the closest to him which happened to be the other teams running back. You now probably get the general idea about the kind of speed that East Highland had. Speed was Coach Scissum's concept of team that he built with, it all started with speed. The Indians didn't have many big corn fed milk drinking lineman types though there was a few like Hickey, Big Joe Pope, Slick Morris, Boot Pratt, Wally Russell, Fatso Odum, Bliss Shealy and Danny Morris' little brother Slick Morris. The Indians high powered offense relied on lineman that could run and pull opening up holes for scat backs like Jerry and Jessie Hale, Jimmy Walker, Alvin Griffin, Tootsie Thomas and Cecil Leonard and of course Lightning Threatt and also, big bully backs like Derry Lee, Holtzclaw Lee, Bull Buford, and Billy Robuck Smith. In Sylacauga, Coach Scissum found a mother lode of talented kids that could run. One of the more intriguing things about the Indians speed was how they nurtured it. They did not have the facilities that some other schools had as far as track was concerned so I guess it was all God given practicing on grass. From Billy the

Jet Harrison and Paul Hubbard in the fifties to Sonny Oden and Cecil Leonard to Alvin Griffin and Lightning Threatt, Coach Scissum always had a game breaker. Sonny Oden signed with the Florida A&M Rattlers after high school and played for Coach Jake Gaither. He played quarterback as a freshman and the first two times he touched the ball he ran for 80 and 65 yard touchdowns. He also ran first leg on the Rattlers record setting 440 yard relay team. The team featured the world's fastest human bullet Bob Hayes, the Olympic 100 meter champion and Dallas Cowboy wide receiver. Griffin ironically was the first black division on scholarship signee from the county who signed with the Missouri Tigers of the big eight conference. In 1966 he was dubbed the fastest freshman on the team by the Missouri head coach. Griffin, as would have many other Indians probably would have signed with Alabama or Auburn in the state had they been to sign him because of Bear Bryant knew about him but couldn't sign him because of segregation. But, it was something about that Indian uniform that transformed a kid into a player something that made them play with heart against every opponent no matter what the class. I don't if it was the fact that they was representing the Indian community in Sylacauga or that Coach Scissum motivated them to believe that nobody no where was better than them from class to class starting in 1952 the year he arrived until closing time in 1970 Coach Scissum kept the being blessed with kids with speed. I guess it was in the breeding after all. Lineman and running backs ends and quarterbacks they all waited their turns to come off the hill and help Coach Scissum write history with the first and only high school team he ever coached the mighty Indians of East Highland High School.

The Hill

There was a hill in the Drew Court Housing Projects that over looked the Indians practice field. On every given day of football practice from the beginning of spring drills to the opening of fall practice that hill would fill to over 200 people mostly young ones with many adults to watch Coach Scissum put the Indians through their drills, running the tries, hitting the sleds, tackling dummies, and live tackling then scrimmaging new players with the veterans. On many a day if the team was late hitting the practice field and we were down at the swimming pool on a hot summer day in late August, we would hear the hitting down the street which was so physical and loud you could hear the pads popping from the contact. Back in those days it only cost a dime to swim so a kid, if he had a quarter which was hard to come by could buy some Humpty Dumpty cookies which cost a nickel at Mrs. Argo's Store which was ran by white lady right on the edge of the projects. Mrs. Argo had a fence separating her house from the projects but the store was in the projects facing the front door but the back part of the store was located on her property fenced in from the projects Mrs. Argo never had to set foot in the projects to sell to her black customers but that old lady made a lot of money off of us, selling that thick bologna that you cut off of a log and many drinks and cookies. Plus if you didn't have to any major grocery shopping Mrs. Argo's was where you went for small items like a loaf of bread, milk, and eggs. And you didn't have to worry about encountering racism. She was okay to us I guess but any way that quarter also allowed you to buy a soda pop. I once picked cotton for a whole day just so I could have some pocket change to swim and buy Humpty Dumpty cookies. But that cotton picking voluntarily was not for me as I could not stand my hands getting bloody and bruised. But after hearing the Indians pads popping we would rush from the pool and soon the hill would fill up. In those days if you had a brother or a cousin playing you would brag on and take pride in the fact that he was an Indian player playing for Coach Scissum. Now just about every player that ever played for Coach Scissum started off on that hill watching the Indians practices 4th, 5th, and 6th graders waiting for their chance to come down off the hill and wear the blue, white, and red and help Coach Scissum, write Indian history. It was a known fact in the community that East Highland practices were very exciting physical and extremely competitive more so than their games. Some of the hardest hits Lightning Threatt received, he once told me came from his own teammates. Every body was trying to catch Coach Scissum eye and other than speed, mean aggressive play was what did the trick. The physical play and nature of Indian practices was such that Billy Robuck Smith, Indian fullback stud once told me that Lee the Bull Buford once bloodied his nose with a vicious hit which prompted Coach Scissum to as Buford to take it easy on his young freshman. Buford responded, "if he can't play, he doesn't need to be out here." That was East Highland football Baptist and initiation by fire from the Indians established players on the rookie wanna be's. Strangely as rough and tough as Buford was, once while running up the middle in a game for a touchdown on a 25 yard run, saw a defensive back approaching from the left, changed direction and ran straight at the defensive back and over him for the touchdown. As physical a guy as he was at 6 feet and 225 pounds of granite heavily muscled, he was allergic to bees and a bee sting once almost killed him. Thus was the nature of Indian football practices highly competitive and rough. We all know that there are only 11 positions on the field on both sides of the ball and competition at East Highland was always stiff to be first string. Throw in the fact that the Indian didn't have a junior high or B team so if a kid wanted to play football he had to be good enough to make varsity. If not, he waited until he got older and tried again. Joe Nathan Hickey Indian legend played varsity football beginning in the 6th grade. Hickey played so long that once he got to high school many people thought he was too old. Coach Scissum dressed about 38 players unusual and competition was brutal to earn a football jersey. Unlike today, where a kid might go out for the team and be kept to add numbers to a team while riding the pine if you earned an Indian jersey you played because Coach Scissum believing in playing all of his kids. Every body contributed which probably explains why he never rebuilt a team but just reloaded. I think one of the reasons Lightning Threatt broke so many long runs was because he knew Coach Scissum was not going to let him carry it but a few times. If you were good enough to make the team and mentally handle the grueling rigorous Indian practices, than you were good enough to play. Many a joker that thought back on the hill only the best that the community had to offer played for Coach Scissum. He was so demanding that you give your best. The

Indians did not have any scrubs on their team. Seeing an Indian jersey on a clothes line in the projects back in those days the school didn't was your football stuff, your mama did and mama made sure that your game jersey didn't get burnt and messed up by a hot iron. That jersey hanging on the clothes line meant respect to the person that it belonged to. They were our heroes and we knew them by their nicknames. Any body that was somebody and worth their salt back then had one. It usually had something to do with a physical trait or your athletic ability. But most times it was earned and christened on you. There was Lightning, Robuck, Slick, Tootsie, PA, Beattie, Chock, Tip, Bliss, Big Joe, and Calvin The Russian, give that name because of his rugged play in the trenches. Cecil Leonard dubbed Son, by Coach Scissum and call Sip by his Tuskegee teammates was another player with a colorful nick name. Not every kid was blessed enough to be an Indian and represent East Highland which made it that much more special for the kids that did. Sixty-five kids competing would be the normal number for the Indians 38 jerseys. If you was young and didn't make it, you would probably be encouraged to try again next year, but, if you were a senior to be and didn't make it, to bad. I can remember one incident in 1967 when the late Clarence Kidd himself, no slouch as an athlete, was running the football for the scout offense against the Indian's hard hitting vaunted first defense, with line backer Deluxe Mike Homer Bledsoe. The quarterback gave the ball to Kidd who wanted no part of the defense and took off toward the hill. He gave the ball to him again and again Kidd took for the hill. They gave it to him a third time and this time Kidd ran straight into the hole that was occupied by Bledsoe, an Indian linebacker with a mean streak who met Kidd head on with shoulder pads to ribs and wiped him out with a lick so violent that Kidd's cleats left the ground as he was driven violently into the grass with a lick so hard that you could hear the pop all over the hill. This drew a large of whoosh! from those of us sitting on the hill. This was the physical nature of Indian practices. You knew that if they hit their own teammates this hard and they liked them, you could imagine what they were going to do to players in different so much that Coach Scissum used to get on him for hitting people when the team was supposed to be going half speed. If you performed in practice, you got a jersey. If you name was called, you became a part of the Indian family. Joe Hickey, as I mentioned earlier from the invincible Indian era of 1963 to 1965, the 36 straight game winners, the group that defeated Cobb three times in a row, was the youngest kid to ever earn an Indian uniform. Hickey a big strong rugged pulpwood looking kid with natural, strength unmatched by an Indian player back then was exceptional. Sitting on that hill watching the Indians, a lot of kids who couldn't afford the seventy-five cents admission charge to get in the games could see some of the best

Closing the Show

football that most people didn't see for free. We were always amazed at what we might see at Indian practices. Incidentally, back then when you went to a real game downtown at Legion Stadium, the city kept a big ole military looking tarp all the way around the fence surrounding the field so anyone not paying could get a good view of the action on the field. Well, somebody from the hood had dug a gopher hole under the fence next to the drainage ditch across from Rumsey Lumber Yard. It was secluded from public view. On game nights when the Indians were playing fifteen to twenty kids would sneak under that fence through the gopher hole one at a time with the game plan of scattering in all directions once we got inside. Depending on who was working the games from the police force that night, we knew what our chances were. If Monkee Lee was one of the officer, we know there was no way in hell he was going to catch anybody, slow as he was, but if you did get caught they would escort you out of the stadium. Many of the Indian fans who paid would be rooting for us to make it. If some did make it and integrated into the crowds, no one would tell on you. East Highland football brought so much excitement that young kids were willing to try the police to get in. Obviously, nobody was taken to jail. To us, if we didn't have any money it was worth the risk to see what we had witnessed on the practice field being executed on players from other towns. Rarely was we disappointed in our team. Also, watching the Indian practices from the hill, you might witness some of the comical stuff that accrued during practices under Coach Scissum. For instance, you might see Coach Scissum kick a player in the behind for missing a blocking assignment or he might paddle an unsuspecting lineman while he was down in his stance. I think Coach Scissum about wore his foot out in Charles Curry's behind. Curry was a big strong kid on the lazy side and Coach Scissum was determined to make a player out of him, which he did. This kind of discipline worked because it was Coach Scissum administering it and he was well respected in the community and also because kids wanted to play for him and be a part of the mighty Indians. Because the hill had many trees, we were in the shade most of the time and it was slightly cool. The heat didn't matter to us because we wanted to see the exciting hitting of Indian practice. It brought us many action packed moments for free. Coach Scissum's house, along with Coach Showers, Principal Lawsons, Principal Davis, and other faculty was located right across the street from the practice field in the very spot that it stands today. The misconception that most people, mostly outsiders, got about the Drew Court Housing Projects was that it was some kind of small town ghetto. Actually, this was far from the truth. Not only did many outstanding people erupt from this community, but it also had a neighborhood of houses that people built right smack in the middle of it. Kids use to risk getting whippings from their parent to go to the projects. So many kids were happy when their single parents moved out to their water toting outhouse bearing rat infested shacks into the projects which were modern. I think in the Jim Crow south of the 50's and 60's, that black people really felt safe in it at a time of much civil unrest in the south. Living in the projects was almost like living in a little city within itself away from the racism that you would experience in downtown Sylacauga and much of the surrounding areas. It almost made us feel like we were living very quickly when we ventured into downtown Sylacauga, it made us feel like we live in a world absence of racism. I remember as a six year old having to sit in the balcony in the colored section at the movie theater amid colored and white only bathrooms and water fountains. My mama had a job working at the Trailways Bus Station briefly as a 20 year old before she like so many young black people seeking opportunity for a better life bolted for New York City. At that Trailways Café, I remember having to go to the back of the building to see my mama and get a small hamburger. It really did a number on my psyche to know that my mama was cooking in a place that she and I was not good enough to be served. Usually a kid didn't experience racism until he or she journeyed outside the boundaries of safety in the projects. The projects also had paved roads and street, and running water in the apartment which explains why so many teachers freshly graduated from Alabama State and Tuskegee, chose to live and build there. There were so many black households within the city limits of Sylacauga that didn't have running water for baths and cooking in homes. They had to walk down to what was commonly called branches which usually were underground springs that were dug up and kept clean. You know you had to share them with the tadpoles and other critters that ventured there, but they were always kept clean. Some people had wells that were dug and relied on rain water. The toilets were outhouses, unless you had a septic tank which was not good if you didn't have running water in the house so you had to come up with primitive ways to gain water. Of course, you risked getting bit by a snake or some other wild animal toting water at night. In Drew Court Projects, you had access to running water from faucets and indoor toilets with bathtubs in apartments overseen by the housing authority that the federal government had build so Negroes would have better modernized housing. In the early fifties, you had the safety of knowing you didn't have to use the infamous homemade outhouses and the outside the city limits did have to use these kinds of facilities. In Drew Court, you had the safety of knowing that you didn't have to worry about getting bite in the butt by a snake, a spider, or some other crawling creature when you went to the toilet. The maggots down in the hole from the toilet seat in the out house that you sat on was always a disgusting experience along with the stench that you had to smell. The paved roads were significant because all the paved roads in the city started and ended in the white neighborhoods. In spite of black people paying taxes, we had very little or no representation in city and county government. There were those apparent to us that were hell bent on keeping us in second class status in society. A prime example of an unpaved road in the city could be found on what is now called Hammett Avenue, right smack in the middle of affluent white neighborhoods but light years away from modernization. Hammett Avenue, right smack in the middle of affluent white neighborhoods but light years away from roads that plagued black neighborhoods all over the deep south. Like leprosy, dusty and dirty when dry and muddy and unavailable when wet. It was even nicknamed read road because it ran all the way from US Highway 280 to Main Street Sylacauga, right next to white neighborhoods that had fully paved roads and running water conveniently short of ours. When it rained, many cars got stuck in places that they ordinarily shouldn't have. We might as well have been living in some third world country when it came to modernization. The paved roads and running water that the city supplied to it citizens, stopped in the white neighborhoods in spite of the taxes that black citizens paid. Talk about taxation without representation, I see why so many blacks moved up north. Drew Court was like a culture center for us and many black kids that visited there. You had a public library, a swimming pool, recreation center fully equipped with a basketball gym, a skating rink, playground, park, little league baseball field, and pony league baseball field for the older boys. This was where other teams surrounding Sylacauga came to play against the project teams. Huge crowds would gather in the bleachers surrounding the field and just as many would sit on the hill by the swimming pool. Cars would park on the hill next to Mountainview Elementary School. Old Mabelle, wearing men pants, looking like Pearl Bailey with a strong voice for a black woman, almost masculine, a voice that told the story of a strong black woman who had survived some difficult times, sold peanuts from a big croaker sack that she carried over her shoulder and dared anybody to steal from her. She would also sit on that hill and sell snow cones by the blind store that was ran by Willie and JP, two blind men from the Talladega School for the blind located in Talladega. This is the same school that produced the world famous Five Blind Boys of Alabama Gospel Group. I swear those two guys could feel paper money and tell you what you were paying them with. Five, ten, twenty, fifty, or one hundred dollar bills, you couldn't cheat them. That school in Talladega did a wonderful job. But, old Mabelle, I was convinced that she was Pearl Bailey's sister or something.

Little league baseball which Coach Scissum along with Principal Lawson, was established for black youths, was very popular back then. I think Coach

Scissum used it as a farm system to culture future Indian football players. Almost all of them played it as youths and it has been said that if you can play baseball you can play any sport because of hand eye coordination. Jimmy Funderburg, Snow Brownfield, and Rufus Farriss along with John Henry O'Neal also coached and helped bring out talent and leadership skills in black youths. That little league was the launching pad for many great Indian football and basketball players. As I mentioned earlier, old Mabelle would sit on the hill by the swimming pool and sell snow cones and peanuts, some of the best I have ever tasted. Those were summer favorites back then. Sometimes on the way to our little league games and to Indian football games, those of use who didn't live in Drew Court would be chased by white teenagers in cars while we were venturing through Ogle Tree Plaza. They would call us niggers and sambos while trying to terrorize us. The police would always look the other way. If for some reason those that were sworn to protect and serve all of the citizens did happen to stop a car load of white teenagers, they were scolded and sent on their way and we were told that they were just kids having a little fun with us. Those officers probably knew those kids parents or were their neighbors or something. Sometimes, I wonder if our parents really knew the danger some of us faced. They probably did, but just prayed and trusted that God would protect us and keep us out of harms way. Never the less, we knew that we had the Indians in the safe haven of the projects, our big brothers. Our Indians could whip their schools if they dared play. The resentment that we faced back then would transform any black kid's mind growing up in segregated conditions. On our way to school, we passed through white neighborhoods which always seemed to be the best kept. Their neighborhood made ours look like we lived in some place that got lost in time. In town we had a colored area called the block which is now named the Shephard Shopping Center. It was named in honor of Reverend Shephard who pastored Rising Star Baptist Church, the most prosperous black church in town in those days. School teachers, brick layers and other phosphorous blacks attended that church. Reverend Shephard was the pastor there for forty years. The block was the place where we went to get hair cuts from the likes of Fuller Russell and Cliff Hale. It also was where all the black men gathered to share small talk and casual conversations, in other words, to shoot the bull. They also talked about community things. The talk in the fall of the year always centered around what was Coach Scissum going to have this year. Also, on the block was where you could find some of the best greasy hamburgers and cheese burgers that you ever tasted in the world, cooked by Frank Dudley at his restaurant. If you happened to be a bachelor looking for a good woman for a wife, the barbershop was the place to hang out. Many good women that had been fooled by the pillow talk and jive of a trifling brother, while being left with the responsibility of raising a baby boy could be found there getting little Johnny his first haircut.

Back to the hill, I can still remember a particular sweltering hot August day when Coach Scissum irritated with his team's execution, denied them a water break. Cooney Russell standing on the sideline taking a break, told my cousin to pick up a towel without letting Coach Scissum sees him, wet the towel and throw it down on the grass behind him. My cousin told him the towel was dirty and Cooney replied, "I don't give a damn, wet the towel lil nigga!" My cousin wets the towel and dropped it behind Russell, who when Coach Scissum wasn't looking grabbed it and sucked the water out of it. My memories of the hill is still vivid to me as it was when I was a nine year old sitting on the hill with other kids my age and a little older. As we sat on that hill we knew that we would never play for Coach Scissum and never get the chance to be Indians, but we loved the Indian program and though we didn't have much in those days, we had East Highland and we would be on them against anybody any where. No matter how big or small you school enrollment was, it was the Indians one mo gin another victim another win. Any place any time our house or yours. They won so much, in fact that on the rare occasions that they did lose it was like a death in the family. I remember my cousin Ricky who played in the baddest little band in the land as an 8th grader, coming home in 1968 after the Cobb game in Anniston, crying saying they cheated on us. Many Indian fans that attended the game swear to this day that time had ran out in the game before Cobb scored the winning touchdown. The officials held time on the field saying that the clock had malfunctioned. The game ended after Cobb scored the winning touchdown. The fact was, the hill was the best seat in the house to view some good Indian football. You could get close to the action without Coach Scissum rejecting you. That hill in Drew Court right above the East Highland practice field sits desolate now forty years removed from the last Indians' practice, forty years since Coach Scissum barked out his last instructions to his final team, perhaps his greatest. If I close my eyes and sit on that hill alone on a given day, I can still see and hear Coach Scissum and his troops coming out of the dressing room running down the hill and holding practice, practices that made us all proud to be East Highland Indians.

Prelude To The 1969 Opener

1968 was the year Dr. Martin Luther King was assassinated and the year that Senator Robert Kennedy, probably the next presidential candidate with vision and hope was murdered. The Olympics were going on and John Carlos and Tommie Smith, two world class athletes who were black and happened to be sprinters on the United States team were about to make their famous or infamous protest depending on what side of the social issues of the times you were on back then. It was the times of an unpopular war, Vietnam being staged and Jim Crow in the south was regressing and on its last leg. Though change was coming ever so slowly in the south years after George Wallace, the Governor of Alabama, had stood in the doors of the University of Alabama and proclaimed segregation now, segregation tomorrow and segregation forever. Clearly, he was playing to the masses of people whom ideas he championed and who had been taught that they were superior to black people and that if you happened to be born black, it was their privileged right to rule over you and their was no rights that you possessed that white people had to respect. I had a white friend who was a co worker of mine at Avondale in the 1990's. He told me that when President Kennedy was shot and killed, in Dallas in 1963, the principal of his elementary school made the announcement over the intercom that the president had died, he and the rest of his fourth grade class cheered loudly, as well as the rest of the student body at his school, which was segregated. This was clearly a reaction from things that had been taught to them by parents that were reluctant to change and probably because they did not like the stance that the Kennedy brothers had taken during the Civil Right Movement. It always seemed to amaze me how some people could call themselves Christians and still have so much hatred. When John Carlos and Tommie Smith raised their black gloved fists to the air on the winners podium at the 1968 Olympics after finishing first and third in the 200 meters finals,

Closing the Show

this represented a sort of black power message to protest to the world that people of color refused to take second class citizenship anymore. This protest against social injustice in America no matter what side you stood on in 1968, the oppressed or the privileged had to raise consciousness to injustice all over America. And you had to admit that it took courage on the part of those two world class athletes who, undoubtedly had been training for years for this special moment that only comes every four years to risk throwing away their gold and bronze medals in a matter of seconds for a cause that they believed so strongly in. Thus, after this protest in front of the whole world, they were forced to give up the precious medals that they had been training for all their lives. The incident portrayed them as heroes to black America and villains to white America. As I sat there in 1968, as an eight year old watching perhaps the best Olympic games I had ever seen, my mind didn't fully grasp the concept of what I was witnessing. For one thing, black athletes wearing red, white, and blue uniforms performed and dominated track and field events for a country in which some citizens didn't appreciate and clearly under valued their worth in. I thought about my cousin, Winston McElrath Jr., who had graduated from East Highland High School in 1967 and voluntarily joined the Marines. How he had fought valiantly against the Viet cong and how at the age of 19, on his way out of the war zone, he stepped on claymore mine and lost his life defending a country where he was thought of as nothing more than a second class citizen. As I tried to grasp all of these things in my young mind, little did I know that East Highland High School was getting ready to write a chapter of sports history in the State of Alabama that would never be duplicated. In the city of Sylacauga and the state of Alabama it was fifties and sixties. In the perilous times that black people faced during these times, the Indians were always something we could brag on. So, in this 1968 year, little did I know it would be the last time East Highland would not only lose a fame in football but also the last time they would face old nemesis Cobb Avenue of Anniston. In 1968, the Indians were one season away from their final year of football and facing their old rival the 4A powerhouse that the Indians had slain many times over the years. The name Cobb meant something to Indian fans as they were always good and usually the team on the Indians schedule that would be the most difficult. During Hickey Holtzclaw Griffin era of the invincible Indians when the Indians ran off thirty-six straight victories, the Indians had beaten their bitter rivals three straight years from 1963 to 1965. It would be their longest win streak over their powerful rivals. Lately the Indians had seen their fortunes change in the rivalry. The Indians still dressed out just as many good players as they had when Griffin Leonard Holtzclaw and Hickey played. The team they were getting ready to face, Cobb, always possessed outstanding talent and speed equal to the Indians. This game was usually the most hyped and difficult test on the Indians schedule. Throw in the fact that Cobb was a 4A school with more players to choose from and you had the makings of a true David and Goliath story. Cobb didn't look at the Indians as a small school, they looked at the Indians as rivals equally able to defeat them. The team that won this game usually ended up going undefeated. The Indians had sent Cobb into many championship games with a loss. This game generated so much excitement in the community that former Indian players would come back to Indian practices during Cobb Avenue game week to fire up current Indian players. Coach Scissum also used this game to gauge what kind of season he expected to have. In the years since, the invincibles graduated, Cobb had beaten the Indians two straight, in very close games. In fact, Cobb had beaten the Indians in the 1967 game at Legion Stadium 18 to 14 scoring in the last minutes to snatch victory from the jaws of defeat in a very emotional, hard hitting game that left the Indian fans heart broken. While giving the Indians one of their rare home defeats, I can't begin to describe to you the excitement that game had generated with both crowds reaching a fever frenzy as time ran out in the game with the Indians in possession of the ball on the Cobb five yard line. Cobb had once again pulled a game out of the fire against the Indians that East Highland had led all but one minute. I can't tell you how big of a heart breaker that was for the Indians and their fans. Since 1952, the year Coach Scissum arrived at East highland, the Indians initially had played Cobb in 1951, losing to them in the inaugural game of the heated series. Though the Indians would be on the short end 9 to 8 in victories against Cobb, Coach Scissum would actually break even with his rivals, going 8 and 8. The two rivals had met 16 times with East Highland winning 8 and Cobb winning 8.

Prelude Cobb 1968

It was a virtue Mexican standoff. The Indians in fact, had let Cobb 8 games to 6 when the invincibles of Hickey Holtzclaw and Griffin graduated. As good as this soon to be class of 1970 was many of whom were born the year Coach Scissum arrived in Sylacauga wee they had never tasted victory over Cobb. Lightning Jay Grimmett, PA Young, Beattie McKinney and Billy Robuck Smith had never beaten Cobb. Only Cooney Russell playing as an 8th grader in this class had beaten Cobb. So, here we were October 3, 1968, a Thursday night game at Memorial Stadium in Anniston, trash talking on both side as Cobb and East Highland always brought out the best I each others fans. As the Indians football team and band buses rolled into the stadium. I'm not going to say the good people of Calhoun County didn't like their neighbors from Talladega County, down highway 21 south or that they had total disdain for the smaller school from Sylacauga, but, the Indians having beaten Cobb a few times over the years let's just say the Cobb fans knew that this was a rivalry game and that the Indians were totally capable of beating them. There had been few blowouts in this rivalry dating back to 1951. Christmas would come early for Cobb this year with the Indians giving them the perfect gift, a football game. Cobb would defeat the Indians 19 to 13 in a game full of emotional highs and lows on both sides, it would be the only game the Indians would lose all season and thus, break up the Indians bid for a perfect season. In fact, if Cobb hadn't defeated the Indians in this game, Coach Scissum would have had five unbeaten teams in ten years in the 1960's. In the game, the Indians made Cobb look anything but like the 10th ranked 4A team in the state for a full 3 quarters and all but on minute and 22 seconds of the fourth quarter. East Highland won every statistical battle except one, the scoreboard. It was the same dramatic ending as the 1967 game when Cobb scored in the last minute to win 18 to 14. Again, this year they scored in the final 60 seconds. Typical East Highland and Cobb battle high energy and intensity and great athletes and coaching from both sides. It took seven fumbles, three interceptions, and a fourth down call by Coach Scissum that didn't work in the final two minutes for Cobb now satisfied with a 9 to 8 advantage in this brutal rivalry would choose not to play the Indians ever again. I wonder did the fact that the Indians would have a team stacked with twenty-four seniors have anything to do with that decision. Something that makes you want to go hum! Back to the game, to open it, the Indians were fired up, eager to get the monkey off their back and drove sixty-eight yards for a touchdown the first time they had the ball. Billy Robuck Smith and Lightning Threatt did most of the damage with Smith busting up the middle from 3 yards out to put the Indians on the board first. Ten minutes and one second was left in the first quarter. That would be all the scoring for the first half in this hard hitting contest between the two gladiator schools. The Indians should have scored two more times before halftime and it probably would have put this game out of reach but Cobb's proud Panther defense rose up in front of the home crowd and forced an Indian fumble on the Panther thirty yard line. With the Indians driving for another touchdown, another Indian turnover caused by a fumble came on the Cobb forty-one yard line and killed another Indian drive. I guess you can see that this was no ordinary game but a very physical hard hitting affair. Just before halftime with the Indians strong defense shutting down Cobb's mighty offense, they handed the ball back to Jay Grimmett and the Indians offense and Grimmett on his first pass attempt was intercepted by Panthers all district defensive end Charles Tolliver at the Cobb's goal line and returned forty yards to stop another Indian threat. To start the second half, 3 fumbles and a pass interception all inside the Indians thirty gave Cobb 4 golden opportunities to score in the third quarter. They made good on two of them. Anybody who played ball knows that turnovers will doom a good team playing on the road in a hostile environment. The Indians were already outsized by Cobb and playing right into their hands. Cobb's first score in the game came with 10:57 showing on the clock in the third quarter after Threatt fumbled the kickoff return. Cecil King, the outstanding Cobb full back, then busted up the middle from a yard out for the score. The second Panther score came with 2:02 left in the quarter when Panther quarterback, Ed Heath, hit end, Charles Tolliver in the end zone from nineteen yards out. There would be no more scoring in this quarter of the hand hitting affair. The Indian fans had to see the momentum shifting in this game and feel like it was slipping away from them. Cobb primed to find some kind of voodoo magic to work against the Indians one more time as they had done in Sylacauga last year. In the fourth and final quarter, the Indians excited their fans and roared back driving sixty-one years against Cobb's stingy defense and scoring with less than 4 minutes remaining in the game. The famous end reverse pass play executed by Sylvester Beattie McKinny to PA Young, gained forty-one yards to the Cobb's twelve yard line. From there, the Indians would score the touchdown with Lightning hitting pay dirt. It would be the last time the Indians would ever score against Cobb ever. The Panthers were stopped on their next series by the mighty Indian defense with time dwindling down on the Panthers with the Indians clinging to a 13 to 12 advantage. The excitement in the game was almost unbearable with hearts thumping fast and lumps in throats. Surely this was not a game for the faint of heart. On the line was the pride of two cities. Cobb of Anniston and East Highland of Sylacauga. Two counties, Calhoun vs. Talladega, north vs. south, what would in less than two minutes and twenty-two seconds. The end would come to one of the greatest high school rivalries played during segregation that the state of Alabama had ever seen. With integration looming large on the horizon and immanent in the a year and both schools destined to be shut down and turned into junior highs, the Indians had the ball facing fourth down and less than a yard to go for a first down. The ball was on the Indians forty-four yard line with a minute and twenty-two seconds to go to gain a first down. Coach Scissum then made the make or break decision of the game. One minute and twenty-two seconds to go to ride off into history with a 9 to 8 advantage. In the series for the Indians over Cobb. But, it was not to be as Coach Scissum gambled that his offensive line now dog tired in this hard fought physical game between the two epic schools could knock Cobb off the ball and the line of scrimmage far enough for Lightning to gain the first down and thus run out the clock. For some unknown reason Coach Scissum chose not to run full back Bill Robuck Smith known to drag would be tacklers for extra yards. Maybe he was thinking he would decoy Smith hoping the defense would jump all over him, and Threatt could possibly break one and secure the game for the Indians. Faith would once again turn on the Indians in this fabled series as Coach Scissum chose to go for it with Threatt running it and Cobb stopping him for no gain. The Panthers took over on the Indians forty-four yard line with Cobb crowd cheering wildly at the great defensive stop and the Indians crowd stunned that the usually reliable Lightning was stopped for no gain on less than a yard. Some would leave the game stunned that Robuck didn't get the call. But, now the crowds on both sides of the stadium was standing with time running out in this game, a game that surely it was a shame that some one had to loose.   Cobb went to work from the Indian forty-four yard line with quarterback Heath hitting two successful passes for first downs. The last one moving the ball to the Indians sixteen yard line. Now, less than a minute remained in the game and from there he threw one incomplete and was dropped for a 3 yard loss by the mighty Indian defense fighting hard and proud trying to bring home the victory for their fans. Seeing how hard they was fighting makes you wonder why Coach Scissum didn't just punt the ball away and make the Cobb offense have to drive further to score. You don't question the judgment of a Hall of Fame head coach. Especially, one of Coach Scissum's caliber, who won over 78% of his games. Coach Scissum did explain to a reporter after the game that his thinking was that if Cobb got the ball back they could score from anywhere on the field with a bomb and he didn't want to give them the chance. Never the less, on third down from the nineteen yard line, Cobb quarterback, Ted Heath found flanker Robert Cook in the back of the end zone for the touch down that was the ball game. Cooks touch down set off a wild celebration on the Cobb side of the stadium. Once again delivered heart break to Indian fans at the game and at home in Sylacauga. Not only that, but the Indians fans, band, and football team had to literally fight their way out of the stadium to the buses. One Indian majorette got slapped and the buses were rocked as one guy even got on top of the hood of the Indian band bus. The team and band ended up being escorted out of town by the police. All of this did not take away from the fact that those of us blessed to be alive to witness this final game in this magnificent series had seen quite a show put on by these two fine negro schools. The Indians needed Cobb like Ali needed Frazier, Cobb needed East Highland like the Lakers needed the Celtics. Every great team needs an equal great opponent to bring out the best in one another, the two certainly did that. It would be the last time the mighty Indians would ever loose a game in football. Seventeen games played between the two schools dating back to 1951. Only one game separated them. Cobb 9 wins East Highland 8 wins. It would be called a draw if it was a prizefight. Though the Indians would be denied the opportunity by Cobb to even the score in 1969, the Indians had fought with guts and heart and laid it all on the line. Surely, the many Indian classes that did defeat Cobb could brag until eternity. East Highland vs. Cobb what a game! What a series!

Fall 1969 Sept: The Final Season

Players on the "Big Blue" team are, left to right, front row: Managers Dewitt Simmons, Jerry Houser. Kneeling, second row: Alphonza Olden, Greg Holtzclaw, Aaron Moon, Gary Oden, Sylvester Shealey, Lynn Foster, Jerry Holtzclaw, Terry Bledsoe, Jay Grimmett, Albert Oden, Neil Hart. Standing, third row: Head Coach Scissum (deceased); Reproter Jerome O'Neal; Lamar Prater, Wilbur Wilson, James Odum, Robert Williams, Billy Smith, Anthony Walton, Richard Threatt, Gill McKinney, Jessie Powell, Thadeus Darby, Coach Bernadean showers, Coach Dwight Duke. Standing, fourth row: Nathaniel Williams, James Williams, Sylvester McKinney, Calvin Drake, James Player, Ruben Parks, Anthony Russell, P.A. Young, Wayne Harris, Darnell Williams, and Danny Morris. This 1969 team was undefeated, untied, and the defense was never scored against. The total score for the year was 498 points, averaging 55.3 points per game. Only one touchdown was scored against them on a fumble in the endzone on the third string offensive team.

There is nothing during the year like the excitement that high school football brings to small towns all over the south in the fall of the year. For us East Highland fans especially, Indian football, the smell of fresh cut grass on the practice field. The site of testosterone charged teenage boys in mint condition crashing into one another. Yes, football season is special around these parts. Maybe the only thing that could compare to it for me was when I was a child growing up on Christmas Eve anticipating something good under the Christmas tree. Well, welcome to the hottest ticket in town in Sylacauga, Alabama, in 1969. The East Highland High School Indians would generate Christmas Eve kind of excitement to their fans in this final year of football for the legendary black school. The Indians fans and spectators were going to fill Sylacauga's Legion Stadium to maximum capacity and overflow status in this final season that anyone would ever see the Indians play organized football. Each of the home games that they would play in the stadium in this final year. The crowds would be diverse with blacks a majority and whites scattered amidst the huge crowds of people who were to see the Indians play and close the show on the number one hit in town for eighteen years. The Indians high scoring offense and touchdown denying defense was electrifying and awesome over the years that Coach Scissum coached them. From 1952 to 1969 Coach Scissum had put East Highland football on the map all over the State of Alabama. The players that Coach Scissum was blessed to have in Sylacauga came from a talent pool that was made up mostly of kids from the projects. The Indians also drew talent from a variety of neighborhoods in Sylacauga such as: West Park, Oakland Heights, the Goodwater Highway, Overbrook South Highland, the Quarry, Coaling Road, Sunrise, and Walco. One player even traveled fourteen miles from Goodwater, Alabama to play for Coach Scissum and the Indians. Under Coach Scissum, people who had not seen the Indians play in person had read and heard about the Indians in the newspapers. Under Coach Scissum, very few football prognosticators ever picked against the Indians. They knew the Indians were a small school powerhouse with a reputation that was cemented in the fact that they were always well coached, disciplined, and a hard hitting scoring machine under Coach Scissum. If you ever witnessed an Indian football practice, you would see why their games were thought to be easier than their practices. Coach Scissum would often deny them water breaks until practice ended. Once as a young Marine Reserve drilling in Montgomery in the early 1980's, I was approached by the company gunnery sergeant who walked up to me while I was in formation and proceeded to ask me if I was from Sylacauga. I told him that I was and he asked me what ever happened to the school named East Highland? I told him after integration in 1970, they shut it down and made a junior high out of it. He just shook his head as in amazement and then told me something I already knew in my heart like a true Marine, he said, "man they use to play some kick A… football. One year they came down here to Lafayette and beat us 44 to 0." I was too startled to respond to him because I didn't know that the Indians had played against the gunnery's alma mata. I just smiled with pride because growing up, I knew almost all of those players on the Indian teams in the late 1960's. I usually got that kind of conversation when ever I wore the East Highland alumni t-shirt in most places in the state. Such was the persona of the Indians under Coach Scissum. Respect even from among the many opponents that they had defeated over the years. Coach Scissum and the Indians brought pride and joy to our little community in Sylacauga every time they won. He, along with his many out standing players, have given us a lifetime of memories to treasure and many reasons to proudly wear the East Highland moniker on our t-shirts over the years. So, here we were in the final season of fall practice for the Indians amidst the

Closing the Show

smell of sweat soaked practice jerseys and grass stained football pants that usher in the sweet aroma of fall football practice coming from the Indians locker room. As we stood nearby both amazed and fascinated by the players and Coach Scissum as they emerged to take the field we knew as black youths in Sylacauga that Coach Scissum knew what he was doing coaching. If you busted your tail you were going to win playing for Coach Scissum and enjoy the thrill of victory. Those of us that were too young to play while sitting on the hill watching practice, wished that we were old enough to play for him. The excitement of the first day of live hitting to the soreness that the players expressed from the physical hitting. Only a true football fan would understand. From the two a day practices to the regret we felt as youngsters knowing that soon the practice field right below the schools would soon be voided of activity forever. The memories of all the great players that had been initiated to Indian football on this field would soon be a distant thing of the past and burned into my memory forever. The popping of the hard hitting Indian player pads, the unmistakable voice of Coach Haywood Scissum barking out instructions, and the sight of kicking someone in the behind or paddling them for messing up a play. All this would soon be no more. As my mind grasps the concept of that shark reality I also embraced the moment that was now. Knowing that I was blessed to be alive to witness the greatness of Coach Scissum and the Indians during this special moment in time in Sylacauga and Alabama prep sports history. In his eighteen years as coach of the Indians, Coach Scissum had taken us to this magnificent roller coaster ride of emotional highs of ups and downs. Ups in the victories that he brought us which were staggering, and downs in the emotion we felt in the close losses to Cobb and Westside that were few in number. If you didn't lose sometime to an opponent, where would the joy in victory come? Think of Michael Jordan ands the bulls struggling with the Celtics and Pistons before they finally kicked the door in on those two franchises. You get an example about what I am talking about. Not that the Indians lost that many times to those teams I mentioned but, you get motivated and hungry for victory when you loose. A majority of the people getting ready to watch the Indians close the show in this final season still remember the Indian's greats from the past. Players like Derry Lee Holtzclaw, Billy the Jet Harrison, Paul Hubbard, George the Ohio Dortch, Sonny Oden, and Andy Red Foster from the early fifties. From the early sixties, Clarence Foster, Harold Looney,, Frankie Hart, Gene Brut Gamble, Cecil Leonard, and Dewey Munn. The invincible of Hickey Holtzclaw and Griffin. The children that were born from 1955 to 1962 that were old enough to witness the Indians play but not old enough to play for Coach Scissum, they were about to witness history that would over the years to come, be swept under the rug and hidden from the grand children and great grand children of Indian players and student that attended the school. The excitement of Indian football always was the center of the talk in the barber shop on the block. What is Coach Scissum going to have this year people asked? Parent and students alike could not wait for Coach Scissum to unveil his team for the coming season no matter what calendar year it was. Coach Scissum never suffered a losing season in his eighteen years of coaching. In fact, 6 wins was considered a losing season at East Highland where the standards were always high. More times than not, Coach Scissum delivered. Over the years his teams have been noted for having explosive offenses while being very stingy on defense. Imagine a team scoring forty on you but not letting you score anything. That was the Indians under Coach Scissum. He delivered bragging rights to Indian fans and students against many schools. This year was especially special for it would be the last time the Indian fans and students would be able to cheer on their beloved Indians. In just 9 short months the federal government ordered integration of the public school system in Alabama. In a few months East Highland would be relegated to merely a junior high school. Some people in the community were excited and some despondent about the decision. The excitement was about the possibility of young black children learning alongside white children in schools which was about to become a reality. The disappointment was in the fact that we were about to loose many dedicated black teachers that loved and cared about black children, if whether or not they received a good education to be successful in life. The loss of East Highland as we knew it in the south where we had been brain washed to believe that everything black was bad from our skin color to our hair as well as all of the bad diseases from diabetes to high blood pressure. You name it, we as black people supposedly had more of it though we were only about twelve percent of the population. East Highland made us feel good about ourselves. It represented every thing that was good to us. Good teachers, good principals, good coaches, and great sport teams. We knew we could always brag on our Indians. In this final season, Coach Scissum and his players had high expectations coming off a nine and one season a year ago. A season that saw there only loss come at the hands of Cobb of Anniston, in a game that the Indians led until the last minute and twenty-two seconds. In fact, the Indians had dominated the game statically but came up short on the scoreboard. The Indians were returning twenty-four seniors to the team that had finished ranked 10th in the state in 1968. A good number of talented veterans for any class in the state. They had barely missed the playoffs and were a solid favorite to win it all by the local newspaper in 1969. With all their major scoring weapons returning; Lightning, Robuck, PA Beattie, Jay Grimmett and Terry Bledsoe, the Indians were stacked offensively. They also had ne blood in Anthony Walton, Greg

Closing the Show

Foots Holtzclaw, Weechie McKinney, Wayne Cow Head Harris and veteran Jerry Chic Holtzclaw. The defense was loaded down with all star candidates at most every position. Cooney Russell and Beattie McKinney at the ends. Robert "Big Un" Williams and Neil Hart at the tackles; Danny Ace Morris at nose guard; Aaron Moon and Lyn Foster at the linebackers. Sylvester Shealey, Lightning Threatt, Billy Smith, Foots Holtzclaw, Chic Holtzclaw and a host of other subs that could have started for other teams. Coach Scissum had a loaded deck and he knew it. Maybe that was one of the reasons Cobb chose to scratch the Indians off of their schedule in 1969. Maybe thinking the Indians were still fuming about their close loss to them in 1968 and with a loaded team in 1969, they were primed to avenge the loss at home. The Indian fans were buzzing and excited anyway about the start of football season and the prospects it brought of a state title in 2A football with East Highland scheduled to be shot down next year, Coach Scissum couldn't have picked a better team to go out with if he wanted to. The Indians never rebuilt any way, they just reloaded and this team was stacked to the teeth. The only thing to Indian fans in 1969 was not whether the Indians were going to win but by how much What better way to close out the show for Coach Scissum and his Indians and what a show it had been for seventeen years. If the Indians were a play on Broadway it would have been a number on hit for eighteen years. As a kid I remember always leaning over the rail in the stadium in Sylacauga sitting up high to get a glimpse of the Indian players as band drummer Monkey Wrench led them on the field beating a war path drum rhythm. As they came down the tunnel and out the entrance leading to the field, I scooped out the number on the back of my favorite players. They were forty, thirty-six, fifteen, eighty-four, fifty, eighty-three, forty-six, seventy-six and ninety-four. As the Indians reached the field of play, my mind grasp the thought of what I was about to witness. I thought of how lucky I was that my Aunt Bessie thought enough of me to take me to the game. At the time, I didn't realize how special they really were. These Indians were getting ready to write history enjoy the ride. The Indians were getting ready to open their final season of football in the season opener against Hudson High of Selma, a 4A school. Hudson High had a student enrollment of 1600 students, a count today that would make them one of the biggest high schools in Alabama playing 6A football. This was a black high school with a student body of 1600 students playing against the 365 student body count that they had against East Highland. In the days leading up to this game, Coach Scissum had only been able to schedule nine games, a problem that the state would use against them in a controversial point system at the end of the season. This void was left when Cobb Avenue of Anniston decided not to play the Indians for fear a loss to the 2A power house would diminish their chances for 4A post season play.

Michael Catfish Smith

Coach Scissum had called out to all the schools locally 1A through 4A to play, but could find no takes for a 10th game. Hudson High, a large black school competing in the state's highest class of 4A and a regular opponent on East Highland's schedule was up first. I have heard it said that a good 4A school is supposed to beat a good 2A school any given day. East highland was not your ordinary 2A school. Little did fans visiting from Selma know what they were about to witness. Though we colored folks as we were called back then could sympathize with the city of Selma, a great civil rights movement city of social change in the 1960's and we wept about Bloody Sunday on the Edmund Pettus Bridge along with the rest of the nation. Old Hudson High was about to become the biggest victim of an Indian massacre since General Custer's last stand at Little Big Horn. It was said that in 1965, Coach Scissum was being interviewed by a local newspaper reporter the week of the big Riverside game in Tuscaloosa. The reporter said to Coach Scissum probably in a doubtful way, the coach of Riverside has over 1800 students, grades 9 through 12. Coach Scissum thought about it for a minute and then said yeah, but they can't put but 11 out there at a time. The Indians went on to defeat Riverside 44 to 0. A team that incidentally featured future Pittsburgh Steelers great John Stallworth. Coach Scissum always knew that he had talent and his East Highland success was a mixture to two things. First of all, a great coach with a great offensive mind and second, great talent and the ability to know how to use that talent. In times now when you usually see a high school have as many as ten coaches on a staff, Coach Scissum had only himself, Coach Showers, and Coach Dwight Duke. He personally knew what kids abilities were as well as their limitations. He also was not burdened down with the politics of having to play a kid because of who his daddy and family were or how much money was he donating to the quarterback club. Throw in the fact that East Highland didn't care how big a school enrollment was, just sign on the dotted line. The Indians felt like the bigger they were, the harder they would fall. In fact, the Indians usually treated the bigger schools worst than they did the smaller one. The Indians would often show mercy to the little ones by calling the dogs off, so to speak. So, here we were on a Thursday night September 4, 1969, in Sylacauga's Legion Stadium with two other high schools, B.B. Comer, a county school and Sylacauga High, a city school like ourselves. I sometime got the feeling while growing up the two other schools didn't feel like the Indians had any rights to the stadium. Never the less, some of the most exciting high school football played in that stadium and some of the largest scores on the board were put up by the Indians. The crowds that the Indians played in front of were largely black but there was always a scattering of white high school fans mixed in the crowds with some of the local high school white coaches perhaps scouting the Indians to see what kind of plays Coach Scissum was going to run. None of them signed on to play the Indians. They really just wanted to see the offensive show of the Indians with their stingy defense amid their athletics and speed. Anyhow, on this particular night, East Highland was getting ready to take a giant step toward the 2A playoffs, something that they narrowly missed in 1968 after a 9 and 1 season. The Indians were about to crush Hudson 50 to 0. The Indians wasted little time as the game started showing why the pre season publicity proclaiming them as 2A state championship contenders was not wasted. The Indians scored in two plays after receiving the opening kickoff. Like a machine hitting on all cylinders, the Indians offense scored twice in the first quarter and once in the second. The Indians would go on to roll up 449 yards in offense to 101 yards of offense for Hudson. The Indians made 17 first downs to Hudson's 6. Hudson, the larger 4A school against East Highland the smaller 2A school could never get anything going against the Indians' vaulted defense. Hard hitting and probably still mad that Cobb refused to play them one last time, the Indians wanted to show the state what they were about. Three of Hudson's first downs against the Indians came because of penalties. Hudson had only 23 total yards in the first half against the Indians first defense. In fact, Hudson would get most of their 101 total yards against the Indians young second and third teams. This well after the starters had retired for the night. The pride to hold opponents out of the end zone ran deep with the Indians who played like they had a chip on their shoulders. They guarded the end zone like a Fort Knox soldier guarded gold. East Highland fans were cheering early and often as the Indians took the opening kickoff and scored in one minute and four seconds. On the first play from scrimmage, right end Sylvester Beattie McKinney fired a long pass to left end PA Young for 42 yards and a first down on the Hudson Tigers' 29 yard line. On the next play, Lightning Threatt took a pitch out from quarterback Jay Grimmett and swept ground right end and flew untouched into the end zone. Terry Bledsoe, the other halfback scored the two point conversion. Hudson received the ensuring kickoff and was stopped cold by the nasty Indian defense in three plays and was forced to punt. They suffered a bad snap from the center who was put under tremendous pressure by an Indian lineman(oops upside the head) and East Highland took over on the Hudson 36 yard line. From there, five plays later and the Indians were in the end zone again. It was Lightning Threatt again going up the middle cutting back against the grain for 22 yards and the touchdown. The try for the two point conversion failed and with 6:02 left on the clock, the Indians were in control. After the Indians held Hudson again forcing them to punt the Indians offense went to work. This time it took only 4 plays. On the first play of the drive Jay Grimmett faded back deep he then dumped a screen pass to Lightning Threatt on the left side with the blocking perfectly set up. Threatt on a marvelous run in which he changed directions 3 times eluding what looked like two would be tacklers, he went all the way but an unfortunate clipping penalty wiped out the score. The Indians were not to be denied, gave the ball to fullback Billy Robuck Smith on the 33 yard line and he rammed the ball straight ahead 3 times, the last 3 yards for a touchdown. The Indians would pick up two more points on a safety. With 6:06 remaining in the second quarter, Anthony Cooney Russell, defensive end, tackled Tiger quarterback Chapman Smith in the end zone. Following a punt by Indians' PA Young that rolled dead on the Tigers two yard line, it seemed that the Indians could do nothing wrong in this game. The Indians would score once more in the first half. Terry Bledsoe capped a 45 yard drive in six plays with a three yard score. The route was on and in the second half on the Indians first possession reserve quarterback, Gill Weechie McKinney, a 10th grader, hit PA Young with a 3rd down scoring strike for 63 yards out. The two point conversion was good. A minute after the Indians scored, the youngsters now playing defense held the Tigers. Then again, McKinney and Young hooked up this time on a 27 yard touch down strike. The two point conversion was good again. Most of the 4th and final quarter was scoreless as the Indian youngsters playing in place of the starters refused to give up real estate to Hudson. Neither team could mount any drive of significance. Somebody from Hudson must have started talking because Coach Scissum sent his first team back onto the field with five minutes remaining. I don't know if Coach Scissum was trying to prove a point to Hudson that he could have beaten them worst that he did or what, but the starters instantly marched 76 yards in eight plays on a death march that would have made Geronimo proud. Billy Robuck Smith took a 14 yard pass from a host of running backs and 3 passers in its balanced attack. The Indian stats read like this: 226 yards passing and 223 yards rushing. Lightning Threatt was the night's leading rusher gaining 80 yards on only six carries, he also caught a pass of 60 yards and had scored twice. Billy Smith had 76 yards rushing on 14 carries with one touch down. He also caught a 14 yard touchdown pass. PA Young was the top receiver with 3 catches for 132 yards and two touchdowns. Coach Scissum had praise for everyone after the game but he signaled out Lightning Threatt and reserved quarterback Gill McKinney for special praise. He said, "I told every body that Threatt was playing with a pulled muscle last year but nobody believed me. He is back to full strength now, as you can see." Coach Scissum asked, "What did y'all think of my young quarterback, McKinney? If I had known that he could throw like that, I might have started him. I can tell you this, he will be playing some this year." McKinney threw two times for 90 yards and two touchdowns. The Indian coach also mentioned the play of his offensive line which was starting two new guards. The blocking on the

Closing the Show

line was fine with Robert Williams and Cooney Russell manning the tackles from big Danny Morris' little brother of Roland Slick Morris, the only junior starting on the line at center. The two new comers on the line both guards, Fatso Odum and Gary Oden did an outstanding job. They opened gaping holes in the Hudson defensive front all night. They also protected the quarterbacks who didn't take any hits as they were given plenty of time to throw. On the defensive side of the ball, bug Robert Williams was in on 14 tackles with 8 individual stops and 6 assists. Other stand outs on defense were Danny Morris, Doug Williams, James Odum and Smith at corner back. Final score, East Highland 50 Hudson 0. On Monday morning, Coach Scissum had nothing but praise for his team that had just put up half a hundred points while giving up 0. "They all played well," he said. Its hard to single out any one that didn't play as well as I expected. Coach Scissum said that all his backs ran well even the second string back field that played most of the second half. He had special praise for senior half back Lightning Threatt. Threatt scored the first 3 times that he carried the ball. Threatt carried six times for 80 yards. Good for an average of 31 yards a carry. He also caught one pass for 6 yards, making his total for the night, 140 yards. Full back Billy Robuck Smith also turned in a good game by rushing for 76 yards on 145 carries and caught one pass for 14 yards and a touch down. He had 90 total yards on the night. Half back Terry Bledsoe and second teamer Anthony Walton gained 42 and 32 yards respectively. Coach Scissum was also well pleased with his passing game as the Indians threw for 226 yards. On only 10 attempts completing 6 of them with 3 touch downs giving Coach Scissum the balanced offense that he craved. Coach Scissum was very proud of his defense which only yielded 101 yards of total offense. They didn't give up any points. His response to this was the defense must have been up for the game and done a good job because Hudson didn't score did they? Coach Scissum said that he had been worried about his defense more than anything about how they would react in a game because his only loss from the 1968 defensive squad had come in the line. He singled out tackle Robert Williams a two way starter and defensive end Anthony Cooney Russell also a two way starter as the top defensive performers. Williams had 8 individual stops with 6 assists while Russell had 4 stops and 7 assists. Coach Scissum expressed surprise at several developments. One was the score with Hudson being a 4A school and East Highland a 2A. He said that he was surprised at the margin of victory. He said, "I was hoping for a one or two touch down margin of victory, I never figured that we would beat them any where near 50 to 0." Coach Scissum said his only complaint was that the defensive secondary did not intercept any passes. "We had a couple chances but missed them," he said. There are some new boys back there and they will get better with time,

Michael Catfish Smith

they better, he said or we could be in trouble against a passing team. I'm just tremendously proud of all my boys and I hope we can keep up the good work he said. So, on with the season one that Indian faithful and certainly hope will be special in the coming weeks.

Reputation Earned

Under Coach Scissum, the Indians had this reputation of not only being a good home team, but also a good road team. The Indians seemed to feed off the other team fans enthusiasm to see them defeated. Most teams can usually play well at home in the friendly confines of their home stadium where thy usually have a home crowd advantage and riding a wave of emotion might be fired up and enjoy a call or two from friendly officials commonly called home cooking. Where you really prove your metal is in front of hostile away crowds who usually out number the amount of fan support that you might bring with you. With the exception of Cobb Avenue a few times and Westside of Talladega couple of times, the Indians usually took away home field advantage from opponents and made their stadium their home away from home. Usually by half time of most Indian away games, the home crowds were silent now not expecting a win but somehow hoping that their team could at least score and keep the Indians from embarrassing them at home. The Indians were always a well prepared hard hitting bunch under Coach Scissum and very confident believed that they could whip you anywhere. Your stadium, their stadium, or a cow's pasture for that matter. The Indians' games that they did manage to lose on the road to the likes of Cobb and Westside were always close action filled that went down to the wire and more than a few were decided by the ill fated calls of an official's whistle. Some people to this day that still reminisce about the Indians still believe that the officials held time on the field in the last Cobb game in 1969. A game in which Cobb scored the winning touchdown while coming from behind in the last few seconds of the game to again deliver heartbreak and defeat to the Indians one more time. It was a defeat that incidentally caused Coach Scissum and the Indians an undefeated season. It would be the only game the Indians would lose all season. Maybe it was some payback for all the times the Indians had spoiled Cobb's undefeated seasons. Often times when leaving hostile places like Westside of Talladega and Laurel of Alexander City, Coach Scissum would instruct his players to leave their helmets on until they boarded the bus because some irate fans upset because their teams was on the losing end of a lopsided score. Not that Coach Scissum was deliberately running up the score on opponents because he once in a game against Laurel in the early sixties, instructed his players to do everything but fall down to keep from scoring in a 57 to 7 game that Laurel was clearly out gunned. These big scores despite Coach Scissum pulling his starters early in the second quarters of most games. How could you tell a youngster playing second or third team not to score if he got a chance considering how brutal the Indians practices were? After all, playing in a game is a reward for hard work in practice isn't it? The fact was that Coach Scissum was an offensive genius way ahead of his time. I have seen film of the Indians from 1969 and saw them run some plays like the middle screen that teams still execute now in college and in the pros. I also saw them execute some plays that a lot of teams can't duplicate today. The famous end reverse pass play that the Indians ran with, precision timing, I have not seen any high school duplicate. The Indians always a deep bunch, had kids running second and third team that could have started for most other schools. There was a song that the Indians used to sing on the bus when they were traveling. It went like this:

Everywhere we go, everywhere we go, people want to know, people want to know, who were are, who we are, and we tell them, and we tell them, we are the Indians, we are the Indians, the mighty mighty Indians, the mighty mighty Indians.

And when they arrive in your town it was ut, oh, here they come. The fans of the opposing teams knew that the Indians were a well coached hard hitting high scoring bunch under Coach Scissum with a lot of talent and when they got off the bus they meant business. Over the years, the tribe had made believers out of many opponent fans. They knew that their team would have to play their best to have a chance against East Highland and often times their best was not enough. As was the case at big 4A Riverside of Tuscaloosa in 1965 and 1967. The Indians massacred them both times by the scores of 44 to 0 and 46 to 0. This despite Riverside having a larger school enrollment with over 1600 students to the Indians 365. Laurel High of Alex City also received a lopsided beat down in 1969 losing 68 to 6. Some how the Panthers of Alex City always managed to score at least once on the Indians to avoid a shut out. In this case, in the 1969 the only points that the Indians would allow all season. Don't think for one minute that these were some cream puff, no talent teams that the Indians were doing this to. Laurel featured high school All American Willie Carl Martin who excelled in college and went on to Coach Benjamin Russell High School of Alex City to a state championship after integration. Laurel would brag about a least scoring one time imagine that! Imagine in your mind a big high school like Hudson High of Selma or Cobb of Anniston or Riverside of Tuscaloosa and putting East Highland on your schedule. Just the mention of that name on your schedule would generate such a buzz of excitement in your town anticipating the week when the Indians would arrive in your town. They knew that they were to see a good offensive show and that the Indians were a hard hitting well coached bunch under Coach Scissum. With this fierce bunch of Indians they also knew that even if their team did somehow prevail that it was going to be a very tough physical game for them to win. So confident were the Indians and their fans that they would win was on the rare occasions that they did lose to other schools it was like a death in the family the sadness level especially to Cobb who spoiled a few Indian undefeated seasons. Winning under Coach Scissum spoiled folks in Sylacauga who loved the Indians and always expected them to somehow win and have bragging rights against other schools. Such was the fierceness or the Cobb rivalry was that it was rumored that after Cobb narrowly escaped a scalping by the tribe in 1968 game Cobb came back from behind 13 to 12 to win in the last minute 19 to13. A Cobb player slapped an Indian majorette who was upset after the on going defeat and it nearly set off a riot between the two legendary black high schools. The Indians' buses had to be escorted out of town. Indians fans always expected to win under Coach Scissum as he had done since he stepped foot in Sylacauga on the East Highland campus in 1952. More times than not he usually did. What a reputation to have and what a legacy Coach Scissum and his Indians left us. East Highland what a name what a school on the east side of town located on high ground!

THE FOOTRACE

A footrace between two star Indian athletes was about to happen. One was a past star and Indian icon who was a present day pro football player and star from the early 1960's, Cecil's son Leonard or Sip as he was called by his Tuskegee team mates. The other was present Indian star Richard Lightning Threatt. Cecil now an established NFL football player with the New York Jets was home for the off season and reportedly called Lightning out. Leonard was a very cocky confident athlete dubbed son by Coach Scissum. He love to compete and win and actually he won at everything he did. Cecil was very competitive so competitive in fact, that it once almost cost him his life. In a pick up basketball and known for its roughness many a boy had been initiated and turned into a man. Cecil once roughed up a youngster named Clarence Kidd, who was a future Indian player himself, took the rough housing personal. He was younger than Leonard and certainly no match for him physically. In those days older boys did not take it easy on you because of your age no matter what the sport. It was a sort of toughening up in sports where you had to prove that you belonged. Well, Cecil roughed Kidd up pretty bad in the pick up game and Kidd because he was probably scared of Leonard knowing that he could not whip Cecil in a fist fight head up, waited for Cecil in a trail and stole him with a brick upside the head. It was a blow that almost killed Son who had to have a metal plate inserted in his skull. Now, this rough housing in basketball was not uncommon back then especially in the projects, Danny Ace Morris starting center on the Indian football and basketball teams, a former Indian great himself, once told me that as a 14 year old, he once went up against Indian legend Joe Nathan Hickey rough and rugged and as physical a ball player that East Highland ever turned out, known to back many a joker who thought that he was tough out of the paint. In the paint, was where guys would rough up the younger guys pushing and jockeying for position with a well placed elbow to the chest or a forearm to the back of the neck or head for that matter. This kind of play would lead to my fist fights if you thought you could win, you had to prove your manhood in the paint. Well, Hickey bloodied young Danny up but couldn't back him down. Danny held his own. It brought the young future Indian star instant fame for the next day in school people who had witnessed the debacle told other students and pointed him out saying that's the one who hung in there with Hickey. It was a big deal because so many students knew what a legend Hickey was and stood in awe of him. I said that to say this Cecil competed hard like all winners did with East Highland bloodlines did back then. It was the only way he knew how to play. Far as winning was concerned, Son certainly seemed to have the Midas touch on it. I remember one summer when he was home from Tuskegee on summer break, he took over as coach for the Indians little league baseball team which was in last place at the time. Though it was some talent on the Indians, the former coach couldn't seem to motivate them. Leonard in his fiery competitive style, took over and led them from worst to first, and the championship. Such was Leonard's persona not only could he play, but he could coach also. As Indians quarterback, he let his team to a 29 and 1 record. With one tie in the three years that he started. The one loss came when Cecil raised a Seventh Day Adventist couldn't play in a rare Indian Friday night game. The Indians usually played on Thursday and Saturday's with an occasional Tuesday thrown in. Reputation was everything back then and I guess Cecil wanted Lightning to live up to his nickname that Coach Scissum had given him. Now it wasn't unusual back then for guys to call out other fast guys in a footrace especially if you had that reputation of being fast. This was in a neighborhood that was blessed with speed and a big deal to be deemed the fastest of them all. So, this race was definitely special. I don't know what Lightning was thinking because he was usually quiet and not the braggadocios type, he let others brag on him. As Leonard was getting ready to test his fleetness, I did know that Lightning was fearless and I didn't see fear in his eyes this day either. Lightning was just as much an accomplished athlete as Leonard was. Before I get to the race, let me take ya'll back a minute. Depending on whom you talked to and from what era some say that two fastest Indians of all time might have been Sonny Oden and Alvin Griffin. Griffin was a 9.6 one hundred yard dash man legit. Lightning ran a 9.7 as a freshman but averaged around 9.9 and 10 flat for his career. I don't know what Sonny Oden's fastest times were but I do know that he ran first leg on the world record setting Florida A and M 440 relay team that was anchored by back then worlds' fastest human and Olympic one hundred

Closing the Show

meter champion in 1964, Bullet Bob Hayes. You had to be stepping out to be a part of that team. Sonny, as a freshman on the Rattlers football team scored the first two times he touched the football as a freshman Rattler quarterback running 65 to 80 yards for touchdowns while playing for legendary Rattler Football Coach Jake Gaither. Griffin was all world playing on Indian teams that won 36 straight games quarter backing most of them. They also conquered rival Cobb Avenue in three straight games. He also conquered Riverside of Northport and pretty much everybody else that the Indians played against. Billy the Jet Harrison and Paul Hubbard could also step out. With a nick name like the Jet, I am pretty sure that Harrison could fly playing for Coach Scissum in the early fifties. But, he played in the early fifties and his legend was not known by present day Indians who were busy being born when he played along with Paul Hubbard. Coach Bryant, at the University of Alabama, knew about Griffin and the many other great Indian football players from the 1960's but he couldn't sign them. Jim Crow laws and segregation prevented it in those days. Griffin instead signed with the Missouri Tigers of the big eight conference and became the first black player for East Highland and Talladega County to sign a division one scholarship., These five guys might have been the fastest Indians of all times, I don't know for sure, but one thing I do know is that Lightning was definitely the fastest Indian of his era dubbed Lightning by Coach Scissum after blazing to a 9.7 one hundred dash as a freshman running track for Coach Scissum. Threatt was captain of the Indian track team which won back to back state 2A championships in 1969 and 1970 after the state opened up competition to the black schools to compete with white schools.

So, here we were in the street in Drew Court in 1968, Leonard and Threatt squaring off in the mother of all foot races in Sylacauga in a 60 yard dash. High School All American versus New York Jet corner back for bragging rights in Sylacauga and probably the county. Old East Highland vs. present East Highland. Reputations on the line, they got down in their stances as we crowded around to watch with people choosing sides on who we thought would win. Someone hollered on the mark, get set, and go! They took off! Side by side it was a good start with both men coming out of the hole smoking! Shoulder to shoulder, not one of them giving an inch halfway through, it looked like Lightning was surging ahead, but Son Leonard, being the competitor that he was, was running on sheer guts not giving away an inch. If this was a one hundred yard dash, Lightning might have been a clear cut victor or it looked like he was getting ready to kick it in another gear when the race ended. Suffice it to say that it was a dead heat, to close to call. One thing for sure was that even though they were from different eras, both of them left with their reputations intact. Old school vs. new school! Both of them left their mark on East Highland and their place in Indian folk lure is legendary.

THE OLIVER OF FAIRFIELD GAME

Indians Scalp Oliver 40 to 0

For the second straight week the Indians have defeated a 4A school, this time the victim being Oliver High School of Fairfield. EJ Oliver, formerly Fairfield Industrial, was scheduled after the loss of Riverside and Chilton County on the Indians schedule due to court decisions. It was hardly a contest with the Indians of Sylacauga grabbing a quick 14 to 0 lead in the first quarter then adding on the points. The Indians elected to receive, after winning the coin toss to start the game. Coach Scissum had said that this was what you call going into a game blind. Not really knowing anything about

Fairfield because they were a replacement game with no game film, were a 4A school much larger than the Indians in enrollment. He had to respect the fact that Oliver was brave enough to take on the powerhouse Indians from Sylacauga on such short notice after it seemed like someone was going out of their way to spoil the Indians last season ever with the cancellations of Riverside and Chilton County. As the game started before the fans could even settle down good in their seats, Lightning Threatt electrified the crowd as he took the Oliver kickoff all the way back for a touchdown. Clearly Fairfield either didn't know about Lightning or they just wasn't scared by their actions of kicking the ball to him but, after this run back for 6, you could bet your last dollar that they wouldn't kick it to him again. Never the less, it was called back because of the eagle eyed official who said that he stepped out of bounds on the Indian's 10 yard line. On the Indians first play from scrimmage, end Sylvester Beattie McKinney threw a long pass to end PA Young, who uncharacteristically dropped it. The usually glue fingered young would prove to be a bad omen for Fairfield with his dropped pass. It would just be the calm before the storm. The Indians on third down had Beattie throw again this time to Lightning who gathered it in for a 25 yard catch to the Indian's 35 yard line. On the next play, Lightning struck for a 65 yard run and the Indians first touchdown. Terry Bledsoe, Lightning's partner in crime added the pat and the Indians led 8 to 0. I don't know if the good people of Fairfield, Alabama, had ever heard of East Highland or even ever played the Indians in anything but one thing I do know is that they were not going to forget them after this game. The Indians kicked off and the Hornets took the ball on their own 40. They were about to learn what Hudson High of Selma had learned in the Indians opener two weeks ago, that you can't run the ball with success on the Indians defense. The stable 11 forced the Hornets to punt on their first series of downs. Threatt then returned the punt 7 yards to the East Highland's 20. Two plays later Lightning carried the ball 32 yards to the Hornets 36 yard line. Then Billy Robuck Smith, the Indians fullback extraordinaire made one of the most magnificent runs that you will see on any level. He took the ball at the 36 yard line and toted half of the Hornets with him on a ride to the four yard line. At least 8 or 9 players had a shot at him as Robuck bounced off tackle after tackle attempting to keep his balance as he ran over two other would be tacklers and was finally tripped and lost his balance on the enemy 4 yard line and was tackled. Such a determined run had never been witnessed by the Oliver fans and especially the head coach who said after the game, "I didn't know when signed on to play East Highland that they had Jim Brown playing for them." Billy later scored on a one yard drive. You have to credit Coach Scissum for staying with Robuck and rewarding him for his hard running by giving him the first chance to score

Closing the Show

after his magnificent effort. Often today you will see one kid do all the work to get to the goal line and then the coach will give the ball to some other kid to score so that he can get his name in the newspaper. The pat failed and the Indians now led 14 to 0. Fairfield was not going to go away without a fight playing on their home field in front of their fans in Birmingham. After receiving the ball from the Indians kickoff, the Hornets managed to move the ball into Indian territory against the magnificent 11 then Anthony Cooney Russell broke the line and dropped the Hornets quarterback for a loss. Such plays were routine for the all state defensive end Russell who had a knack for making the big defensive plays for the Indians. The quarter ended with the Indians leading the Fairfield Hornets 14 to 0. If the home crowd was not shocked by now they soon would be for they were about to find out what many schools and towns had found out over the years that Coach Scissum coached the Indians, that they score big on you but you don't score on them at all. To start the second quarter, the Hornets punted but got off a bad one and the tribe took over on the Hornets 38. Five plays later, Threatt scored on a ten yard run. The pat failed and the Indians now lead 20 to 0. The Indians kicked off and once again the Indian defense failed to yield any real estate to Fairfield and they were forced to punt. The punt landed on the Indians 37 yard line. Lightning then set up another touchdown on a 45 yard scamper that was set up by the outstanding blocking of the Indians offensive line lead by Morris, Russell, Williams, Odum, Oden, Young, and McKinney who allowed Lightning to do his thing. Jerry Chic Holtzclaw, the bowlegged wonder, then scored on a 13 yard run in an act that clearly showed that Coach Scissum liked to reward his players for hard work in practice and spread the wealth, for Lightning or Robuck could have easily got the call and scored. The hard hitting Holtzclaw, brother of Indians' great Willie Holtzclaw or the famous Holtzclaw family of Indian athletes certainly earned his right to score. Anthony Walton added the pat and the Indian's led 28 to 0. After the kickoff, the Hornets started at their 31 and moved the ball to the Indians 39 yard line. From there the Indians defense stiffened and stopped the drive on the Indian 39 yard line where the Hornets cold not muster another yard. Chic Holtzclaw then made a beautiful 25 yard run just before the bands entered the fray. The half time score East Highland 28 Oliver 0. As the bands played you had to wonder what was on the minds of the Fairfield players and their fans. I would have loved to have been a fly on the wall for a few seconds in the locker room of the Hornets to hear what kind of pep talk their coach was giving them to motivate them to get back in the game. Either way, the home crowd certainly had been taken out of this game. One had to wonder if the Hornets felt like they had done the right thing by singing on to play the Indians. After the bands had finished, the Indians kicked off to start the second half. The Hornets returned it to their own 38 yard line. Two plays later the Indians hard hitting defense forced a fumble that was recovered by big Neil Hart and his 280 pound body. On the next play, sophomore sub quarterback Wayne Cow Head Harris fumbled at the Indians 38 and the Hornets recovered this play seemed to fire up the Hornets and the home crowd sensing a opportunity to do what no one had done thus far in the season against the Indians defense get on the scoreboard. But, the optimism was short lived as on the very next play the Hornets offense turned the ball back over to the Indians as they suffered a bad exchange from the center who was put under pressure by big Robert Williams(oops upside the head) and fumbled the football which was recovered by line backer, Aaron Moon on the Hornets 18. Two plays later, Cow Head Harris threw to PA Young for 16 yards and the touchdown. The pat failed and the Indians now led 34 to 0. The teams would exchange punts before Moon would intercept an errant pass and run it back to the Hornets 19. The quarter ended with the score Indians 34 Hornets 0. The opening seconds of the fourth quarter fans from the home side of the football stadium surrounded the football field. If this was meant to intimidate the Indians, it was to late. On the first offense play, PA Young fumble a reception after a big hit and the Hornets stopped another Indian scoring drive by recovering the fumble at their own 11. Robert Williams affectionately called "Big Un", the Indians unblockable defensive tackle, then dropped a safety, punted and learned what many an opponent has learned about the Indians that there is no safe player to punt to on the Indians return team as end Anthony Cooney Russell received the punt and ran 37 yards for a touchdown. Noted here that though Cooney played end on the defense and tackle on the offense, he was faster than most teams running backs as he was the anchor leg of the Indians two time state champion 440 relay team that defeated all challengers no matter what class. A 4.4 forty man Russell was a force to be reckoned with. The pat after Russell's touchdown failed and the Indians led 40 to 0. Indian rookies played the rest of the game. By this time the DJ Oliver fans knew that the little school from Sylacauga was a legit 2A state championship contender in 1969. After manhandling the 4A Hornets by the final score of 40 to 0. Coach Scissum was tremendously proud of the Indians for the very fine win. He had high praise for Richard Lightning Threatt who he says has to be an all state and All American back this year, speaking of Threatt, the senior sensational tailback gained 183 yards his best this season in only 7 carries with 2 touchdowns. The incomparable Mr. Threatt usually only plays about 2 quarters of offensive ball for the highly talented Indians offense. One has to wonder what his numbers would look like if he carried the ball at least 25 times a game. Anthony Cooney Russell played his best game of the young season as he had 10 solo stops on defense with 7 assist from his defensive end position. He also scored on a 37 yard punt return. Outstanding backs joining Threatt were Billy Robuck Smith, Terry Bledsoe and Jerry Chic Holtzclaw. Other outstanding defensive players were Robert Williams, Aaron Moon, Darnell Williams, Neil Hart and Sylvester Beattie McKinney. Every body that dressed played. The Indians play host to Ophelia Hill of Munford next.

THE OS HILL GAME
INDIANS EXPRESS ROLL MERRILY ALONG

The East Highland High School Indians playing in their final season won their third game of the season Thursday night rolling over the OS Hill of Munford Wildcats to the tune of 36 to 0. The Indians were held to that margin in the game which is amazing in itself when a team can score 36 points in a game while holding the opponent to 0 and it's called an off game. Such are the expectations of the Indians and their fans where most coaches would love a five touchdown victory margin in a game the Indians had their fans expect more. Grown accustomed to big victory spreading games, once the big blue offensive machine gets going, the fans usually see the Indians scoring like a pack of sharks in a feeding frenzy smelling blood. Coach Scissum said after the game that he was disappointed, not in the score but in the overall play of his team. It must be said that the Indians did not play impressive football but, as Coach Scissum pointed out and it was a valid point when you can look as poorly as we did out there tonight and still win by 36 points then you must have a pretty good team when you're on. The area scoring leader, Richard Lightning Threatt played only a quarter and a half but managed to pick up 14 points in his brief appearance. He scored the first two touchdowns for the Indians. In his pre game statement coach had stated that he expected a hard fought game with OS Hill and he was right. For almost the whole first quarter the tough hard hitting defense of Hill kept the Indians offense in check forcing them to punt twice in a row without even making a first down. The pin point accuracy on his punting by PA Young, kept OS Hill bottled up offensively. His first kick went out of bounds on the Hill's 8 yard line. His second punt rolled dead on the Wildcat's 3 yard line. In Indians big blue monster defense playing its usual unpenetrable style with equal hard hitting as Hill's forced them to punt for the second time near the end of the first quarter. Lightning looking much like his idol, the other number 40, Gale Sayers and living up to his nick name, struck like a thunder bolt and showed why he was an all state player and potential All American when he gathered the Jacobs point in and 63 yards later took it to the house and crossed the goal line for the first Indian points of the night. Little Terry Bledsoe cat quick ran over the pat and the Indians led 8 to 0 with 3:43 left in the second quarter. The tough defense that the Indians always played this 8 to 0 lead probably would have held up and been enough for the Indians to win their third game of the season, but they were not done yet. In fact, they were just getting started. Lightning scored with 1:46 left in the quarter on a 25 yard run. The score was set up by a pass interception by halfback Anthony Walton. The pat was good and the score was not 16 to 0 in favor of the Indians. As the second quarter begin Jacobs of Hill again punted after Hill could not muster anything against the Indians' defense. He punted to the Wildcats 47 yard line. Then Billy Robuck Smith, running with his usual reckless abandon sprinted 35 yards to the Hill 12. Then he carried 12 more yards for the touchdown. It was nullified by a call holding penalty. Two plays later quarterback Jay Grimmett threw a scoring strike to end PA Young and Threatt ran in the pat with 8:53 left in the half, the rout was on. There would be no more scoring in the first half as Hill punted again and it seemed like the Wildcats was trying to wear Jacobs leg out. As the second half begin, the reserves would play almost all the second half with the first stringers seeing action only on defense for the Indians. Coach Scissum made numerous changes in the lineup on offense and defense. As the Indians offense took over they moved the ball to the Wildcats 28 yard line where the OS Hill defense stiffened and took over on their own 28. On the very next play, Indian linebacker, Aaron Moon recovered a fumble after a hard hit at the OS Hill 24. From there the Indians could not score and Hill took over on downs at the 4 yard line. The Hill offense still could not muster anything and Jacobs punted from the 26. Then fullback Billy Smith showed his speed and ran it back 60 yards for a touchdown. The pat failed and with 8:33 remaining in the third quarter, the Indians now led Hill 30 to 0. As his team failed again to move against the Indians stingy defense, Jacobs punted as it seemed like he was going to set a record for punt in this game. The ball landed on the Wildcat 47. Then Indians sub quarterback sophomore Gill Weechie McKinney little brother of Beattie took over the helm of the Indians offense. He promptly directed the Indians on a 53 yard drive that ended with Jerry Chic Holtzclaw capping it with a 7 yard run for the score. The pat again failed and with 2:03 left in the quarter, the Indians led OS Hill 36 to 0. Many of the Indians deep reserves played in the last quarter. The high light of

Michael Catfish Smith

the quarter was a 51 yard drive engineered by sophomore quarterback Wayne Cow Head Harris., The game ended and the Indians had won game number two. On the night Threatt carried 4 times for 32 yards and a touchdown. The mighty Indians defense was led by rising star Aaron Moon. He had 8 tackles from his linebacker position along with 3 assists. Anthony Cooney Russell had 7 tackles from his end position. Big Neil Hart Junior defensive tackle had 5 tackles and 1 assist. Beattie McKinney, end had 3 tackles and 4 assists. Next the Indians journey to Alexander City next Saturday to play the tough Hornets of Laurel High School, go see the Indians in action.

East Highland and Shelby County in the To 20

The Daily Home
October 1969

Montgomery- according to the latest rankings of football teams by the Alabama High School Athletic Association released Friday. East Highland of Sylacauga and Shelby County of Columbiana are the only are teams in the top of their respective classes. Shelby County is 8th in class 3A, a drop of one position from last week. The Wildcats are 4 and 0 on the year. East Highland also 4 and 0 jumped for 20th last week to 14th in this weeks 2A ranking. Childersburg undefeated with a 2-0-1 record moved up to 22nd position from 25th in 3A. Other area schools and their rankings:

3A - Sylacauga 32nd and B.B. Comer 58th

2A - Clay County (Ashland) 23rd; Talladega County(Lincoln) 47th; Munford 48th and Winterboro 59th

1A - ASD is ranked 44th

You will note the two predominantly white schools in the county are ranked lower than the Indians the black school in the polls at this point. Sylacauga at 32nd with one loss and Childersburg at 22nd both in class 3A.

10 Indians Score as East Highland Stings the Hornets 68 to 6

Alex City- The East Highland High School Indians of Sylacauga played the Laurel High School of Alexander City in their last meeting ever in football last night. This Laurel team had fell on hard times against the Coach Scissum Indians since his arrival in Sylacauga in 1952. The Hornets had only been able to defeat the Indians one time. This heated rivalry between the two schools had definitely become one-sided in its nature as the powerhouse 2A Indians had taken the measure of the number 3A and sort of took the sting, so, to speak, out of it. But tonight the Hornets faithful were optimistic that their team could end the losing draught against the Indians in this last meeting ever between the two Negro schools targeted for shutdown next school year in 1970. The hornet fans never ones too shy to boast and voice their opinion was fired up as ever when the Indians team buses rolled into Tallapoosa County. Laurel always had very good athletes but Coach Scissum was the factor along with his excellent talent that they couldn't get around Everybody knows that if you put the right coach with the right talent, it usually spells success. This stadium at Laurel in Alexander City was one of the places the Indian players had to keep their helmets on after a game on the way to the team buses. One didn't want to get hit in the head by a flying object on the way to the team bus. Now, I am not saying all the Laurel fans were guilty of this but you always have a knuckle head or two at every school that can't take the agony of defeat. Also, in Alex City was one of the stops on your schedule where you knew the fans had a hair trigger mentality when it came to fighting. This edition of Laurel their last one an outstanding lineman in the name of Willie Carl Martin who had never beaten the Indians. On with the game.

East Highland Stings the Hornets 68 to 6
10 Indians Score

Alex City - Each time the Indians go against Laurel of Alex City with a string of zeros on opponents the Hornets always seem to find a way to score on the Indians to avoid the shutout. There seems to be a jinx or something on the Indians against them. Now understand this, this is not about the victory which the Indians under Coach Scissum seems to always get against Laurel. About the shut out on the scoreboard, spoiling perhaps a point against them. This is only the 4th game of the season. So, we will see how the rest of it goes. All of the Indian players were unhappy about the touchdown. But, I guess some things just can't be stopped. With only one Hornet scoring the Indians saw 10 individual players put points on the scoreboard for East Highland. Lightning had 14 points; PA had 12; Terry Bledsoe and Jerry Hotzclaw had 8 each; Billy Robuck Smith had 6; Anthony Walton had 6; Wayne Cow Head Harris had 6; Jay Grimmett 2; Cooney Russell 2; Rueben Parks had 2. I know this sound like basketball stats but no, they are football stats. Threatt, now has a 4 game total of 52 points. Young has 36 and Smith 30. To start the game, the Indians received the opening kick-off and ran it back to the 40 yard line. After 1 first down, Lightning then broke loose for a 30 yard run. The play netted them at the Hornets 7 yard line. On the following play, little Terry Bledsoe quickly blasted around the right end for the score. Threatt then ran in the two point conversion, and with 10:34 remaining in the 1st quarter, the Indians led the Hornets 8 to 0. After the Indians kick off, the Indians brick wall defense went to work as usual and kept the Hornets offense in check, forcing into a 3 and done situation. The Hornets punt landed on their 50. At this point in the game the Laurel defense seemed to rise behind the urging of the partisan home Alex City crowd. They forced the Indians to punt and Prince Albert boomed one to the Hornets 7. So much for field position for the Hornets. The Indians unpenetrable defense again refused to bulge any real estate and again the Hornets punted to their 33 yard line. Lightning Threatt then sprinted 33 yards for his first score of the night. The incomparable Mr. Threatt, the best running back seen around these parts in either county Talladega, Clay Coosa, Tallapoosa or Calhoun was just getting started. The pat failed and with 2:40 remaining, the Indians led 14 to 0. Cooney Russell, the versatile one, kicked off to the Hornets and the ball traveled to the Hornets 2 yard line and the Hornet return man was stopped in his tracks right there and didn't go any further. To bad for Alex City to have start on their two yard line against the stingiest defense in the state. The Hornets had the ball as the quarter ended with the Indians leading the home standing Hornets 14 to 0. On the opening play of the 2nd quarter, Richard Lightning Threatt intercepted a Hornet's errant pass and returned it 12 yards to the Hornets 35. Several ball rushes by full back Billy Robuck Smith carried the ball to the Hornets 5. From there, Coach Scissum rewarded the hard running fullback by allowing him to carry the ball over the enemy goal line. Quarterback Jay Grimmett ran in the two-point conversion. With 9:41 remaining in the half the Sylacaugans in blue and white had pretty much took the Hornets out of the game once again in Alex City leading 22 to 0. Now, I don't have to tell ya'll reading this book thus far that the Indians defense already had enough points scored by the offense to win this last outing against their Tallapoosa rivals. The Hornet offense once again tried to put something together and once again they were denied by the stout Indian defensive 11. The Hornets punted to the 44 and minutes later Grimmett threw to Young for a 29 yard strike and the all state end pulled it end for the touch down. With 6:30 remaining, the Indians now led the Hornets 30 to 0. If Alex City was indeed going to make a game of this affair tonight they had to find a way to answer the mighty Indians. The 2A powerhouse was once again having their way with their 3A counterparts. Coach Scissum decided to let his youngsters play at this point and brought in the Indian young reserves. I often wondered what would happen to a lot of Indian youngsters after this final season. For in season past, Coach Scissum knew that he was building for the future. But after this season there was no future for the Indians. Sophomore quarterback Gill Weechie McKinney on his opening drive at the helm, had a pass intercepted as the play ended. At the half, the bands did their thing and the Alex City faithful got their last peak as East Highlands' famous best little band in the land and its beautiful majorettes with the prettiest legs in the state. As usual the Indians had took another home crowd out of the game in their opponent's stadium leaving the

Closing the Show

home team feeling neglected again. As the bands finished and exited the field, the Indians had to feel pretty good about their chance to win this game. What with a 30 point lead and knowing that no one had scored on them thus far in the season. Heck no one had even penetrated inside their 10 yard line this season. To start the second half the Indians kicked off to the Hornets and they started on their own 26. But once again the Indians defense did not bulge and the Hornets were forced to punt once again. They punted to the Indian 25, a good punt. From there, sophomore field general Gill Weechie McKinney still commanding the Indians offense took over. But as faith would have it, he fumbled the ball in the backfield on the quarterback exchange from center and couldn't find it. But an alert Hornet player did and scooped it up look what I found and took the gift 24 yards for the score. Hard to believe in a game the Indians had broke open long ago and were dominating so thoroughly that this score would break so many people hearts. But, lo and behold it did. The pat failed and with 5:45 remaining the Indians led the Hornet 30 to 6. The mishap seemed to ignite the Indians and especially Lightning Threatt because on the Hornets kickoff he showed the Alex City fans and Hornets the back of his number 40 jersey one last time as he grabbed the kickoff and sprinted 71 yards pulling away with his state champion 100 yard dash sprinters speed. The touchdown electrified the Indians fans from Sylacauga in attendance and stunned the Laurel faithful. Terry Bledsoe ran in the two point conversion and with 5:45 remaining in the 3rd quarter the new score Indians 38 Laurel 6. The score took away any little hope the Laurel fans had that their team could get back in this game. On the 1st play of the last quarter Lyn Project Foster, 2nd team fullback, showed his speed as he dashed 54 yards to the Hornets 9 yard line. On the next play he scored on a 9 yard run but as luck would have it and eagle eyed officials threw a flag nullifying the score. So on the next play Coach Scissum called the number of another one of his stable of good young running back as he gave the ball to Anthony Walton who sprinted 14 yards for the touchdown, Jerry Hotzclaw ran in the pat. With 11:20 remaining in the game the Indians now led 46 to 6. It's hard to say that the Indians were punishing the Hornets for scoring on their offense because Coach Scissum was playing everybody that dressed for the Indians, all 34. The Hornets received the kickoff and returned it to the 29. Their offense fizzled as it did all night against the Indians defensive 11 and they punted to the 50 yard line. Later in the quarter, Sylvester Beattie McKinney gave the Alex City fans one last look at the famed Indians end reverse pass play as he threw to glue-fingered end PA Young who hauled in the aerial for a 28 yard score. Anthony Cooney Russell the versatile one ran in the pat. With 7:15 remaining the Indians now led 54 to 6 over their Tallapoosa County rivals. On the Indians kickoff, a Hornet back fumbled after being stung no-pun intended by an Indians tackler and Darnell Williams recovered it at the Hornets 12. Jere Chich Holtzclaw recovered another Hornet fumble on the 28. The Hornets had fallen apart, wilted in the desert sun against the Indians. The Hornets defense jelled and stopped the Indians 3rd team at the 15. The Hornets offense fizzled again and they punted to the 29. Sophomore quarterback Wayne Cow Head Harris set up a 1 yard drive. Rueben Parks another youngster ran in the pat and the Indians had defeated Laurel of Alex City 68 to 6. Coach Scissums 34 warriors all saw action. Reserve backs who played well were Jerry Holtzclaw, Lyn Foster and Anthony Walton. Third team quarterback Wayne Harris led two scoring drives. The tireless Indians defense was led by the Williams brothers, Darnell and Robert who had 8 tackles and 3 assist apiece. Anthony Walton had 5 tackles from his strong safety position. The Indians have now won 17 straight games against Laurel dating back to 1953 and 2nd year as head coach of the Indians for Haywood Scissum. Before Coach Scissum arrived Laurel had beaten the Indians 4 straight. This would be the last time the two rivals would ever meet in football. The Indians defense once again did not allow 100 yards rushing

Final Stat:

Indians first down	11
Yards rushing	391
Yards passing	69
Total offense	430
Penalties	60 yards

Friday October 3, 1969
The Daily Home

The following article ran in the daily home the local newspaper for the Talladega and Sylacauga area in an article written by Dan Rutledge.

The 1969 football season is now 4 weeks old and the high school football picture is beginning to come into focus. Like a bottle of milk the cream is beginning to rise to the top and at this point about a third of the way through the schedules the cream of the crop seems to be East Highland, Childersburg and Shelby County High Schools. These three are the only undefeated teams left of the 18 schools in the daily home area. Shelby County is undefeated and underscored on in 4 games and is ranked 8th in the state in call 3A by the AHSAA. The Wildcats should make it 5 and 0 against Pell City (1-3) Friday night. The Shelby County defense is tough and the secondary especially tough. The Wildcats have scored 4 of their 10 tds in 69 on pass interceptions. East Highland was the only county team in the top twenty in last weeks rankings, rated number 20 in class 2A. The Indians are now 4 and 0 and should have moved up a couple of notches. East Highland is easily the most offense-minded team in the area. The Indians have scored 194 points in 4 victories, an average of 48.3 per game. The offense is led by halfback Lightning Threatt; a 9.7 speedster who has crossed the opponent's goals for 8 td's thus far this season. He also has a two-two point conversion giving him 52 points and a big lead in the county scoring race. Threatt is aided by three other senior backfield members. Quarterback Jay Grimmett, halfback Terry Bledsoe, and fullback Billy Smith, along with senior end PA Young, who has caught 6 touchdown passes thus far. The Indian defense is led by tackle Robert Williams and defensive end Anthony Russell has done pretty well so far. East Highland has had 6 points scored against them this season.

Michael Catfish Smith

A defensive back for Laurel scooped up a fumble and scampered into the end zone for the score. Childersburg was close to the top 20 last week rated number 25 in 3A and could move up a notch or two this week with the 10 to 0 victory over Pell City. You will note after this first report of state rankings in the daily home after 4 weeks, that East Highland was the highest ranked team in the county at number 20 in the polls. Sylacauga was not on the radar and Childersburg had not cracked the top 20 in class 3A.

Offense vs. Defense
Indians to Play Westside Tonight

The East Highland Indians will face their sternest test to date against powerful Westside of Talladega. Westside is not only the arch-rival of East Highland by competition but also a natural rival. These teams have played each other for many years and the game seldom goes true to form. The Panthers have a fine 3 and 1 record coming into tonight's game. Their lone loss came at the hands of the number two team in the state in class 2A, the St. Jude Pirates of Montgomery. St. Jude took the measure of the Panthers early in the season and could not muster a score in the second half against them. Needless to say, both teams have improved and our Indians will be hard pressed to score on the defensive minded Panthers who have scared the daylights out of St. Jude, the handily whipped 3 other opponents. The Indians have a schedule that is marred by open dates and other things. Last week was such a date, Coach Scissum when questioned about open dates, said the he prefers other teams to have them. They serve no good he said. So, the battle is tonight. Jay Grimmett will send Billy Robuck Smith, powerful fullback; Terry Bledsoe, halfback and the incomparable Lightning Threatt, tailback; at the Westside defensive line. Where can you see better players or play? Add to this the circus the catching of PA Young and Beattie McKinney. The line will be anchored by Anthony Cooney Russell all county defensive end and big Robert Williams defensive tackle. Aaron Moon, Lyn Foster, Darnell Williams, and Anthony Walton promise to back the line with ferocity. Put it all together offense vs. defense football Indian style mister, that's what it's all about. I wouldn't miss it for the world. See you there!

Jerome O'Neal

Indian Beat Writer

October 23, 1969
East Highland Remains Undefeated with a 46 to 0 Trouncing of Westside

The Indians were getting ready to face rival 3A Westside of Talladega for the last time. Westside scheduled for closing also after this year, would soon merge with Talladega High School. The funny feeling I get thought is that this year you could have put Westside and Talladega together and they still could not have stopped this Indian juggernaut. After the game, Westside's Head Coach Duncan would be asked to comment on the game. He said that there is not much to say. They are a good team with 24 seniors that know how to play, and play well together. Not much you can expect a coach to say about their bitter rival inter county that has just beaten you by 7 touchdowns and two-two point conversions. Westside has a bigger school in enrollment than East Highland in the same 3A class that Sylacauga High School played in along with Childersburg. They were commonly called the big schools in the county. Like Coach Scissum once said to a reporter in 1965, you can't put but 11 out there at a time no matter how big your enrollment. Poor Westside probably wished that they could have put 13 out there at a time this night against the Indians. So on with the final meeting for the fierce old black high school rivals.

It was a game for a quarter or maybe a quarter in a half. But, by half time, East Highland had turned the battle for the independent county championship into a laughing matter for Indian fans. The so-called black version of the county championship for Westside's supporters was like the old Ray Charles song crying time again. The final score was 46 to 0 and it could have been worst. The Indians offense was just getting crunked up good in the

Closing the Show

second half when the game ended. The first half was pretty much a defensive battle between the two schools. Westside came in as a defensive minded team and certainly played stubbornly in that area early on. But like Muhammed Ali throwing jabs at an opponent, you knew sooner or later they were going to take a toll. The Indians defense known for ferocious hitting and touchdown denying aggression was on top of its game tonight. In the first half each team could only manage 3 first downs but, the Indians defense proved to be tougher. In addition to holding the Panthers to 1 yard of total offense in the first half, the Indians defense accounted for two touchdowns. Real estate was not for sale or given away tonight as the Indians were playing as if they were punishing Westside for old crimes against them. Surely this was not personal against Westside but, just business as usual for the powerful Indian's defense. The 1st quarter score came with 9:58 left in the quarter. Without running a single offensive play. On a 3rd down and 25 from his 7 yard line, Westside's quarterback Johnny McKinney attempted to throw to halfback Jesse Sawyer in the flat. East Highland junior defensive back Anthony Sayers Walton read the play beautifully and broke perfectly in front of the intended receiver and sped into the end zone untouched for the touchdown. Terry Cat Quick Bledsoe ran over the 2 point conversion. The second score came on a 48 yard drive some two minutes deep in the second quarter. The Indians moved the distance in 5 plays with fullback Billy Robuck Smith bulling his way the final 9 yards up the middle. It would be a long time before the city of Sylacauga would ever see a fullback the caliber of Robuck again, if ever. At 5 feet 9, 175 pounds, Billy played much better than his size. Refusing to be tackled by 1 or 2 and sometimes 3 players, you had to gang tackle or trip Robuck up to get him off balance and off his feet. The defense got the 3rd score with 1:53 left in the half. McKinney of Westside was again back to pass when he was hit on a vicious tackle by defensive end Sylvester Beattie McKinney no relations to the quarterback, I think the ball popped loose and was grabbed in midair by the Indians other outstanding defensive end Anthony Cooney Russell also in the pass rush for the Indians. Russell grabbed the ball and using his 4.4 forty yard speed he motored 32 yards to score with no one even coming close to him. Grimmett ran over the pat and the score stood at 22 to 0 at the half time break. You had to think that this was not the way Westside envisioned their last meeting ever against the Indians. I can image that coach Duncan of Westside was telling his team in the locker room to motivate them to come back and play better against the Indians in the second half. Westside had never beaten the Indians in Sylacauga's Legion Stadium and had a hard row to hoe in southern terms to get back into this one. Meanwhile, the Talladega side of the stadium was noticeably quiet. These fans probably knew coming down highway 21 south that their teams was going to have trouble against the mighty Indians but probably held out hope. No matter how slim, could they possibly pull off an upset of the 2A power house Indians? What ever Coach Duncan of Westside told his troops at halftime didn't work because to start the second half the Indians got two more td's in the 3rd quarter. The first was set up on a defensive play by Cooney Russell who always had a nose for the football which probably explains why he was the only one in this class of 1970 to play 5 years of varsity football for Coach Scissum starting in 1965 with Hickey Holtzclaw and Griffin as 8th graders. Russell recovered the fumble by the Panthers halfback Jesse Sawyer on the Westside's 29. The Indians marched the 29 yards in 4 plays. Half back Lightning Threatt got the td from one yard out. Threatt also ran over the two pointer. The next score came with 1:14 left in the quarter. Threatt carried for 49 yards on this drive and it seemed like poor Westside's defense was taking jabs from them like Muhammed Ali pecking away at an opponent who could nothing to stop him. He carried 4 straight times scoring from 14 yards out where he out ran the Westside secondary to the end zone. Surely, the Sylacauga faithful was watching an All American back at work tonight. The last Indians score came with only 14 seconds left on a 22 yard pass from quarterback Jay Grimmett to all world end PA Young. Threatt got the pat. The Indian defense already in control of this game, they have been against everybody this year, was being led by big Robert Williams with 8 tackles and Cooney Russell also with 8. The 8 big Robert Williams got from his tackle position was high numbers for his position. This was not your ordinary hole plugger. This guy could motor and get after a quarterback. PA Young and linebacker and guard Gary Oden also had fine nights for the Indians. Westside did not get outside their own 34 yard line for 3 quarters. It had to be frustrating for them to get hit in the mouth so many times by the Indians and not be able to answer on the score board. But, the Indians did this too many opponents over the years. Its like in boxing when somebody hits you pretty hard and immediately you want to retaliate, but you can't hit what you can't catch and Westside could not catch these Indians. Their only venture into Indian territory came in the 4th quarter of play when McKinney hit halfback Bobby McCargo for 33 yards. It netted them a first down at the Indians 38. Tut, the mighty Indians defense stiffened and in the final meeting ever for the two schools with East Highland sending the hometown fans home happy for eternity with a 46 to 0 victory over Westside. Richard Lightning Threatt, who once again rushed for over 100 yards against Westside, finished with 117 yards against the touch Panther defense. Billy Smith bulled his way to 78 touch yards and little Terry Bledsoe scouted for 48 yards. A good night for the Indians triplets in the back field. Westside's Bobby McCargo finished with 68 yards. Not bad, because very few backs ever rush for a 100 against the Indians defense anyway. The Panthers top performers on defense were Charles Calhoun and Bobby McCargo. The Indians next game will be at home against Darden of Opelika, in the homecoming game, the last homecoming game for the Indians ever. East Highland is now 5 and 0 for the year.

Final Statistics

	East Highland	Westside
First downs	16	8
Yards Rushing	272	68
Yards Passing	39	47
Total yards	313	115

The Daily Home
Time out for Sports
Dan Rutledge

Keep your fingers crossed- It's beginning to look like Talladega County or at least the surrounding area has a good chance of getting a team into the grid playoffs this year. East Highland, Shelby County, Childersburg and Sylacauga all have a good chance at this point in the season. East Highland is considered to have a good shot. The Indians are 5 and 0 ranked 18th this week and are one of only 7, 2A school that can reach 80 points if they go undefeated. Childersburg moved up to number 14 in 3A rankings. Coach John Cox's Tigers have been tied once but can still finish with 75 points if they win the rest. From the head man of the AHSAA himself, Bubba Scott gave the opinion yesterday that Childersburg has a real good shot at post season play. There are 8 teams left in class 3A that can. The maximum 80 points and 4 of these squared off against each other Friday. Shelby County can get only 64 points with and opponents either Shelby County or Childersburg chances will be greatly lessened after Friday when they play at the Tigers homecoming. The Tigers don't have an easy road either if they get by the Tigers coming October 24 is 3rd ranked Walter Wellborn. Sylacauga still has a good chance. The Aggies were beaten 21 to 0 by Childersburg earlier this season but can get 70 points with a 9 and 1 finish. Last season two 9 and 1 teams and one 8-1-1 team made it to the playoffs. The 49 to 2 victory last week over Talladega as evidence it seems like Tom Calvin's team is really rolling.

Note- You'll notice that in this weeks poll from the state, Childersburg Tigers predominantly white, moved ahead of the undefeated and untied Indians of East Highland in playoff position in the polls. Inner city counterpart

Closing the Show

Sylacauga the once beaten Aggies, are also gaining momentum with Bubba Scott and his pollsters. It was pointed out that the Indians because of their strength of schedule where they played 6 opponents larger than themselves could gain the maximum 80 points by going undefeated. We will see in future weeks.

INDIANS TAKE SIXTH WIN OF SEASON

The Indians were getting ready to play their last homecoming game ever in Sylacauga's Legion Stadium against ole opponent 4A Darden of Opelika. They had just watched the best little band in the land parade up Broadway in downtown Sylacauga for the last time. And what a parade it had been for the Indians fans. Now it was on to the game where at halftime Rhonda Player would be named or should I say crowned as the last beautiful young lady to be crowned as homecoming queen for the Indians.

The East Highland High School Indians added win number 6 to their 1969 record by defeating Darden High School of Opelika. The Indians are currently untied, undefeated and ranked number 11 in state 2A class. This win should move the Indians into the top ten. A step or two closer to the

Closing the Show

top. Before the game Coach Scissum worried that his Indians might become to lackadaisical which would eventually lead to a defeat. Saturday night was always the Indians realized the job at hand and proceeded to win. To start the game the Indians won the toss and elected to receive. The Panther's kicker Clifford Bowen kicked to the Indians 9 were Lightning took it. Bad mistake for Darden who should have learned something from scouting Indian films, don't kick the ball to number 40, Lightning Threatt. But, lo and behold they did and Lightning promptly struck as he took it back 91 yards for a touch down and made the home as well as visiting spectators come to their feet and stand up once again. Terry Bledsoe ran in the pat, and with the game just 18 seconds old the Indians led 8 to 0. The Indians kicked off to the panthers and the receiver was stuffed at their own 17. Then on their first offensive play, a Panther back was hit hard and fumbled as Cooney Russell recovered it on the Panther's 14. Darden just found out that for a running back playing against East Highlands vaulted defense trying to run no where to hide. Three plays later and Threatt was in the end zone again on a 2 yard drive. Field general Jay Grimmett added the pat and with 8:48 remaining in the 1st quarter the Indians led Opelika 16 to 0, Cooney Russell kicked to the Panthers offense then moved the chains for one 1st down before the big blue 11 shut them down. Panther punter James Driver booted the ball to the Indians 44, the Darden Defense then rose up and held the Indians offense in check forcing the 1st punt of the night for the Indians. Prince Albert Young boomed the ball 45 yards to the Panther's 5. Displaying his usual pinpoint accuracy, the Panther offense was running into a big blue wall and could not move the chains this time and was again forced to punt. They punted to their 25. The quarter ended with the score East Highland 16, Darden of Opelika 0. On the second play of the 2nd quarter, little Terry Bledsoe went around his left end and hit pay dirt from 23 yards out. Grimmett threw to Beattie McKinney for the pat. With 11:54 left in the half, the Indians were in control of this final homecoming game 24 to 0 to the delight of the partisan home crowd. Seeing that their ground game was founded by the Indians defense, the Panthers decided to go to the air. PA Young intercepted the aerial and returned it 29 yards to the enemy 26. A penalty however put the ball on the 38. On the next play, Albert Young to Sylvester McKinney as they swapped roles with McKinney on the receiving end, this time for 38 yards and the touchdown. Billy Robuck Smith added the pat and with 9:04 left in the half, the Indians were making a laugher out of the homecoming game leading 32 to 0 over 4A Darden. After receiving the kickoff the Panthers again went to the air. Wrong answer again as this time little Terry Bledsoe intercepted a pass and scampered it 34 yards to the Panthers 9. At this point in the game I am sure Opelika was hoping to just get halftime without East Highland scoring anymore points on them. An eagle eyed official perhaps having mercy on Darden called a penalty and they got the ball back with a 1st down. The panthers then put a drive together which stalled at the Indians 46. James Driver punted to the Indians 16. Then Opelika's defense stiffened and held the mighty Indians at the 20. On Opelika's 1st offensive series a running back was bucked by Ly Project Foster, Indian linebacker as the other linebacker Aaron Moon, always Johnny on the Spot when it comes to turnovers recovered it. On the next play, Gill Weechie McKinney, sophomore quarterback in for Jay Grimmett, threw a bomb for 82 yards which landed in the sure hands of PA Young for a touchdown. The play thrilled the Indian fans and shocked the Panther's secondary. Gill threw to his big brother Sylvester for the pat and at halftime the Indians led in their homecoming game 40 to 0. The halftime show was a thing of beauty as usual by the best little band in the land under the direction of Mr. Larkins. As the second half started, the Indians kicked off to the Panthers but again the Panthers found no offense against the Indians 11 and punted. Greg Foots Holtzclaw returned it 13 yards to the panther 40. Once again a penalty moved it back to the Indians' 40. But no matter because Gill Weechie McKinney once again led his team toward pay dirt. He later scored on a 7 yard quarterback keeper. Lyn Project Foster added the pat and with 6:48 left in the 3rd quarter. The Indians let 48 to 0, as the Indians went on defense. The Panthers were still canceled on offense and had to punt. The Panthers punter driver punted to the Indians 34. The Indians then started another drive. The quarter ended though with the Indians up 48 to 0 over Darden. Billy Robuck Smith scored the final Indian touchdown of the last homecoming night in the 4th period on an 8 yard run. The pat failed and the Indians led 54 to 0 in their last game ever with Opelika. Terry Bledsoe intercepted another stray Panther pass and returned it 32 yards for a touchdown. Lo and behold the merciful eye of an official wiped this score out. Darden got the ball back but to no avail. Clifford Dowdell fumbled after a big hit from the Indian youngsters playing in mop up time and the Indians recovered it on the 40. The Indians then drove deep into Panther territory and were threatening for another td, but the clock ran out. The Indians had won their last homecoming game ever as the clock struck zeroes 54 to 0 over Darden of Opelika. Bright spots in the scoring department were: Lightning Threatt, Terry Bledsoe, Billy Smith, Jay Grimmett, Gill McKinney, Sylvester McKinney and Prince Albert Young. The 1st defense saw only limited action. A little sophomore Wilber Wilson caught Coach Scissums' eye as he made 5 individual tackles in the final quarter.

Montgomery – Early Word from Montgomery
The Daily Home

A talk with Bubba Scott, President of the Alabama High School Athletic Association, Thursday morning revealed that Talladega County almost has 3 teams in the top 10 in their respective classes. Scott said in the new rankings which were released that Childersburg is ranked 11th and Sylacauga 13th in class 3A. East Highland is ranked 12th in class 2A. Childersburg came up 3 places from 14th with its 32 to 0 pounding of Shelby County. Sylacauga made the biggest jump from 25th last week to 13th this week after its 45 to 14 win over Alex City. East Highland moved up to 12th from 18th by blasting 3A Westside of Talladega 46 to 0. Scott said all 3 had a good chance if they keep winning. East Highland has to be figured to have a slight edge on the other two. If the Indians of Coach Haywood Scissum can amass the 80 points for going undefeated. John Cox's Childersburg Tigers go if they can get to 75 points and Tom Calvin's Sylacauga Aggies have a possible 70 points.

Note- The two white schools are gaining more momentum with Scott and his pollsters than the undefeated black school East Highland despite their impressive wins. East Highland was the only school in the county predicted to have a chance for the state championship before the season started. Also, the only one that had finished ranked in the top ten last year in 1968.

Indians with 7th Game of Season Downs TCTS 52 to 0

East Highland Plays Second and 3rd Teams
By Dan Rutledge

Sylacauga- Using second and third stringers for the last three and a half quarters undefeated and untied 6th ranked in class 2A. East Highland crushed county rival Talladega County Central Training School 52 to 0 Thursday night in Sylacauga. For the first time this season county scoring leader Lightning Threatt failed to score a touchdown as he and the other Indian regulars took an early exit to the bench exiting the game with 9:38 left in the TCTS quarter following the Indians 1st score on the 1A Tigers. Junior halfback and second string Greg Holtzclaw seeing unlimited offensive action for the 1st time this season was the offensive star. He scored on runs of 46 and 1 yard. He was the games top rusher finishing with 136 yards on 15 carries. It was Foots' as the Indian players called him, busiest night on offense this year for the Indians. To start the game, Threatt intercepted TC quarterback Gene Elston's pass early in the 1st quarter on the Indians 37. After a 25 yard run by little Terry Bledsoe had put the ball on the Tigers 6. Fullback Billy Robuck Smith ran for the Indians first score. He would not carry the ball again this night. Threatt ran over the two point conversion. At this point the first offensive unit retired for the night. They would not be needed for the second string took over and there was little difference. Fullback Lyn Project Foster got the second score and the pat. Jerry Chic Holtzclaw the bowlegged wonder and cousin to Greg Foots Holtzclaw got the 3rd score. Foster again ran over the pat. Third string halfback Rueben Parks then got into the act as he broke loose for a

Closing the Show

47 yard score his longest run from scrimmage this season. The touchdown came right before halftime to make it Indians 30 TCTS 0. The famous East Highland band, the best little band in the land performed at halftime and put on their usually outstanding show. With the band getting down and the Indian majorettes the prettiest anywhere did their thing delighting the East Highland faithful and the visitors from TC. As the second half begin it was more of the same for the Indians. Greg Foots Holtzclaw got his second of two tds in the 3rd quarter and sophomore defensive end James Blair blocked a punt in the end zone for a touchdown. Linebacker Aaron Moon also blocked a punt. Besides Greg Holtzclaw leading Indian rushers were Rueben Parks with 68 yards in 9 carries and Jerry Holtzclaw with 59 yards in 9 carries. Only one pass was thrown by Indian quarterbacks. From second string QB sophomore Gill Weechie McKinney to second string end Lamar Prater, a sophomore. The Indians rolled up 399 yards on the ground and 10 more passing for a total of 409 yards for the evening. They made 16 first downs. TCTS top performer was Elston who had several good runs on the evening. One for 25 yards that he almost broke for a touchdown. East Highland is now 7 and 0 on the season and is at home next week hosting powerful St. Jude Thursday night. The Pirates, last season's 2A state runner-ups are sporting a 5 and 2 record thus far this season. Losing only to inner city Montgomery rivals and powerhouses Carver and Booker T. Washington ranked 7th in class 4A. Both schools are class 4A and only beat the Pirates by very close scores. The Pirates notable local wins came against Westside of Talladega 17 to 0 and Laurel of Alex City 47 to 0.

Tiger, Indians and Aggies Advance in AHSAA Rankings

Montgomery- All three of Talladega's county teams advanced closer to the top spot in their respective class rating in the latest rankings released by the Alabama High School Athletic Association. Childersburg moved from the number four spot to the three spot in class 3A with the big 31 to 22 win over Wellborn. The tigers are not 6-0 in the year. Sylacauga downed USM Wright of Mobile 40 to 27 and moved from eight to seventh in class 3A. Tom Calvin's Aggies are now 6 and 1 on the year. East Highland rolled over Talladega County Training 52 to 0 to preserve its perfect slate and advance from 9th to 8th in class 2A. With the Alabama High School Football season drawing to a close the standings found Etowah, Russellville, Abbeville and Excel leading in the four classifications. However, the first four spots in each classification become more important each week since those are the teams that will enter into championship playoffs at the end of the regular season. One of the biggest drops came in the 1A classification where powerful Lowndes Academy dropped from 5th to 11th after losing to 4A Lee of Montgomery. The Academy has a record of 73 and 3 over the past several years and has started playing big schools since it has had difficulty scheduling school in its class. The academy rebels are the defending 1A champs and have defeated Columbus Miss already this season. It takes on another big school power Meridian Miss this week.

Mighty Indians Poised
October 30, 1969

St. Jude Here Tonight
By Jerome O'Neal

The game that all of you have been waiting for is finally here. The King Pins of 2A football last year and sporting a fine record this year amidst a number two ranking in the state the St. Jude Pirates are here. The Pirates have hopes of upsetting the blue warriors of East Highland. Now blue warrior denotes only our school color and not our mood. The Indians have looked as though they have awaited this game since it was scheduled. There is a quiet confidence in the eyes of our gallant warriors and I feel that their full fury is about to be unleashed tonight. In the previous 7 games, I have seen Coach Scissum call in his warriors in an attempt to hold down the scoring on out manned opponents. A case in point was the last game played when the only touch down scored by a starter was made by fullback Billy Robuck Smith. I am sure that it must pain Coach Scissum to have to take out the pony backs of Grimmett, Bledsoe, Smith, and Threatt to hold down the score. But that is exactly what he did. The score in the TCTS game mounted to 52 to 0 on the strength of 2 tds by Greg Holtzclaw, 1 by Jerry Chic Holtzclaw and 1 by third team fullback Rueben Parks. 10 points were made by fullback Lyn Foster 6 by starting fullback Billy Smith a two point conversion by Lightning and a 2 point conversion by sub sophomore quarterback Gill Weechie McKinney. A blocked kick was recovered for a touchdown in the end zone by James Player. So there you have it. The score mounted without the Indians starting backfield or offensive line getting into the scoring act. The big blue was restricted to only defense. Tonight though, the Indians will be able to put it all together. The defense will have to play as it played against 4A Oliver of Fairfield and 3A Westside of Talladega. The offense is usually on but must have its best night of the year. So the stage has been set and this should be the biggest game to come to Sylacauga this year for the Indians. The defensive and Beattie McKinney watched them. Big Robert Williams must play inspired ball at tackle as he did against Westside. He must get better play from his running mate at tackle Neil Hart. Linebacker Aaron Moon and Darnell Williams must give more at their positions. Corner back Lyn Foster and strong safety Anthony Walton must defend with enthusiasm. Halfback PA Young and Terry Bledsoe have been steady ball hawks and allowed no completions in their zones this year. Safety Lighting Threatt must be vigilant as ever at his post. Sound like I am coaching? You better believe that I am trying. We can use you too. There is speculation and sneaky suspicion that our backfield maybe the best in Indian school history. It might just be the best backfield that high school fans have ever seen in the state of Alabama. The school spirit is high and the Indians and their fans are motivated because Birmingham morning show radio personality Tall Paul of the number one station in Birmingham WENN 107.7, has been saying this week that the city boys from Montgomery were going to come to Sylacauga and teach the plow boys of East Highland how to play some football. I know this game will be a classic see you there tonight!

Big Game Tonight
By Dan Rutledge

East Highland vs. St. Jude
Thursday, October 30, 1969

Sylacauga- For the second week in a row there is a big game on tap for weekend high school football. Of course, every game is big to the teams playing them. But there are some that are something special. Like last week's Childersburg-Wellborn contest that vaulted winning Childersburg to second place in the 3A football rankings and almost assured them a playoff spot in November. This week's East Highland - St. Jude match is as big to Coach Scissum and his Indians as was the Wellborn game to Coach John Cox and his Tigers. East Highland is currently 7-0-0 and ranked 8th in the 2A state polls and a win over tough St. Jude can go a long way toward a playoff spot for them. St. Jude is 5 and 2 this year but have lost only to 4A powers Montgomery Carver and Booker T. Washington(BTW). BTW is undefeated and seventh in the state in class 4A. St. Jude like East Highland has a habit of winning. In 1967, the Pirates were undefeated. In 1968, they were also undefeated in regular season play ending with an 11 and 1 record and second place in the state in 2A. They lost in the finals to Gordo but downed Clay County of Ashland in the semi's. East Highland has really had no trouble this year in winning 7 games. The closest game was a 36 to 0 win over OS Hill of Munford. Their biggest margin of victory was 68 to 6 over Laurel of Alexander City. And that six points is the only points they have had scored on them all year. The Indian defense led by tackle Robert Williams (270) end Anthony Russell (180) and linebacker Aaron Moon (175) has allowed no points. In fact, no one has been allowed inside of their 10 yard line. The one touchdown scored against them was a loose fumble picked up on the bounce by a Laurel defender and ran 26 yards for a score. The Indians are far and away the highest scoring team in the area averaging 49 points per game. The potent offense is led by halfback Lightning Threatt, fullback Billy Smith, end PA Young and offensive leader quarterback Jay Grimmett. Threatt is the leading scorer in the area having 82 points on the year with 12 touchdowns. Smith is the hardest runner on the team who had rather go through defenders than around them. He has scored 50 points with 8 tds. End PA Young has caught 8 touchdowns for 48 points. Grimmett does not score a lot but throws the passes that let others score. He runs the team very well and is the field general that seldom makes costly mistakes.

This is Jays second year quarterbacking the Indians. Except for the two games they lost, St. Jude has given up no points. No points to anyone in their own class and they have scored 140 points this year. Of common opponents between the two St. Jude downed Westside of Talladega 17 to 0 and Laurel of Alex City 45 to 0. East Highland whipped Westside 46 to 0 and Laurel 68 to 6. The Pirates leading ground gainer is Calvin Leashores. Their leading scorer is fullback Gary Rodgers. Two quarterbacks run the team both youngsters junior Robin Jeeter is known as the passer while sophomore Lester Rodgers likes to run. Two defensive starts for St. Jude were out in the Booker T. Washington game. Which means in the close 15 to 6 loss they could have possibly made a difference for St. Jude. They will both return for East Highland. They are linebacker and team captain Ricky Brown and tackle Eddie Calloway. East highland Assistant Coach Bernadean Showers and Pirates Coach Ostel Hamilton have opposed each other before. Hamilton was the basketball coach at Laurel of Alex City from 1960 and 1965 before going to St. Jude. The Alex City team took the Indian round ballers 4 of the 5 years and showers is hoping for revenge Saturday night. It will be the first meeting for the two teams in football. Coach Scissum reported Wednesday that Smith, Young and Grimmett will be slowed by minor injuries sprained ankles but reported no major ills and said the starters will play. Our spirit is high we know what this game means to us. We want a shot at those playoffs Coach Scissum said.

Closing the Show

THREATT ON MOVE — East Highland's Richard Threatt (15) and Gary Oden (65). Coming up for stop is Jude's Franklin moves for yardage here during Thursday night win over St. Oliver (70), Johnathan Powell (84) and Eddie Calloway (88). Jude of Montgomery. Other Indians in play are Jay Grimmett

Indians Blast St. Jude 70 to 0
October 30, 1969

Sylacauga- The state championship inspired East Highland High School Indians played at least that well last night against St. Jude of Montgomery. St. Jude came to town on luxury buses rolling into Sylacauga with the billing as the first real test for the Indians. I have never seen such a flamboyant team in my life. As they took the field, the Pirates looked like a small college team compared to our Indians. They were decked out in all white uniforms and each player had capes over their shoulder pads. They were a sight to behold. Many people expected this game to be a classic and it was for Indians fans. It was close for only one quarter. After scoring 8 points in the 1st quarter the Indian unleashed its power and exploded for 30 unanswered points in the second quarter. Never had I seen such an offensive show in high school ball as I was witnessing tonight in Sylacauga. This score stunned everybody at the game Indian fans and Pirates too. For this was the St. Jude team that had played for the 2A state title just months ago and lost a close battle to fellow Montgomery School and 4A power house Booker T. Washington 15 to 6. St. Jude was supposed to be as fine a team as East Highland. But they had just given up more points to the Indians 38 in one quarter than they had in six previous games altogether. I think the scoring barrage by the Indians stunned the Pirates like a boxer getting stunned by a good power shot, Jay Grimmett, the little general who has played hampered by injuries most of the year had his biggest night. As he ran for 2 scores and threw for another, he completed

8 of 12 passes for 160 yards and 2 scores. He also picked off 4 interceptions from his defensive back position. Richard Lightning Threatt had his biggest night point wise. He rushed 19 times for 149 yards and 3 touch downs. He also made 5 two-point conversions for a total of 28 points on the night. He now has 110 points for the season. To start the game the Indians received the opening kickoff and Lightning almost broke it but was pulled down at the Indians 48. Then the Indians were unable to get a first down and PA Young punted 50 yards to the end zone. Who knew that this would be the high light of the night for the Pirates stopping the Indians on their first drive. The Indian defense took the field and did just fine as the Pirates also were unable to move the chains and punted. St. Jude punter Williams kicked the ball to the Indians 49. On the Indians 3rd play of the drive, Pirate James Brown, linebacker, intercepted Indians quarterback Jay Grimmett's pass at the St. Jude 49. On the Pirates offensive play, Indian linebacker Aaron Moon recovered a Pirate's fumble at the Indians 47 yard line. Grimmett then went to work passing the ball 21 yards to Sylvester Beattie McKinney to the Pirates 28. Then Lightning capped the drive with a 1 yard drive for the score the initial one for the Indians tonight. There would be more to come. The Indians were playing like a team that was hungry for a playoff berth. Jay Grimmett ran the two point conversion in and with 3 minutes and 26 seconds remaining in the first quarter the Indians led the Pirates 8 to 0. The Indians kicked off and St. Jude's Jeeter returned the kickoff to the Pirates 29. PA Young then intercepted a Pirate aerial and returned it 7 yards to the Pirates 30. When the quarter ended, the Indians were knocking on the door at the Pirates end zone again. On the second play of the 2nd quarter fullback Lyn Foster scored on a 1 yard drive. Threatt ran in the two point conversion. With 11 minutes and 15 seconds remaining in the half. The Indians let St. Jude 16 to nill. On the Indian kickoff the Pirates got the ball but could not move against the Indians stout defense. This surely shocked the Pirates of Montgomery because they had been able to move the ball against every team they played this year including 4A teams Carver of Montgomery and powerhouse 4A team, Booker T. Washington also of Montgomery. But, as Joe Frazier once said to Muhammed Ali in their first bout, you ain't fighting Sonny Liston tonight you're fighting Joe Frazier. The Pirates likewise, found out they were playing the Indians tonight and not the two aforementioned teams. A bad punt by the Pirates went out of bounds at their own 16. Lightning later scored on a 1 yard drive. Grimmett threw to Beattie McKinney for the two point conversion with 8 minutes and 1 sec remaining in the half the Indians now led 24 to 0 and were pitching a shut-out on one of Montgomery's finest football teams. Bad luck seemed to be the calling card for the Pirates tonight as on their next possession, Anthony Cooney Russell

Closing the Show

recovered a Pirate's fumble at the St. Jude 22. Turnovers will kill a team as if the Indians needed any help, the Pirates were giving graciously to their hosts. But an Indian penalty moved the ball back to the 46. Then the Indians treated the hometown fans with the famous end reverse pass play when end Sylvester Beattie McKinney threw to other end PA Young for a touchdown. PA, while not the fastest Indian, always seemed to break open 10 yards behind secondaries in spite of them seeing this play on Indian films. Maybe it was the respect that the Indians powerful running game demanded that helped. But one thing for sure Prince Albert was going to catch it. The point after failed for the first time tonight, nobody's perfect not even the Indians tonight. But with 6 minutes still remaining in the half the Indians now led the Pirates 30 to 0. If the Indians were trying impress the pollsters surely this game tonight against such a powerful and respected foe would do the trick surely? After the Indians kickoff the Pirates again failed to move the chains and the hometown Indian fans could sense that the Indians were in control of this game only half way through it. But we certainly expected a tougher battle than this from the 2A state runner-up from a year ago. As the Pirates again punted, it looked like St. Jude was going to wear their punters leg out before the game was over tonight. He punted to the Indian 9 yard line, East Highland's worst field position of the young night. Not to worry. The Indians started marching to pay dirt. Moving the chains behind field General Jay Grimmett as he threw for 17 yards to PA Young. Then Lightning broke loose for a 33 yard gallop to the Pirates 16 yard line. A penalty moved it back to the 24. Grimmett then pulled a rabbit out of his hat as Coach Scissum the sly devil pulled out one of his old Indian Plays from deep in his play book as Grimmett passed 23 yards to Cooney Russell on a tackle eligible play. Grimmett then capped the 91 yard drive with a 1 yard plunge of his own. Threatt added the two point conversion and at halftime, the fans of East Highlands and St. Jude's were shell shocked as the Indians led the Pirates 38 to 0. 38 unanswered points on the team that finished second in the state in 2A last year. The halftime of this highly anticipated match up of titans was very subdued for the Indians fans but across the way, the St. Jude fans were very quiet, never had they witnessed their team being man handled by a rival not even in the state championship game last year to Gordo where they lost but 27 to 6. Not even to inner city rival Booker T. Washington or Carver. St. Jude came into this game expecting to win but now it looked like they were trying to survive if the Pirates didn't come up with something after halftime it was going to be a long quiet 63 mile bus ride down highway 231 south for the Pirates. As the fine East Highland Indians band , the best little band in the land with the prettiest majorettes with the prettiest legs finished performing their fine half time show the Indians made their way along with St. Jude out of the dressing room. If St. Jude thought that the Indians were not going to play with the same fire in the second half leading 38 to 0, they were wrong. The Indians kicked off to the Pirates to start the second half. On their first offensive play, linebacker Aaron Moon, intercepted a pass at the Pirates 41. Three plays later Lightning scored on a beautiful 34 yard sprint. Terry Cat Quick Bledsoe ran in the two point conversion. With 9 minutes and 52 seconds remaining in the 3rd quarter, the Indians led in a romp 46 to 0 over St. Jude. If this was a prize fight the referee would certainly stop it as the Pirates were on the ropes getting hit by power shot after power shot by the Indians of Sylacauga. The Pirates threatened to score once finally when quarterback Robert Geeter connected with Louis Peoples to the Indians 11 yard line. Surely, the powerful 2A Montgomery school would now be able to do what no team had done on the Indians defense al year and scored in the red zone a touchdown, a field goal, or something. But, yet again this threat was foiled when PA Young intercepted the ball that was intended for a pirate receiver in the end zone to end the scoring attempt. The ball was brought out to the 20 yard line. I guess the Pirates were a good team after all. Because thy had driven the ball in making it to the Indians 11 further than any team had been able to do all season against the Indians vaulted 11. We Indian fans thought that our perfect record of not giving up an offensive touchdown or field goal was in jeopardy. But as great teams always do the Indians defense rose to the occasion. Grimmett then connected with Prince Albert Young for 46 yards and another score as the all world Indian receiver electrified the crowd with a one handed circus catch then out ran the Pirates defenders. The play left the crowd going oooh! in amazement at the effort. Young routinely pulled off this act. I now began to sense that St. Jude was ready for their nightmare on broadway for them to be over. Their one and only visit to the marble city was certainly not working out as a pleasant one for them. All the fire that they came up here with was dying out. And some of their fans were even starting to head for the exits. Ones that were staying were the mamas and daddy's because there was certainly no joy in this game for the Pirate faithful. But the Pirates unlike the Indians would live to fight another day in the future. Because they were a private catholic school like Holy Family in Birmingham, they were not being closed down next year. The Indians kicked off again and again the Pirated offense was stuck in neutral by the Indian defense. They punted again. The Indians got the ball on the Pirates 33 and Billy Smith scored on a 4 yard drive. Threatt added the pat and at the end of 3 quarters, the Indians led 62 to 0. Early in the 4th quarter the Pirates put together a drive. However, this stalled and they punted again. To the Indian 29. Grimmett then threw another tackle eligible pass this time to big Robert Williams who rumbled 28 yards to the Pirates 8 yard line. The play seemed to delight the Indian fans among the hand slapping and cheers because they appreciated the fact that big Robert usually opened holes not caught passes. The game had long ago been decided except the final score. And Indian fans were wondering just how much the Indians would score on St. Jude. Grimmett later scored on a 2 yard keeper. He threw to Anthony Walton for the pat. With 6 minutes still remaining in the game the Indians led 70 to 0. The white fans that were in the stands including some well known local coaches had to be very impressed at this final edition of Haywood Scissum Indians. I knew some of them came expecting to see the Indians tested but surely they didn't expect to see the Indians lay 70 points on such a respected. When the Pirates got the ball and realized that time was short in the game. They went to the air. But Young grabbed his 3rd pick of the night and returned it 6 yards to the Pirate 39. The reserves team then fumbled the ball on the Pirates 24. Then Pirates quarterback Geeter desperately threw the ball into the waiting hands of Prince Albert Young who returned it 4 yards to the Indians 47. The Indian reserves Threatt to score again but the clock mercifully ran out for the Pirate ending their nightmare on Broadway as the Indians won 70 to 0. Before the game senior Indian quarterback Jay Grimmett had said the difference between a good team and a great team is that a great team wins the big game. We are a great team and this was a big game. The Indians are a great team and they won.

Final Statistics

	Indians	Pirates
First downs	25	2
Tds Rushing	327	1
Yd Passing	215	80
Total yards	542	86
Yds Penalized	65	36
fumbles lost	1	3

Timeout for Sports
By Dan Rutledge

Talladega County's playoff hopefuls kept rolling along this weekend with East Highland, Childersburg, and Sylacauga all posting big victories over tough opponents. East Highland win must be called the most impressive as they literally slaughtered St. Jude of Montgomery 70 to 0. Now St. Jude is not just any school. The Pirates from the capital city were last years state 2A runner-ups. They have had back to back undefeated seasons were they went 10 and 0. 1967 and 1968. They lost to Gordo in the state championship game last year in 1968 after downing Clay County of Ashland in the first round? They lost in the championship game to Gordo 27 to 6 and finished the 68 season 11 and 1. Scouts from numerous colleges were on Auburn and Kentucky. They got an eyeful as the Indians put on quite a show. Tommy Tollison, Alabama Assistant Coach and Talladega alumni said after the game that he came to see and scout number 40, Lightning Threatt and number 84 Sylvester McKinney. But he said after the game he added number 83 to his list number 83 is senior Prince Albert Young. Young really gave the scouts a performance while putting on quite a show. Thursday night Young caught 5 passes for 147 yards and 2 tds. Three of his catches were one handed circus catches that left the crowd going ooh! in amazement. As good as his offensive out put was, PA's defensive showing was even better. As a defensive halfback he stole four passes from the Pirates one and stopped a Pirate's touchdown in the end zone to preserve the shut out.

Childersburg and Aggies Rated 3–4 in State

Montgomery- Etowah and Russellville continued to hold on to 1st place ratings in their Alabama prep divisions Wednesday. While Susan Moore and Hicks memorial shoved Abbeville and excel over in the other two. In the class 3A ratings Russellville was followed by Bibb County, Childersburg and Sylacauga which jumped to 4th from the 7th spot. At the end of the regular season the top four teams in each class will enter state playoff championship contention.

Note- At this point Bubba Scott and his associates have all but guaranteed the two white county schools Childersburg and Sylacauga playoff spots ranking them 3 and 4 in class 3A. All they have to do is win out and the pressure has been taken off of Sylacauga at this point by moving them from 7th to 4th. The Indians on the other hand are being toyed with emotionally by the state holding them at number six even after they destroyed last years state 2A runner ups St. Jude of Montgomery 70 to 0. Neither Childersburg nor Sylacauga had a win on their schedule this impressive over a contending state championship team. It's becoming apparent at this time that Scott and his associates have no intention of letting Coach Scissum and his powerful Indians in on matter how impressive they are on the field.

Here are the rankings with two weeks left in the season in 1969.

Tigers Indians and Aggies Advance in AHSAA Ratings

Montgomery- All three of Talladega County's teams advanced closer to the top spot in their respective class rankings in the latest rankings released by the Alabama High School Athletic Association. Childersburg moved from the number 4 to number 3 spot in 3A with the big 31 to 22 win over Walter Wellborn. The Tigers are 6-0-1 on the season. Sylacauga downed Ums Wright of Mobile 40 to 27 and moved from 8th 7th in 3A. Tom Calvin's Aggies are now 6 and 1 on the year. East Highland rolled over Talladega County Training School 52 to 0 to preserve its perfect slate and advance from 9th to 8th in the 2A standings found Etowah, Russellville, Abbeville and Excel leading in the four classes. However, the top 4 spots in each classification become more important each week since those are the teams that will enter championship play off contention at the end of the season.

Note- You will notice that now late in the season, both white schools Childersburg and Sylacauga have surpassed the Indians in the rankings. At this point Childersburg is safe in 3rd place in the 3A rankings and only have to win out to make it in. Sylacauga on the other hand is in 7th place and has positioned itself to move up with some help. The Indians can amass the maximum 80 points with a perfect season all they need is one more win.

CHILDERSBURG AND AGGIES RATED 3 AND 4 IN STATE

Montgomery - Etowah and Russellville continued to hold first place ratings in their Alabama prep divisions Wednesday while Susan Moore and Hicks memorial shoved Abbeville and Excel over in the other two. The Alabama High School Athletic Association standings showed Huntsville pulled up behind Etowah in the class 4A ranking pushing Berry down to number three. Followed by Robert E. Lee of Montgomery. In class 3A rankings Russellville was followed by Bibb County, Childersburg and Sylacauga which jumped to 4th from the 7th spot. Susan Moore pulled ahead of Abbeville which had an open date. In the class 2A standings with Aliceville and Addison up from the 6th spot rounding out the top four. At the end of the regular season the top four teams in each classification will enter state championship playoff contention.

Following are the top ten teams in each class

1. Etowah 8-0-0
2. Huntsville 8-0-0
3. Berry 8-0-0
4. Robert E. Lee 9-0-0
5. Decatur 8-0-0
6. B.T. Washington 8-0-0
7. Emma Samson 8-1-0
8. Banks 7-0-0
9. Jeff Davis 8-1-0
10. Woodlawn 7-0-0

Class 3A
1. Russellville 8-0-0
2. Bibb County 9-0-0
3. Childersburg 7-0-1
4. Sylacauga 7-1-0
5. Wellborn 7-1-0
6. Pisgah 7-0-1
7. Lawrence County 6-1-1
8. Muscle Shoals 7-2-0
9. Saks 7-1-0
10. Leeds 8-1-0

Class 2A
1. Susan Moore 9-0-0
2. Abberville 8-0-0
3. Aliceville 8-0-0
4. Addison 8-0-0
5. TR Miller 7-0-0
6. East Highland 8-0-0

The Rankings in Week Number Eight of the Season 1969

Class 4A
1. Etowah 9-0-0
2. Huntsville 8-0-0
3. Berry 8-0-0
4. Robert E. Lee 9-0-0
5. Decatur 8-0-0
6. B.T Washington 8-0-0
7. Emma Samson 8-1-0
8. Banks 7-0-0
9. Jeff Davis 8-0-0
10. Woodlawn 7-0-0

Class 3A
1. Russellville 8-0-0
2. Bibb County 9-0-0
3. Childersburg 7-0-1
4. Sylacauga 7-1-0

5. Wellborn 7-1-0
6. Pisgah 7-0-1
7. Lawrence County 6-1-1
8. Muscle Shoals 7-2-0
9. Saks 7-1-0
10. Leeds 8-1-0

Class 2A
1. Susan Moore 9-0-0
2. Abbeville 8-0-0
3. Aliceville 8-0-0
4. Addison 8-0-0
5. TR Miller 7-0-0
6. East Highland 8-0-0
7. Oneonta 7-1-0
8. Collinsville 8-0-1
9. Washington County 8-0-0
10. Holtville 9-0-0

Looking at these rankings class 2A to 4A, I can only imagine what a great tournament it would have been if the state would have let the top 10 teams duke it out in each class in a playoff for the state championships. They went to an 8 team format the very next year any way. But, how times have changed now. With the state in the 2000's allowing teams in the playoff that don't belong there. Example Talladega High School had a 1 and 7 overall record in 2008 going into their last region game in class 5A region 4. A region that also included rival Sylacauga Aggies who had a 7 and 3 record but lost to Talladega in a region game where the Tigers had an overall region record of 1 and 4. This article ran in the Talladega Daily Home Newspaper written by sports editor Heather Baggett explains what I am talking about. It's been quite a few years since the Talladega Tigers had hope of making the playoffs when week 9 of football rolled around. But that's the position the Tigers find themselves in, Baggett wrote, as they traveled to Birmingham to face John Carroll tonight. A win over John Carroll and some help from other teams would put the tigers in the playoffs for the first time since 1995. The kids have been real excited Talladega Head Coach Bill Granger said Thursday. They've done the best that they could this season. Imagine that a coach wins one game and he says they have done very good. Baggett went on to write in her article here at the very end we have a chance to make the playoffs and they are real excited about that Granger said. A 1 and 7 record overall and 1 and

Michael Catfish Smith

4 in the region and they were excited about possibly entering a tournament that they had no chance of winning. The state of Alabama now rewards mediocrity. The Talladega team did not make the playoffs in 2008 but the state does let many weak teams into the field that once only the elite were a part of. The Indians certainly were ahead of their time, I wonder sometimes how many state championships Coach Scissum and his Indians would have won under this present system. One can only wonder!

East Highland Close Childersburg Sylacauga Keep Playoff Positions

Montgomery- Childersburg continued to hold on to 3rd place and Sylacauga 4th place in the state 3A rankings according to ratings issued by the Alabama High School Association Tuesday. East Highland also moved up to 5th place from 6th in this weeks rankings in class 2A. In 2A, Susan Moore has completed its season with a perfect 10 and 0 season. It is followed by Abbeville, TR Miller and Aliceville.

Note- You will notice in this poll announcement that TR Miller the team that would eventually win the state class 2A championship in 1969, their schools first in history has slipped or been skipped up to number 4 in the state rankings. While the Indians move up to 5th shy of the magical number 4. You will also notice that East Highland and Booker T. Washington the two highest ranking black schools in the polls are securely locked out of the playoffs in their respective classes of 4A and 2A in the 6th and 5th positions in their respective classes. No, I am not trying to imply the state was racist in its positioning of the two powerhouse black schools in this poll but the facts speak for themselves. With both schools being shut down next year in integration they are both destined to be shut out of the playoffs. If the state hadn't been so stiff hearted and made this playoff, the top 8 teams among them knew they were already going to make next year in 1970 the Indians and Booker T. Washington would have been able to compete for a state championship. As it is the Childersburg Tigers lost to rival Talladega late in the season and got knocked out of the state playoffs. As for Sylacauga they won their first and only state championship on the

Michael Catfish Smith

field in 69, defeating number one ranked Russellville. But forty years later they haven't won another.

Final Game, The Calhoun County Game

Pre Game

As the Indians players sat in the dressing room that they called home in Legion Stadium being perhaps the finest single season team that Coach Scissum had ever assembled. There was a touch of sadness in the air as Coach Scissum surveyed the faces of his troops perhaps for the last time as Indian players. As he looked around the room at his final edition of Indians who had enjoyed the highest scoring season in school history, he could see the look of uncertainty on their faces. Not about the opponent they were about to face, but an opponent that they could not whip on the playing field. The one with the power to say whether they go to the playoffs or stay home. Whether they had done enough on the field to earn enough votes to move into the top 4 ranked teams in the state to qualify for the class 2A football playoffs. It had been quite a ride for Coach Scissum and his Indians in 1969. Along the way, they had played and destroyed 2 - 4A teams. Dominated 4 -3A schools, humbled 2 - 2A schools and toyed with 1 - 1A school while smashing scoring records in the county, Sylacauga and the state in class 2A. Some which probably still stand today in Sylacauga and Talladega county. As he looked at quarterback Jay Grimmett, his last field general and tackle Anthony Cooney Russell perhaps his most versatile player end PA Young the best receiver to ever wear the blue white and red fullback Billy Robuck Smith and tailback Richard Lightning Threatt and the other seniors in this marvelous class of 1970 that were perhaps getting ready to play their last game ever. He wondered if they had done enough or was this outstanding season for the record books about to come to an end? Inside of his heart, I Believe

Coach Scissum knew that they were not going to let his team in. Not with the high scoring touch down denying defense playing Indian team he had. This was not some St. Jude team that had played Clay County and Gordo in 1968. These were the East Highland High School Indians that routinely beat up on 4A and 3A schools. And if the Indians were allowed two more games they would certainly shatter the state scoring record while averaging 55 points a game. I can only image what they would have done in the states five game playoff format of today. But Coach Scissum held out slight hope that one of the teams ranked in front of them might slip up and lose. If so the Indians might face TR Miller of Brewton themselves a powerhouse in the making from the southern part of the state. Would this possibly be the Indians swann song? Would this be the last time that anybody would pull the Indians blue and white jerseys over their shoulder pads and play a game? Coach Scissum in addressing his team before the game told them that he was proud of them and that they had represented themselves, the school, the community and the city well as they had done all they could on the field. It was now out of their hands albeit the task at hand of defeating the Calhoun County of Hobson City team. In front of them one last time. It was left up to other to decide their fate. If this was to be the last game ever for the Indians at Legion they were prepared to close the show with a bang. The love that these players shared for one another would become even more evident as the years would past by from decade to decade. The hard practices of being denied water breaks until the end of practice. The intense hard hitting in the hot Alabama sun with humidity so thick you could cut it with a knife. The hero treatment they received from little kids in the community. The respect they garnered from classmates and foes alike. The envy they got from rival schools and people that wished they had played for Coach Scissum and the Indians. They were family. East highland High School football players. The best that Sylacauga had to offer. A proud fraternity of people that very few would ever be able to claim to be. A Haywood Scissum player. A winner on the field and in life. The lessons learned by these young men from Coach Scissum would teach them how to be men. Good husbands good citizens and good fathers. Molded from boys to men to become future leaders in this community and communities all over America. As these Indians sat in this locker room perhaps for the last time that only housed the Indians when they came down town to play. This locker room that many, many, many times had came in from the field of battle jubilant as they were filled with the joy that only the thrill of victory that a victorious locker room always brought after annihilating another opponent. A locker room that also had known the pain and agony of defeat amidst the disappointment of losing a rare home game to the likes of Cobb or Booker T. Washington in games that the Indians were oh so close to winning but let slip away in the last minute. The locker room where Coach Scissum had fired up and motivated many Indian players with pep talks before games and at halftime when they were not playing up to his standards. This locker room would soon be vacant for all eternity. They sat in this locker room for the last time getting ready to face a decent Calhoun County team with a winning 6 and 3 record. But certainly no match for the Indians. This Calhoun County team had beaten Westside of Talladega but lost to old Indian rival Cobb. Was about to face the highest scoring team in East Highland High School history with the stingiest defense. As the Indians got ready to take the field for the last time. The Legion Stadium crowd that were about to witness this historic event rose to its feet as supreme drummer Monkey Wrench Corbin led the Indians out of the tunnel for the last time. The crowd was loud and excited as they trotted onto the field perhaps for one last curtain call. Looking like gladiators decked out in white helmets navy blue jerseys and white pants the Indians looked ready for battle one last time. Certain of victory but by how much. Knowing in their minds and their fans minds that not only were they the best in Sylacauga and Talladega County. But they were the best in the state! Lets play some football.

Lightning Strikes for the Last Time East Highland end Season with 82 to 0 Blast of CCTS

Sylacauga- The East Highland High School Indians finished a near perfect season here Thursday night by blasting Calhoun County of Hobson City 82 to 0. It was an offensive show and explosion that the city of Sylacauga had never seen and probably won't for many many years to come. The Indians close out their high scoring show in Sylacauga by finishing the year with a near perfect record going in 9-0-0. The season was near perfect for a number of reasons. One being they gave up a 6 point touch down scored on their offense to Laurel of Alex City. And number two reason it now looks like the Indians will miss the state playoffs in spite of earning the maximum amount of 80 points accumulated in the states controversial point system. Barring a defeat by one of the teams ranked ahead of them this is indeed the last game they will ever play on the grass field of Legion Stadium. According to Coach Scissum himself the season was near perfect because of the 6 points scored on them by Laurel. To start the game the East Highland attack worked so smoothly Thursday night almost methodically against the 3A Calhoun County visitors. The Indians never punted in the game giving Price Albert young the night off in his final game as the Indians punter. The Indians high powered offense never had a drive stopped. Each time they had possession of the ball they scored in an amazing display of offense that the city of Sylacauga had never witnessed before. The only time they didn't score at the end of the second quarter was when a pass to Sylvester Beattie McKinney slipped off of his finger tips in the end zone as time ran out in the quarter. Senior scat back Richard Lightning Threatt striking for the last time scored 5 touchdowns and ran in two 2 point conversions. He amassed a total of 34 points for the night.

Lightning's performance was the best single game performance in the county for the season and the best the fan in Sylacauga saw all year. It over shadowed Lincoln's David Hendrix show against Wedowee 4 weeks ago by 4 points. It also widened Threatt's already large lead in the area scoring race. Threatt now has a total of 144 points scored for the season. Several college scouts were on hand to view the Indians performance while they closed out the show in Sylacauga. Calls concerning Threatt have come from as far away as Michigan and from every school in the state of Alabama. The game was really no contest as the Indians kicked off and 3 plays later recovered a Calhoun fumbles on the Tigers 1 yard line. The quarterback Jay Grimmett starting in his last game under center for the Indians, scored on a 1 yard sneak over right tackle. Halfback Terry Bledsoe ran in the pat. With 2:48 left in the 1st quarter, East Highland made it 16 to 0 with Lightning scoring on a 6 yard run. The score capped a 6 play 47 yard drive. Grimmett passes to Bledsoe for the 2 point conversion. The Indians unstoppable scoring machine mowed through Calhoun County's defense like a John Deere Tractor through high grass as they scored 3 more touchdowns in the second quarter to take a 36 to 0 halftime lead. Too bad for Calhoun County that they had to be the last school the Indians dropped the hammer down on. It didn't matter that they were a decent 3A schools with a decent record because they were receiving the full brunt of East Highland's awesome power amidst the wrath they felt of knowing they were not going to be let in the playoffs. But if the Indians were trying to send a message to those who left them out of the playoffs then what a message it was. As the Indians band the best little band in the land or the baddest little band in the land, Indian fans like to say, performed in front of the home crowd for the last time ever. What a show it was with them dropping their smooth Motown sound with the Indian majorettes performing immaculately while flashing pretty smiles. As they exited the field for the last time under the directions of Mr. Larkins it really then dawned on me that I had seen them perform for the last time as a unit. Some of the underclassmen's would never wear a band uniform ever again in high school. As the second half started Lightning got 2 more touchdowns as the Indians added 3 more as a team. By this time the Calhoun County fans knew that this was little more than an exhibition of East highlands power against the out manned rival from Calhoun County. This same Calhoun team had been beaten 50 to 0 by old Indian rival Cobb Avenue early in the season. Maybe the Indians were sending a message albeit it a late season one to Cobb that the 4A Anniston school did the right thing by dropping them this year. Lightning scored on a 1 yard drive and on a 7 yard pass from quarterback Jay Grimmett. Billy Smith ran in the pat. In the 4th and mercifully final quarter for Calhoun, the Indians added 4 long distance touchdowns. As the Indians continued to close the show in football by giving the fans something that they would not soon forget. Second team fullback Lyn Project Foster left his mark by breaking a 62 yard run for a touchdown. Little Terry Cat Quick Bledsoe broke his longest run from scrimmage ever for the Indians with a 82 yard jaunt. Lightning caught a 45 yard bomb from Grimmett. PA executed the famous Indians end reverse pass play to the other end Sylvester Beattie McKinney on a beautiful 83 yard bomb for a score that brought the Indians faithful to their feet one more time. If you know of two better ends anywhere they must be playing pro football. The number 83 to 84 and 84 to 83 combination the like of would never be seen in the city of Sylacauga ever again. The 2 point conversion after the scores were run in by Lightning, Terry Bledsoe, Anthony Walton who perhaps was not playing in his last high school game being a junior he would go on next year and play for the Sylacauga Aggies in the state championship game that the Aggies lost 23 to 16 to Valley. The final 2 pointer was scored by field general Jay Grimmett. Of course it goes without saying that the Indians line of Cooney Russell, Fatso Odum, Danny Morris, Gary Oden and Robert Williams were blocking their tails off as they had done all year opening up gaping holes while escorting their running backs 5 and 10 yard up field before they were even touched. Haven't seen a line like them in 40 years from 1969 to 2009. As the game ended with the final score East Highland 82, Calhoun County 0 on the Legion Stadium score board. It was the highest score ever recorded on the home score board while flashing a 0 for the opponent. The game leading rusher with 111 yards on 8 carries was Lightning Threatt. Terry Bledsoe had 100 yards in 5 carries clearly his best effort ever as an Indian. The toughest little running back and player I've ever seen in a football uniform in Sylacauga weighing in at 5 feet 6, 140 pounds soaking wet. Lyn Project Foster ended his Indian career by rushing for 92 yards on only 3 carries. And Billy Robuck Smith Indian fullback supreme left his mark on Indian fans memories by bulldozing his way to 51 yards on only 6 carries. As you can see, Coach Scissum spread the wealth in this last game ever for the Indians. They operated like a well oiled machine hitting on all cylinders as they gave the folks in Sylacauga something to reminiscence and talk about for decades to come. Lightning also caught 4 passes for 90 more yards and 2 tds. It gave him a total of 201 yards for the night. Tops by far in the tough touchdown denying Indian defense was the versatile one, Anthony Cooney Russell who has been a mainstay in the East Highland line all year. He was in on 24 tackles and also blocked a punt for good measure. If Russell was a horse they would have saved his genes by breeding him as a thoroughbred. He played on the Indians varsity for 5 years beginning in the 8th grade. He played defensive end like he was the blueprint for the position. Combining strength speed and game savvy to the position. Linebackers Aaron Moon and

Billy Smith were each in on 11 stops individual. Moon also intercepted an enemy pass. Big Roberts Williams number 94 all 265 pounds of him at right tackle and end Sylvester Beattie McKinney the other prototype end for the Indians had 10 tackles each. Williams also caused a fumble and recovered it. The East Highland defense has not given up a single point all season. Calhoun County got inside the Indians 50 twice. To the 18 in the 3rd quarter and to the 8 yard line in the final period. Thus the East Highland High School Indians close out the final game in their history in Sylacauga by the closing the show in football with their highest scoring effort of the season while again allowing no one to cross their goal line. As the game ended their were many hugs to go along with some tears as every one realized that they had seen the last Indian game as East Highland's journey had finally come to an abrupt and unexpected end with this game. As the players exited the field and headed for the Indians dressing room one last time, I peered over the railings as they headed for the tunnel and looked as I had done many times before scooping out the number on the backs of my favorite players. They were: 40, 36, 46, 15, 83, 84, 76, 50 and 94. As Coach Scissum walked by with Coach Showers and Coach Duke, I saw him flash his million dollar smile at the Indian fans one last time as he savored the sweet taste of another Indian victory heading to a victorious dressing room. Something he did many many many times as the head coach of the only high school team he ever coached, the mighty Indians of East Highland. Stop! Look! And Listen! Here comes the mighty Indians.

Final Stats for the Game

	East Highland	Calhoun County
1st Downs	15	8
Yards Rushing	380	67
Yards Passing	196	-2
Total Yards	576	65
Passes	7-11-0	1-7-3
Penalties	60 yards	95 yards

EAST HIGHLAND HIGH SCHOOL INDIAN INTANGIBLES

Richard Lightning Threatt

Richard Lightning Threatt a recent graduate of East Highland High School and the son of Roosevelt and Mattie Threatt of Sylacauga, has signed a letter of intent to attend Pratt Community Junior College in Pratt, Kansas. Threatt, a 5 ft 10, 165 pound halfback was voted all state, all county, all mid state and most valuable player by his teammates in 1969. The class 2A state 100 yard dash champion also holds the record in class 2A for the 220 yard dash. Chuck Helton Head Football coach at Pratt Junior College had the following comments to say about Threatt. Richard is one of the most outstanding high school backs in the country. He has the ability and the toughness to make the big play that can win the game. We feel very fortunate to have him attending our school as he has a great future in both football and track. Richard was our most sought after running back.

Indian Folklore

Indian saying from graduating class to graduating class who are you!

Football defensive line - the thin blue line!
To defeated opponents near the end of game
It's crying time again!
Nah nah nah nah
Nah nah nah nah
Hey hey hey goodbye!
Indians on the warpath!

Oops upside the head!
Say oops upside the head!
(Repeat)

Everywhere we go!
Everywhere we go!
People want to know!
People want to know!
Who we are!
Who we are!
We are the Indians!
We are the Indians!
The mighty, mighty Indians!
The mighty; mighty Indians!

Indian Intangibles

Richard Lightning Threatt of East highland High School in Sylacauga, Alabama has been included in the inaugural issue of letterman magazine. Threatt is featured in the publications letterman section, a special department highlighting teams and players who have won special recognition or been involved in unusual situations. Publisher Paul Nyburg said that for the first time in history, high school performers will be able to know what is going on in their area of interests. There are over 2 and one half million participants in sports that will not be able to keep up with their peers. They can read about the best in all 50 states. Standards are high in material considerations executive editor Tammy L. Preston said just because an athlete is good isn't enough. We want to tell the story of those who excel both in and out of the arenas. Congratulations to Richard, the son of Mr. Roosevelt and Mattie Threat.

Sylacaugan Wins Grand Prize in State Social Studies Fair

When I was growing up in Sylacauga there was always this misconception talk that a black high school education was inferior to that of a white school that the quality of teaching was a level below that of white teachers. That black kids could not compete on the level with their white counterparts. Well all these theories were put to shame by students and teachers at East Highland

High School. One of the brightest students at the school was Bruce Burney, the state record holder in the two mile event. Bruce the son of the Rev. and Mrs. W.H. Burney was as good in the classroom as he was in athletics. Here lies a story from the Sylacauga Advance printed about Bruce in 1968. There is nothing like setting goals for yourself charting your course and keeping at it nothing of course except reaching those goals. Bruce Burney, a junior at East Highland High School is two thirds of the way with the last third well in sight. When the school year began, Bruce set three goals for himself. He wanted to make the national Honor Society, win the state social science fair and win the two mile race in the state meet. The fist two he has accomplished and he goes to Auburn Saturday to get the third. He is very optimistic about his chances. He has already broke the state record in the two mile race in other meets this year. He even bettered his second goal. He was the grand prize winner at the social studies fair held at Huntsville Saturday. Sponsored by the Sears Foundation, Bruce was given a 50 dollar savings bond for his efforts, along with a book about Alabama. The subject of his entry was integration in Sylacauga in 1969. His teacher is Miss Margaret Newman. He said that he felt that his project showed that a teacher of the opposite race could work with a pupil on a problem which affects both races. He decided last August on his subject and began working on it. He compiled a questionnaire which 11th grade students at Sylacauga High and East highland answered and from these answers he drew conclusions for his project. Some of the questions were would you be willing to have a person of the opposite race as a teacher? Or as a friend? Would you be willing to join a club where the majority are of another race? In addition to the conclusions he gathered from the questionnaire he used pictures of various local groups in his exhibition. When asked how he feels about integration the way it has been handled locally, Bruce said that he thinks the local approach has worked well. I believe we are doing it the right way here he said. He also said that he wanted to stay at East Highland and finish with his classmates of 11 years. However, if the original court order to move his classmates to Sylacauga High had been carried out, Bruce would have adjusted well. Bruce father pastors the Tallahatchee Church in the Kymulga Community of Childersburg, Alabama. He has 3 brothers and a sister among siblings.

Two Indians are Small School Award Winners
By Dan Rutledge

Two East Highland High School Indians have been chosen this week to be honored as the Daily Home back and Lineman of the week. Lightning Threatt wins as the week's best back among 1A and 2A schools for the 3rd time this year, on Fridays' 70 to 0 route of supposedly powerful St. Jude of Montgomery. Threatt scored 28 points. The seasons best one game effort in any class and regained his scoring lead, Threatt now has 110 points to second place David Hendrix of Lincoln 97. Hendrix overtook Threatt a week ago by getting 9 touchdowns in two weeks. He has the top one game performance against Wedowee with 30 points. Threatt scored 3 tds and 5- 2 point conversions for his 28 point effort Friday night. He was the games leading rusher 145 yards. His td runs were for one and 33 yards. While Threatt was impressive end, PA Young was even more so. This week's lineman of the week gained 147 yards on 5 catches. Three of the catches were one handed circus grabs that brought forth oohs! from the crowds in amazement. On defense, Young looked like Auburn's defensive backs defending against Florida. He stole 4 enemy passes, one in the end zone to avert a score. Young intercepted St. Jude passes in the first third and the 4th quarters. Both Indians are seniors. Honorable mention this week goes to Munford's George Brannon, who threw scoring passes of 50, 36 and 15 yards in the lion's 34 to0 route of ADS. David Hendrix and David Redding of Lincoln who each tallied once in the bears lost to Vincent. Winterboro full back Ronnie Harrell who was the Bulldogs leading rusher and scorer 8 points one td and one two point conversion in the win over Wedowee. East Highlands Lynn Foster who was the second leading rusher with 76 yards and was the work horse in most of the Indian drives Friday night. He scored twice. Honorable mention lineman goes to Aaron Moon, East Highland linebacker who had 8 individual tackles and seven assists and also intercepted a pass. Glenn Bishop of Winterboro who intercepted two passes from his line backer position against Wedowee. Mike Minton and Ronnie Foshee of Munford line stand outs in the ASD shut out. Raymond Steele of ASD for his play both ways against a tough Munford 11. Tackle Doug Freeman of Lincoln who played his usual hard nosed game against Vincent and was the leading tackler for the bears.

LIFE WITH THE NEW YORK JETS BY CECIL LEONARD, FORMER INDIAN GREAT

Former Indian Star Receives Honor At Tuskegee Institute

    The week before the college all star game was spent working on the special teams. Every rookie has to be able to occupy some position on the special team. I was placed on five special teams. Kickoff, return, punt return, field goal, defense and the onside kick. There were definite things had to do on the

Closing the Show

on side kick. There were definite things had to do on each team. The most dangerous of the so called suicide teams was the punt return team. The ball hangs in the air for four seconds to five seconds before coming down. I was paired with mike battles from U.S.C. each one of us had the responsibility of telling the man receiving the ball whether to fair catch it or to take it and go. What made the punt return so dangerous was the average player can run forty yards in five or less seconds. By the time the ball is caught the would be tackler is there. The receiver is always looking up and he must never take his eyes off the ball. On the kickoff team each position is given a number and I was a R5. In the R5 position my job was to go with the ball. This position is given to the fastest men on the team. With a kicker like Jim Turner, I had plenty of time to get to the ball carrier. The squad had to be cut to sixty men before the college all star game. There were seventy of us and ten men had to go. The locker room again was very silent as the Turk walked. The Turk, to the unknown of you is the coach who visits your room and tells you to report to the head coach with your play book, you don't want to get a visit from the Turk. That means that you didn't make the team and was cut. I was again passed up by the Turk. So off to Chicago we went. It was a warm night in Chicago and everything was set. This was my first game with the world champion New York Jets. And I was going into it with a maximum effort. We kicked off to the college all stars and from my R5 position. I met Roger Werhli on the ten yard line. By the time he caught the ball. The two biggest thrills of the whole ball game for me was one playing in front of 75,000 people and two being able to catch Altie Taylor from behind on a kickoff after I was pleased with my performance. Knowing this gave me more confidence and will power to fight harder to overcome the Turk and make this team to be continued.

East Highland High School Indian Intangibles

Former Indian Stars Review

Tuskegee Institutes Golden Tigers undefeated and once tied in 7 games gives credit to two former Indians for the fine start. The report that comes to us is that these former Indians are destined for further accomplishments on the gridiron after their college days are done. At East Highland, Cecil Leonard was quarterback and defensive safety. He quarterbacked but 2 losses out of 30 starts from Tuskegee. Captain Cecil Leonard outstanding defensive back, very high on all pro scout's reports, junior from East Highland High School in Sylacauga. Bernard Gunn was a late bloomer at East Highland logging no playing time as a sophomore but coming into his own as a junior. He played guard on offense and middle linebacker on defense for the Indians. Teams always tried to direct their plays away from him. He was all district his junior and senior years at East Highland. The report from Tuskegee Bernard Gunn star defensive back and monster man for Tuskegee, junior from East Highland High School in Sylacauga.

Former Indian Frosh Star at Missouri

Alvin Griffin of Sylacauga was called the fastest player on the Missouri Tigers 1966 freshman football team by Coach Bob Frala. Nicknamed Chock by his East Highland teammates Griffin started on a freshman team that compiled a 3 and 1 record defeating the Missouri B team and the Iowa State cyclones and the Nebraska Corn Huskers Yearling Squad. They lost to the Kansas Jay Hawks freshman 14 to 13. Chock has always been a winner quarterbacking the Indians to a 27 and 0 record as a starting quarterback for

Closing the Show

Coach Haywood Scissum. Griffin was hampered during the season by a knee injury which cut down on his playing time. We worked at both halfbacks and split end positions said Coach Frala. He really has a knack for getting himself open and catching passes. Coach Frala predicts a bright future for Griffin

From the Talladega Daily Home Friday, May 29, 1970
By Dan Rutledge

Sylacauga- It was a tough decision but Haywood Scissum made it. The 20 year head coach of East Highland High School will move on to Alabama A & M next year. Coach Scissum new assignment will be a many faceted one. He will be defensive football coach, track coach, head counselor and head scout. It was a real tough decision to make Coach Scissum said. That's why it took me so long to make it. But in the end the offer was too good to pass up. It would not have been fair to my family to let it pass by. Beside the immediate duties at hand the position also offered something for the future. Although not official, Coach Scissum said, the offer carried with it the future position of head of the Physical Education Department. A & M does not offer a degree in physical education and has no physical education department. But the offer to me was that I go to school in the summer and get my doctorate in a few years. By which time I might be ready to return from active coaching and I would become head coach of the new physical education department he said. I hate to leave Sylacauga and all my many friends here he continued but this new job is a challenge. A challenge that I welcome. Coach Scissum chose the job at A & M over several offers he had including Kentucky State, Tuskegee, Parker High in Birmingham, and Central High in Phoenix City among others. Coach Scissum would not reveal what his new pay scale would be but he did volunteer with a wide smile it represented a substantial increase over his present salary. Coach Scissum takes a long with him to A & M, 3 of his prize athletes. P.A. Young, Sylvester

Beattie McKinney and Donell Corbin. Young was an end on the football team and the county scoring champion in basketball. McKinney was an end in football and center on the basketball team an outstanding shot putter and discus thrower on the track team. Corbin was an outstanding miler in track and very good guard on the basketball team. Richard Lightning Threatt could be the 4th Indian to follow coach to

A & M in Huntsville. Threatt has not decided between A & M and Pratt Junior College Kansas. Threatt a halfback county scoring champion was a 9.9 hundred yard dash state champion. I made the decision to go with regret and I want all my friends to know that I will never forget East Highland or Sylacauga . Both will be close to my heart forever.

Another East Highland vs Cobb Rivalry

**Mountainview Recreation Center
wins all sports day from Anniston
June 1968**

The Mountain view Recreation Center met Anniston in what must be termed an all sports day. They emerged victorious in all events except one. The idea was a novel one and plans were finalized during the dedication of the new recreation center. The program was to have a swim meet from 10:00 a.m. to 12 noon; a box lunch from 12 noon to 1:00 p.m.; dancing from 1:00 p.m. to 2:00 p.m.; girls softball from 2:30 p.m. to 3:30 p.m.; and baseball from 4:00 p.m. until completion. This program was followed with minor changes. The swim meet was captured by the local aquatics by the score of 228 to 182 for the Anniston Rec. The visiting team had no girls team so the Sylacauga lassies were forced to compete against one another. No points were rewarded however. In the senior swim division Jerry Doc Houser took 5 first place blue ribbons. Anthony Cooney Russell, Larry Tinsley and Michael Brownfield took four blue ribbons each. Wayne Gluck Houser, brother of Jerry led the junior division but was closely followed by Terry Lewis Odum, Andre Showers, and Anthony Pig Odum. The local rec team made off with the diving competition also. The baseball game was played between 16 year olds and under. Alvin Griffin who works with the recreation department and manages two of the teams in the Mountainview league sent fire baller Tyrone Stone after Anniston. The heroics of Prince Albert Young, aka PA was the difference in the game. The big first baseman stroked a 410 ft. 3 run homer in the first. A triple in the 4th good for 3 more runs. And added a single he struck out in the 7th. Griffin played all 15 of his boys and the game ended with the Sylacauga Rec team beating the Anniston Rec team 8 to 3. Adding to this wonderful day of recreation the visitors from Anniston challenged the boy from the projects to a game of five on five basketball, This was an unscheduled event. Nevertheless, the Sylacaugans rose to the occasion and defeated the Anniston squad 3 games to 1. Anniston got their lone victory of the day in girl's softball. They trounced McMillian quarters by a large score. Played on the little league field below the swimming pool under the light. This day July 24, 1968 showed what can be done in recreation in the short span of a day. The new recreation center was used for basketball and dancing. The old rec center was used for lunch. The new baseball field hosted the baseball game and obviously the swimming pool for the swim meet. The little league field for the girls softball game. Sylacauga's Mayor Gene Atkinson welcomed Anniston and Talladega to the city at the Mountainview pool. Coach Scissum's wife, Mrs. Scissum served as the director of these events. Mrs. Beth Yates is the Superintendent of Recreation..

East Highland Opponents in the Scissum Era 1952–1969

1. Cobb Avenue of Anniston 4A
2. Carver of Gadsden 4A
3. Riverside of Tuscaloosa 4A
4. Laurel of Alexander City 3A
5. Westside of Talladega 3A
6. Phylliss Wheatley of Childersburg 2A
7. JD Thompson of Coosa County 2A
8. RR Moton of Sycamore 1A
9. Calhoun County of Hobson City 3A
10. Hudson of Selma 4A
11. Parker of Birmingham's 4A
12. Hayes of Birmingham 4A
13. St. Jude of Montgomery 2A
14. Fairfield Oliver 4A
15. OS Hill of Munford 2A
16. TCTS of Howell Cove 1A
17. Darden of Opelika 4A
18. Norris of Attala 4A
19. Jenifer High 3A
20. Chambers county of Lafayette 2A
21. Booker T. Washington 4A
22. Drake High of Auburn 3A
23. Moton of Leeds 2A
24. Clay County Training Lineville 2A
25. St. Clair Training Pell City 3A

26. Chilton County Training Clanton 2A
27. Eufaula Yellow Jackets 3A
28. Ullman High Birmingham 4A
29. Prentice of Montevallo 2A

Coach Scissum and the Indians slighted Again

A slight against Coach Haywood Scissum and his Indians accrued when the coaches in the Talladega County Coaches Association voted him and Winterboro Head Coach Alton Shell as Co-Coaches of the Year in small school competition. Shell in his first year at the helm of the bulldogs, guided them to a 7 and 3 record. Which earned them a share of the small school championship in Talladega County. While Scissum, a veteran of 18 years all at East Highland took his team to a 9 and 0 record averaging 55 points a game while giving up only 6. What I want to know is since when does 7 and 3 equal 9 and 0? Since when does losing 3 games in a season as Winterboro did in 69 equal not losing a game? The Indians were the only team in Talladega county to go undefeated winning 9 games. Where was Winterboro when Coach Scissum was crying out all over the county in 69 for a tenth game on his schedule? They just like the rest of them declined the invitation to play the Indians. Only TCTS of Howell Cove was brave enough to accept. Part of the reason why I have so much respect for them now. Coach Scissum had been the head man at East Highland for 18 years coming straight from Tuskegee Institute after graduation as a 22 year old with no prior head coaching experience. During his tenure at East Highland from 1952 to 1970, was some of the most turbulent and nation changing times in our history. He witnessed the Brown vs. Board decision as the Indians head Coach. He witnessed the voting rights act and the civil rights acts of the mid sixties as Indians head coach. Surely knowing that these decisions would some day shut down his beloved school. But he knew that these decisions would make life better for his people and certainly he embraced them. Coach Shell of Winterboro expressed surprise at being selected as co-coach of the year saying that there were several other good coaches in the area that could have qualified but he was happy to get it. Yeah! But none of them including himself went undefeated as Coach Scissum did and none of them out shined Coach Scissum of East Highland who in 18 seasons of coaching has a 136 wins 27 losses and 11 ties record. I guess those coaches just couldn't bring themselves to a point where they could do the thing in their heart that they knew was really right. After Coach Scissum and his Indians had just had one of the most dynamic seasons that this county has ever seen and that was in his last season ever reward him with Coach of the Year Award! Despite the unanimous fact that the Indians were the top offensive team in the county averaging 55 points a game. The top defensive team giving up only 0.6 a game in 69. This of course while going unscathed. No one else in the county even came close to these staggering numbers. No mater what class. Incidentally last year's Coach of the Year in Small School Competition was Munford's Ken Upton, who by the way shared the award with no one.

1969 Scoring Race Almost Over, Indians Threatt Unofficial Winner
By Dan Rutledge

Unofficially East Highlands' Lightning Threatt has won the 1969 scoring title for Talladega County and the surrounding area. Threatt has a total of 144 points. His runner up David Hendrix of Lincoln has 92 points. The standings are not yet official because Sylacauga High School is still playing in the 3A state playoffs. The Aggies Randy Billingsley is in third place in the standings with 80 points. He has a outside chance to catch Threatt if he has a couple of 30 point games in the semifinals and finals. Threatt just about put his lead out of reach with the fine performance he had in his last game before the home fans as the Indians stomped Calhoun County of Hobson City 92-82 last Thursday. Threatt scored 5 touchdowns and 2 two point conversions for a 34 point night. This was the best individual game performance in the area. It surpassed by 4 points the 30 point evening enjoyed by Lincoln's David Hendrix against Wedowee a few weeks ago. The only changes in the standings came in Billingsley's climb into second place with a td against BB Comer and Childersburg's Mike Allen moving into 4th place. Last years scoring champion Howard Hop Along Bussey of Munford was injured most of the year and missed 4 games due to injury but he still managed to score 58 points. Good enough of 10th place on the scoring ladder. Listed below are the final standings of top 25 scorers in the area.

1. Richard Lightning Threat, East Highland, 144 points
2. David Hendrix, Lincoln, 92 points
3. Randy Billingsley, Sylacauga, 80 points
4. Mike Allen, Childersburg, 76 points

5. PA Young, East Highland, 72 points
6. Ken McLain, Sylacauga, 72 points
7. Steve Robertson, Lineville, 68 points
8. Billy Robuck Smith, East Highland, 66 points
9. Lee Carpenter, Childersburg, 62 points
10. Howard Hop along Bussey, Munford, 58 points
11. Terry Bledsoe, East Highland, 48 points
12. Paris, Talladega, 42 points
13. Mitchell, Shelby County, 38 points
14. Greene, Ashland, 38 points
15. Browning, Ashland, 38 points
16. Elston, TCTS, 38 points
17. Johnson, BB Comer, 38 Points
18. Jenks, Talladega, 38 points
19. Edwards, Lincoln, 36 points
20. Griffin, Ashland, 36 points
21. Ham, Sylacauga, 34 points
22. Watts, Munford, 34 points
23. Carden, Winterboro, 34 points
24. Steele, ASD, 34 points

Popular Songs During the Indians 1960's Era that Indian Students grooved to.
1. Didn't I Blow Your Mind This Time, The Delfonics
2. Shot Gun, Jr. Walker and the All Stars
3. Young and Foolish, NA
4. Back Field in Motion, NA
5. Grazing in the Grass, Hugh Masekola
6. My Girl, The Temptation
7. The Horse, NA
8. Hey Jude, The Beatles
9. Twist and Shout, The Isley Brothers
10. A Change is Gonna Come, Sam Cooke
11. Black and Proud, James Brown
12. Ooh Baby Baby, Smokey Robinson and the Miracles
13. Tears of a Clown, Smokey Robinson and the Miracles
14. Ain't Nothing Like the Real Thing, Marvin Gaye and Tammmi Terrell
15. Pride and Joy, Marvin Gaye
16. Stop in the Name of Love , The Supremes
17. Baby Love, The Supremes

18. My Guy, NA
19. Ain't Too Proud to Beg, The Temptations
20. La La La La La La La La La La La Means I Love You, The Delfoni
21. Sex Machine, James Brown
22. Papa Got a Brand New Bag, James Brown
23. Sitting on the Dock of the Bay, Otis Redding
24. Mustang Sally, Wilson Pickett
25. Hold on I'm coming, San and Dave
26. When Something is wrong with my baby, Sam and Dave
27. Put on You Red Dress, NA
28. Be Young Be Foolish, NA
29. A Talk With My Man Last Nigh, NA
30. Love is Here, The Supremes
31. Too Busy thinking Bout my Baby, Marvin Gaye
32. Dancing in the Streets, Martha Reeves and the Vandellas
33. People Get Ready, The Impressions
34. The Way You Do the Things You Do, The Temptations
35. Love Child, Diana Ross and the Supremes
36. Patches, Clarence Carter
37. I Want You Back, The Jackson Five
38. Who's Lovin You, The Jackson Five
39. Still Waters, The Four Tops
40. Soul Finger, The Bar-Kays
41. Stand, Sly and the Family Stone
42. Dance to the Music, Sly and the Family Stone
43. Every Day People, Sly and the Family Stone
44. My Cherie Amore, Stevie Wonder
45. Stay in my Corner, The Dells
46. Knock on Wood, Eddie Floyd
47. Mr. Big Stuff, Jean Knight
48. Cowboys and Girls, NA
49. Turn Back the Hands of Time, Tyrone Davis
50. Purple Haze, Jimmi Hendrix
51. What I say, Ray Charles
52. I'm in Love, Wilson Pickett
53. When Something is wrong with my Baby, Sam and Dave
54. Super Bad, James Brown
55. The Sweeter he is, The Soul Children
56. Rescue Me, Fontella Bass
57. Cryin in the Streets, George Perkins
58. No Where to Run no Where to Hide, Martha and the Vandellas

Closing the Show

59. Stand by me, Ben E. King
60. Choice of Color, The Impressions
61. Rainbow, Gene Chandler
62. Going in Circles, The Friends of Distinction
    Ain't to Proud to Beg, The Temptations
63. Beginning of my End, NA
    Chain of Fools, Aretha Franklin
    Respect, Aretha Franklin
64. Tears of a Clown, Smokey Robinson
65. Crying Time Again, Ray Charles
66. Hot Fun in the Summertime, Sly Stone

Honor Roll

Indian Football Greats from the Past
Cecil Leonard, Quarterback
Alvin Griffin, Quarterback
Johnny Grimmett, Quarterback
Jay Grimmett, Quarterback
Sonny Oden, Quarterback
Sammy Louis Johnson, Quarterback
French Carpenter, Quarterback
Dale Clark, Quarterback
Andy Red Foster, Quarterback
Manuel Big Joe Pope, Guard
Robert Sleepy Hollanquest, Tackle
Houston Tip Averette, Defensive Back
Mike Homer Bledsoe, Linebacker
James J.D. Thomas, Flank man
Joe Nathan Hickey, Tackle
Robert Bobba Averette, Guard
Charles Curry, Tackle
Lee Buford, Fullback
Jerry Hale, Fullback
Jessie Hale, Halfback
Larry Butler, Halfback
Evander Morris, End
Willie Isome, End
Gene Brut Gamble, Tackle
Richard Oden, Tackle

Closing the Show

Clarence Foster, Halfback
Ray Hubbard, Guard
Paul Hubbard, Halfback
Big Fluker, Tackle
Jacob Midnite carpenter, Guard
John Thomas Harrison, Fullback
Billy the Jet Harrison, Halfback
George the Ohio Flash Dortch, Halfback
Calvin The Russian McKinney, Guard
Clarence Kidd, Halfback
Travis Olden, Halfback
Willie Holtzclaw, End
Jerry Chic Holtzclaw, Halfback
Greg Foots Holtzclaw, Halfback
Derry Lee Holtzclaw, Halfback
Robert Poor Rob Gunn, Linebacker
Anthony Boot Pratt, Tackle
Julius Bobba Finley, Tackle
David Grimmett, End
Larry Tootsie Thomas, Halfback
Jimmy Walker, Halfback
Billy Brown, End
James Hollanquest, End
Willie Whetstone, End
Bo Chambliss, Tackle
Willie Green Knight, Tackle
Homer Pearson, End
Melvin Bardwell, Tackle
Johnny Sonny Cook, Center
Jeffie Hughes, Linebacker
Preston Leonard, Halfback
Preston Leonard, Halfback
Ralph McKinney, End
Frankie Hart, Halfback
Roland Slick Morris, Tackle
Wally Gator Fulks, Tackle
John Gilliam Love, Guard
Clark Cook, Quarterback
Harry Hughes, Tackle
Richard Corbin, End
Jimmy Burns, Ends

Michael Catfish Smith
Eliga Benson, Jr.
Walker Hubbard
Sidney Frank Woodyard
Donald Harrison, Fullback
Verdell Pearson, Linebacker
Ralph Cook, Linebacker
Charles Davis, Tackle
Booker T. Harris, Tackle
Grove Miles, Tackle
Sam Breedlove, Guard
James Lee
Alfred Oden
Gleamon Oden
Jimmy Sexton
Morris Hollis
Odessa Hunter halfback
R. Lasley
Lionel Player
Frank McNealey
Hal McLemore
James Blood Pope
Ricky Player
John McIntyre
Ronal Tinsley
James Williams
Willie Isome
Harry Jemison
Tommy Ackles
Ed Kelly
Donnel Prater
David Dunklin

Final Team the 1969 team and managers

Managers
Jerry Doc House
Eddie Tuna Turner
Dewitt Simmons
Louis Choker Stearns

The Players
Alphonza Olden
Anthony Cooney Russell
Greg Holtzclaw
PA Young
Aaron Moon
Wayne Cow Head Harris
Gary Oden
Darnell Williams
Sylvester Bliss Shealey
Lyn Project Foster
Danny Morris
Jerry Chic Holtzclaw
Terry Bledsoe
Jay Grimmett
Albert Oden
Neil Hart
Lamar Prater
Wilber Wilson
James Odum
Robert Williams
Billy Robuck Smith
Anthony Walton
Richard Lightning Threatt
Gill Weechie McKinney
Jessie Powell
Thadeus Darby
Nathaniel Williams
James Williams
Sylvester Beattie McKinney
Calvin Drake
James Player
Ruben Parks

1969 Here is the total List of Scorers from the Area
1. Richard Lightning Threatt, East Highland, 100 points
2. David Hendrix, Lincoln, 92 points
3. Steve Robertson, Lineville, 68 points
4. Randy Billingsley, Sylacauga, 62 points
5. PA Young, East Highland, 60 points
6. Ken McLain, Sylacauga, 59 points

Michael Catfish Smith

7. Mike Allen, Childersburg, 58 points
8. Lee Carpenter, Childersburg, 57 points
9. Billy Robuck Smith, East Highland, 56 points
10. Howard Bussey, Munford, 44 points
11. Terry Bledsoe, East Highland, 38 points
12. Elston, TCTS, 38 points
13. Browning, Ashland, 38 points
14. Greene, Ashland, 38 points
15. Mitchell, Shelby County, 38 points
16. Paris, Talladega, 36 points
17. Brooks, Ashland, 32 points
18. Calhoun, Westside, 32 points
19. Carden, Winterboro, 30 points
20. Jenks, Talladega, 30 points
21. Jerry Holtzclaw, East Highland, 28 points
22. Griffin, Ashland, 28 points
23. Watts, Munford, 27 points
24. Brannon, Munford, 26 points
25. Steele, ASD, 26 points
26. Elston, OS Hill, 26 points

1969 Football Season
Threatt Regains Scoring Lead in Area

East Highland's premier halfback Richard Lightning Threatt regained the area scoring lead he relinquished last week by scoring 20 points in leading the Indians over St. Jude by an amazing 70 to 0 margin. Threatt tallied on a pair 1 yard drives and a 33 yard burst off tackle. He picked up 10 more by running in 5, 2 point conversions. The Indian star was the games leading rusher with 145 yards on 21 carries. Threatt was overtaken in last week's standing by Lincoln's David Hendrix. The senior golden bear halfback was held to 1 touchdown in last week's lost to the Vincent Yellow Jackets. He now trails Threatt by 8 points. Threatt has a even 100 points total to Hendrix's 92. The one score by Hendrix made an amazing 10 touchdowns in 3 weeks for the Lincoln speedster. Steve Robertson of Lineville although didn't play due to injury maintained his 3rd place pace with 68 points. Randy Billingsley of Sylacauga likewise did not score in Sylacauga's 13 to 6 win over Auburn but stayed in 4th place with 62 points. East Highlands PA Young, the only receiver in the top ten jumped from 7th place to 5th with his 2 touchdown effort against St. Jude. East Highland is the only school in the county with 3 players listed in the top ten scores as Billy Robuck Smith comes in at number 9 with 56 points scored. Here is a total list of scorers from the area and their ranking.

1. Threatt, EHSS, 100 points
2. David Hendrix, Lincoln, 92 points
3. Steve Robertson, Lineville, 68 points
4. Randy   Billingsley, SHS, 62 points

Michael Catfish Smith

5. PA Young, EHHS, 60 points
6. Ken McLain, SHS, 59 points
7. Mike Allen, Cburg, 58 points
8. Lee Carpenter, Cburg, 57 points
9. Billy Smith, EHHS, 56 points
10. Howard Bussey, Munford, 44 points
11. Terry Bledsoe, EHHS, 38 points
12. Elston, TCTS, 38 points
13. Browning, Ashland 38points
14. Greene, Ashland, 38 points
15. Mitchell, Shelby County, 38 points
16. Paris, Talladega, 36 points
17. Brooks, Ashland, 32 points
18. Calhoun, Westside, 32 points
19. Carden, Winterboro, 30 points
20. Jenks, Talladega, 30 points
21. Jerry Holtzclaw, East Highland, 28 points
22. Watts, Munford, 27 points
23. Brannon, Munford, 26 points
24. Steele, ASD, 26 points
25. Elston, OS Hill, 26 points

Indian Elite Players

The Game Breakers
Derry Lee Holtzclaw
George The Ohio Flash Dortch
Andy Red Foster
Clarence Foster
Sonny Oden
Billy The Jet Harrison
Paul Hubbard
Alvin Griffin
Cecil Leonard
Willie Hotzclaw
David Grimmett
Jerry Hale
PA Young
Richard Lightning Threatt
Larry Tootsie Thomas

Closing the Show

The Pass Defenders
Cecil Leonard
Anthony Walton
Greg Foots Holtzclaw
Jerry Chic Holtzclaw
Lightning Threatt
Houston Tip Averette
Travis Oden
Clarence Kidd
Billy Robuck Smith
Larry Butler
Jimmy Walker
David Grimmett

The Impact Players
Bernard Gunn
Joe Nathan Hickey
Robert Gunn
Dewey Munn
Gene Brut Gamble
David Grimmett
Richard Oden
Billy the Jet Harrison
Cecil Leonard
Alvin Griffin
Willie Holtzclaw
Anthony Cooney Russel
Roland Slick Morris
Make Homer Bledsoe

The Run Stoppers
Ralph McKinney
Joe Hickey

Michael Catfish Smith

That gives us a week to get together. I already know most of them Duke said. Five played against us in regular season or in the state tournament and I've got PA Young who was on the all county, all state and all state tournament teams. He had the areas individual high game of the season when he scored 44 points against Talladega County Training early in the season. He set a state record for points 84 in 3 games. Both south rosters show formidable board strength. The 1A-2A team has three 6 ft. 5 boys and one 6 ft. Charles Davis of Marbury High School is the team's tallest player at 6 ft.6 and a half. As all conference and all county performer his specialty is a jump shot along the baseline. He averaged 23 points a game. The 3 best known names on the 3A-4A team coached by Decatur Coach Earl Morris are Andy Ott, Mason Bonner, and Leon Hester. Ott from Tuscaloosa High will be the biggest man in either game at 6 feet seven. He as the states MVP. As selected by the Birmingham Post Herald. He as named to all state all southern and All American prep teams. In his senior year Ott averaged 28 points and 19 rebounds a game. He has signed to play for the University of Alabama. Leon Hester was the two guard in 3A state champion Bibb County's one-two punch of last season be combined with Charles Cleveland MVP and only a junior to lead Bibb to a state title with almost no trouble. At 6 ft. 3 Hester jumps and rebounds like a forward but handles the ball and shoots from the outside like a guard. He averaged 25 points a game and 17 rebounds last year. The 1A-2A game will start at 1:30 p.m. on August 6. When asked if Young would be firing up jumpers from the corner, Coach Duke replied PA can shoot from anywhere he wants to at anytime.

East Highland Cobb and Westside
Cobb East highland and Westside
Westside Cobb and East Highland

Closing the Show

In 1966 the Indians of East Highland High School saw themselves in a rare position. Third in the trilogy that was the Indians Cobb and Westside football series. The Indians 1966 season started off with them pushing the team's unbeaten string from 1963 to 65 even further as they won their first 4 contests of the season against Norris of Attala, Calhoun County of Hobson City, Carver of Gadsden and Laurel of Alex City all four in convincing fashion. There was no reason for Indian fans in Sylacauga to feel that the team would suffer a drop off in 66 after the invincible's had graduated. They met old nemesis Cobb Avenue of Anniston who they had ran 3 straight victories over. After Cobb they ran headlong into Westside of Talladega a team that had defeated Cobb earlier in the season. Westside, a 3A school was a natural rival to the 2A Indians with a few victories to claim over East Highland over the years. But Westside was no slouch this year as their victory over powerful Cobb illustrated. The two teams East Highland and Westside really didn't like each other. Though there was a mutual respect between the two. As the two cities to this day Talladega from the north end and Sylacauga from the south end of the county being the two largest cities in the county are natural rivals. Talladega the county seat has the Talladega 500 race track and calls itself the racing city. Sylacauga on the other hand is called the marble city and boast the finest white marble in the world. They compete against each other in everything. Sylacauga built a Plaza Twin Theater so Talladega one upped them with a Martin Triple. Even blood drives for the Red Cross and raising money for the United Way brings out competitive juices between the two. With Westside representing Talladega and East Highland representing Sylacauga it was an intense rivalry. Westside which drew most of its talent from Westgate of Talladega equivalent to Drew Court in Sylacauga and Knoxville and Curry Court. They had many outstanding athletes especially in basketball and track. The Indian players knew not to venture into Westgate and Knoxville to date girls. And the Westside players knew not to come to the projects in Sylacauga looking to hook up. Both schools were territorial when it came to girls. This stance would soften somewhat after integration with the two white schools in town Talladega and Sylacauga. The Indians like the fastest gun in the west that every loose cannon wanted to challenge to gain a reputation was being called out by a new adversary in 1966, the Phylliss Wheatley Panthers of Childersburg, the new kids on the block. Childersburg was only 10 miles from Sylacauga which also made them want to be a natural rival. Add to this the fact that they had a star player named Larry McKenzie who grew up and lived in the Walco Community that had spawned so many great Indian athletes in the past. McKenzie who started his career at East Highland as a ninth grader had made the varsity basketball team as a freshman. Playing for the Indians 27 and 3 district champions, you had to be exceptional to play on a team that featured Marion Harrison, Joe Hickey, David Grimmett and Willie Holtzclaw to name a few. Football and baseball was other sports that McKenzie shined in and Coach Scissum said that he was the best third base prospect that he had ever saw. He along with David Jones who had brothers playing at East Highland and Walter Sims, Billy Borden, Robert Peterson, James Vincent and the McElrath brothers, James Winston and Willie Lee were all outstanding athletes who could have played for Coach Scissum but chose to drive from the Sylacauga area to Childersburg. In those days, players were not limited to schools in their neighborhood district by the state like they are today. It's a rule that I personally feel has hurt many kids treated wrongly in some school districts by coaches with personal agendas. Anyway, Phylliss Wheatley burst on to the scene winning right away in their brief football history. They only played two football games against the mighty Indians but what a sweet two game series it was. People to this day still talk about it. But it would be one more season before Wheatley would get a crack at Scissum and his Indians. Lucky for fans in Childersburg and Sylacauga it came before whole scale integration. In 67 and 68 the Indians and Panthers would square off in two classic football games one in Childersburg and one in Sylacauga. Both years East Highland and Phylliss Wheatley were outstanding. Wheatley was even undefeated when the two teams met for the first time in 67. Can you believe the strong school from Sylacauga was even the underdog in the first meeting? Due to the Indian lost to strong Cobb I guess. Not bad for a school that only played 3 seasons of high school football. They would not however, get a 3rd shot at the Indians in 69 because they were forced to shut their program down to get ready for integration. What happened in those two meetings between East Highland and Phylliss Wheatley? Read on to find out!

September 8, 1966 East Highland Stomps Norris 34 to 0

The East Highland Indians opened their 1966 season by defeating Norris High School of Attala 34 to 0. On the first play of the game quarterback Sammy Sank Johnson pulled a neck muscle. It was a minor injury and he will be able to continue to play. Captain Frank Williamson suffered a minor injury and may be forced to miss next week's game. Johnson's under study Johnny Grimmett took over the offense for most of the way. The Indians scored the first time they had the ball as Grimmett scored on a 3 yard swoop around right end. Lee Bang Bang Buford scored the second touchdown on a 3 yard plunge up the middle. The conversion failed and the Indians led 13 to 0 at the end of the first quarter. Second quarter action saw the Pirates offense on the move but a timely interception by Travis Olden stopped the drive. After the Indians got the ball short runs moved them deep into Pirate's territory. Odessa Rip Hunter then sprinted 18 yards for a score. Buford converted. The Indians led 20 to 0. There was little scoring in the third quarter. Both teams moved the ball well. But a stubborn Indian defense would not let Norris score. The Pirates had driven deep into Indian territory when Houston Tip Averette intercepted a pass at the goal line to stop the threat. The Indians then moved the ball down field rapidly behind the power running and quarterback Sank Johnson scored on a 1 yard plunge. Tip Averette converted and the Indians led 27 to 0 at the end of the 3rd quarter. The 4th quarter was much like the 3rd with both teams moving the ball well. Still the Pirates couldn't score. Rip Hunter sprinted 35 yards to put the Indians deep in Pirate territory. 4 plays later Rip scored his second td of the night. Tip Averette converted and the Indians now led 34 to 0 in the season opener. On the kick off the Pirates almost scored. But a great effort by rookie

Michael Catfish Smith

Darnell Prater a sophomore first year player saved the touchdown. The game ended and the Indians had won their 34th victory in a row. Outstanding lineman were John Buford, Make Homer Bledsoe, Robert Gunn and Frank Old Hustle Williamson. Outstanding backs were Lee Bang Bang Buford and Odessa Rip Hunter and Houston Tip Averette. Two promising rookies are Richard Lightning Threatt and his cousin Larry Tootsie Thomas. The offense was strong running the ball for 284 yards and through the air a respectable 57 yards, the net total was 341 yards.

1966 Season Indians fall to Cobb 26 to 7
By Jerome Oneal

The East Highland Indians lost their first football game since September of 1963. They ran into a fired up band of Panthers from Cobb Avenue High School of Anniston. They were humbled 26 to 7. For those Indians fans back home in Sylacauga hoping to see the Indians add on to their winning streak started by the invincibles back in 1963 it was not to be. For not only did Cobb defeat the mighty Indians but they also stopped the Indian streak after they started the season with 4 straight victories at 36 straight games the score in the game mounted only because of some shoddy play by the Indians. The first and third quarters were scoreless. The Indians had proven their superiority by holding the Panthers twice inside of their own 5 yard line. It was along the airways that Cobb dented the Indians armor and scored goal after goal. The Indians kicked off to start the game and they swarmed all over the big Panthers. Forcing them to punt in their first series the Cobb punter lofted a long spiral up field that was gathered in by Houston Tip Averette and he was smothered by the Panther defense for no gain. After several smashes in the line by Lee Buford was unfruitful the Indians were forced to punt. Indian punting has been sub par all year and tonight was no exception. They gained about 30 net yards on the exchange of punts. A 30 yard pass play set the Panthers up in good shape. But another pass went astray and Tip Averette picked it off to kill another Cobb scoring threat. The first quarter ended tied 0 to 0. Cobb opened the second quarter by completing a 35 yard pass to set up their first score of the night. A few plays later Cobb scored on a 6 yard pass play and the Panthers led 6 to 0. The Cobb lead was short lived however, because Robert Gunn shot through from his linebacker position and blocked a punt and the Indians had the best field position that they had enjoyed all night. The ball was on the Cobb's 40 yard line. And the Indians were able to loosen up the big Panther defense with their own passing game. Quarterback Sank Johnson who walked in the shadows of Griffin last year broke loose for 23 yards to set up the score. Johnny Grimmett then threw to Tip Averette for the touchdown. Johnson ran the pat and the Indians led 7 to 6. It would be all the Indian fans would have to cheer about all night for it would be short lived. On the kickoff they almost permitted the Cobb return man to go all the way. He was finally pulled down on the Indians 30 yard line by Sank Johnson. This is what causes coaches to have ulcers. Two pass plays later the Panthers were in the end zone and now led the Indians 13 to 7. It would prove to be a lead that Cobb would not vanquish all night. With less than a minute left in the half the Indians received the ball. They could not score and the half ended with Cobb and the Indians in a close game with Cobb leading the Indians 13 to 7. This was a rare half time deficit for the Indians especially during the Hickey Holtzclaw and Griffin years and the soon to be Lightning Threatt led teams. The Indians usually had games decided before the bands played. But this was the mighty Cobb Avenue Panthers they were facing. And Cobb fought the Indians like Joe Frazier fought Muhammed Ali. This was truly an intense rivalry not meant for the faint of heart. Cobb was trying to erase the bitter memories of losing 3 straight years to the Indians. To start the second half East Highland received the ball determined to make something happen on offense, but return man Houston Tip Averette was tackled deep in Indian territory. In defense of the Indians they could not penetrate the stacked 8 man in the box defense Cobb was playing because they could not pass deep in their own territory. A punt was forced, but the Indians defense was also playing inspired ball and Cobb could not make a first down and they too had to punt. The fans were witnessing a typical hard hitting Indians and Panthers defensive struggle with the game still resting in the balance. But if the home town Cobb fans were worried about an Indian come back, they were about to be able to rest their minds. On the Cobb punt which was long and high Indian Odessa Rip Hunter camped under it on the Indian 10 yard line with red Cobb shirts all around him. I saw no fair catch signal and I closed my eyes, you the reader of this page guessed it! He fumbled after being leveled by the Panthers and Cobb had the gift fumble on the Indians 9 yard line primed to break open a close game. Indian defensive Captain Big Frank Williamson called his troops around him and they played tough East Highland defense and thwarted every play that Cobb ran to muster the effort to keep them out of the end zone. Playing with heart as Scissum coached teams usually did men on the line like Dugger Cook, John Buford, Sleepy Mule Hollinquest, and Mike Homer

Closing the Show

Bledsoe stood up and held the strong Panther offense 4 straight downs with the Indians taking over on their own 4 yard line. The Indian fans still had hope. On second down, Sank Johnson lofted a beautiful 40 yard quick kick out of his end zone for no return yards. A penalty against the Indians forced another punt after they had again held the mighty Cobb offense in check. This time Indian Quarterback and punter Sank Johnson got off a squibbler and the Panthers were on the Indians 37 yard line in good field position. If you are reading this book you guessed it bad field position and special teams play were about to turn this game in Cobbs favor. The third quarter ended with the Indians still very much in the game trailing Cobb 13 to 7. But fate was getting ready to turn on the good guys from Sylacauga. It was the change of quarters that saw the Indians completely break down and Cobb break this close game wide open. Sandwiched between a Buford interception was some hard knocking, the Indians were always in poor field position. Cobb scored on a 23 yard and a 30 yard pass. The score now Cobb 26 and Indians 7. The game was much closer than the final score would indicate. Coach Scissum as any winner would be sounding like a man that's not used to taking butt whippings but giving them said simply when you quit, you get killed! We quit and we got killed!. In 14 years of coaching I have only had one other team score 4 touchdowns in a game against me and that was Cobb in 1960. From a reporter's standpoint and eye Sank Johnson played a great game. Tip Averette, Odessa Hunter and Lee Buford did well on offense. Johnny Grimmett was a steady on the line. Captain Frank Williamson was head and shoulders above the rest. Dugger Cook, John T. Buford, Mule Hollingquest and Lionel Player did some hard hitting and had some big plays backing up the line Mike Homer Bledsoe and Robert Gunn were seen often. Clearly the Indians defense did not lose this game. Next week the Indians take on another rival powerful Westside of Talladega who knocked off this very Cobb team in an earlier contest.

Indian Mistakes Give Westside 13 to 7 Win
By Jerome Oneal

The East Highland High School Indians lost their second consecutive game as Westside beat them Friday night 13 to 7 in Talladega. The Indians apparently were not ready to play something totally unusual under Coach Scissum for both Talladega scores came off of miscues by the Indians. Maybe still suffering a hangover let down from the Cobb Avenue game last week. Westside was fired up and ready to play knowing that they had already defeated the Cobb team that the Indians had just lost to. Westside kicked off to the Indians to start the game and Tip Averette fumbled and Westside recovered on the Indians 25 yard line. A carry over of mistakes from the Cobb game last week. Tip was untouched by Westside. The Indian defensive unit was again called upon to bail out the team. The hard hitting thin blue line held Westside out of the Indian end zone without them even registering a first down. But the Indians offense was so deep in their own territory they could not move and themselves attempted to punt out. A bad snap from the usually reliable Robert Gunn, Indian center snapper caused punter Sank Johnson to be caught behind the line of scrimmage. The defensive unit again was called on and again they held Westside without them making a first down. As you can guess the Westside home crowd was fired up and excited about their chances to defeat their bitter inter county rival, the East Highland Indians, something that they had not done lately. This Westside East Highland game was a match up where you could get slapped for running your mouth or hit upside the head with a brick boarding the bus if you was an Indian player. Neither of them enjoyed losing to the other and this was something that would carry over to Talladega High and Sylacauga High by

Closing the Show

the black players after integration. Back to the game the Indians offense took over and started a mild drive that soon ended. Sank Johnson's attempted punt was blocked. For the third consecutive time the Indians defense held Westside without allowing them to gain a first down. From our 10 yard line the Indians started to move the ball but a fumble by Richard Threatt reserve halfback gave the ball back to Westside at our 45 yard line. Again Westside could not move the ball on the Indians stingy defense so the chains did not move and they punted to us with no return as the quarter ended in this intensely exciting old school defensive struggle between the two old rivals. On the second play of the second quarter Indian quarterback Sank Johnson aimed a pass for Tip Averette that found its home in the hands of a Westside Panther. He raced untouched 66 yards for a touchdown. The pat was good and Westside led the Indians 7 to 0. The next kick found the Indians unable to move the ball consistently against the Westside defense and they were forced to punt. Another bad snap by Gunn, the second of four for the night caused Johnson to be caught. Again Westside could not move the ball against the Indians defensive 11 and the Indians took over on downs. Westside only touchdown so far had come by way of their defense on an Indian mistake. The Indians offense completed their first pass and you guessed it he (Lamar Walker) fumbled. Walker was attempting to lateral the ball to Richard Threatt. Again the Indians mighty defensive unit fighting hard and proud as they usually over the years did for Coach Scissum held the Panthers without a first down. Clearly this defense of the Indians was a nightmare for Westside's offense. The first half ended with Westside leading the Indians 7 to 0 in a game that if the Indians didn't have such a tough defense would have been a blowout for Westside. After the bands played the second half opened with the Indians kicking the ball off to Westside and forcing them to punt after again refusing to let them register a single first down. One down later EHHS tried to punt because of bad field position in this defensive struggle and you know what! Johnson was smothered by Westside at the Indians 1 yard line. Now the Indians proud defense was put in an almost impossible position of having to try to hold Westside out of the end zone where they only had to gain 1 yard. It took 3 hard plays but the Panthers finally cashed the gift in for six and they now had a 13 to 0 lead over the Sylacaugans in blue, white and red and they had not registered a single first down. The 4th period found the Indians offense finally arrive at thee game to put the Indians in the game. Richard Threat, freshman running back who certainly was going to have many great years as a Indian runner in the future had the long gainer of 16 yards on the drive and Sank Johnson scored on a 9 yard sweep play. The drive had been initiated by quarterback Johnny Grimmett. The extra point was added on a run by Johnson. The following kickoff found Westside playing the gracious, host now reversing roles with the Indians. They gave the ball back to the Indians. Tip Averette carried the ball to the Westside 9 yard line. But, the play was nullified by a penalty. Clearly the worst call of the game to void Indian fortunes. Time was running out in the game with the Indians fighting fiercely to win. The game ended with the Indians running out of downs on the Westside 19 yard line. Westside won the game in which they could muster only one first down in. Coach Scissum was heard to say it was the worst case of miscues by an Indian squad ever! Of the defensive line he said give the whole bunch credit for their outstanding play. That prevented a Westside massacre. With the Darden of Opelika game cancelled because of bad weather and not scheduled to be made up. It is rumored that Phylliss Wheatley of Childersburg the new kids on the block with a lot of good talent wants a piece of the Indians. They are said to be hungry for a game with the mighty Indians. Be careful what you ask for you just might get it!

1 (note) the Indians would end the 1966 season their first without Hickey Holtzclaw and Griffin with a 6 wins 2 losses and 1 tie record. It was a season in which Cobb Avenue and Westside took out the opportunity to exorcise some demons against the mighty Indians. Neither school had been able to beat the invincible Indians in 3 years and I am sure the victories they gained over Scissum and the Indians brought great joy and thrills to their fans. This was supposed to be a rebuilding year for Scissum and the Indians. But as you can see Coach Scissum did not rebuild at East Highland he just reloaded. Still it was a disappointing season for the Indians under Coach Scissum. Incidentally Phyllis Wheatley would have to wait to next season to get their shot at the Indians.

East Highland Drubs Cobb 19 to 6
1963
By Lawrence Hall

The East Highland Indians upset 3A district champions Cobb High of Anniston in a bitterly contested fray on October 17 at Legion Stadium. The game was a game of inches because the big Panthers line kept breaking through and keeping the Indians from breaking the long bomb on them through out the contest. When the Indians found this out they started one drive that covered 94 yards for a touchdown and another of 96 yards for a touchdown. When the game started the Indians lost the coin toss for the first time this year. The Panthers elected to receive putting a mild drive together. The Panthers moved by land and air to the Indians 37 yard line. The hard hitting Indians defense tomahawked a Panther receiver and forced a fumble. It was big Melvin Bardwell that forced the fumble and pounced on it for the Indians. Then quarterback Cecil Son Leonard took over and put his mates on the move. He sent Jerry Hale into the line for 5 yards Ralph Cook for 6, Alvin Griffin for 3, and this was the story all the way down the field as the Indians continued to sustain the long clock consuming drive to the Cobb 3 yard line. Proving that they not only could strike fast on offense but could drive the ball down a defenses throat. It was here at the 3 yard line that Leonard, on an option play danced into the end zone. The attempt at the conversion filed and the Indians led Cobb 6 to 0. The second quarter found the Panthers driving goal ward on the Indians defense before the thin blue line forced them to punt. Again the like to Jerry Hale, Cecil Leonard, Alvin Griffin and Ralph Cook fullback playing like an all starter tonight moved the football goal ward. From the Cobb 12, Griffin feinted left dodged right jumped over a man and went in for the touch down. It was as magnificent a 13 yard run that you will witness anywhere high school college or pro. The Indians attempted the pat from placement. The snap was high but Son Leonard thinking quickly and using his athletic ability and fleetness ran it in for the two. But the Indians were guilty of an infraction and Leonard had to try the kick from the 17 yard line. It was off to the right. At the half the Indians led Cobb 12 to 0. In the second half the Cobb score came on some poor playing from the Indians. From the 43, the Panthers quarterback shot a pass to his big end. Two backs went for the interception for the Indians and two went for the receiver but he broke loose for the touchdown. The pat failed and the Indians now led 12 to 6 over Cobb. This Cobb score seemed to arouse the Indians for they put on a powerful drive that drove the nail in Cobb's coffin. The Indians offense alternated hand offs pitch outs and fake pitch outs to Hale Cook and Griffin. It was on this drive that fullback Ralph Cook showed the Indians the way. Playing with an injured shoulder that will probably cause him to miss some playing time. He continually plowed into the Panther line for first down yardage. This was not a night given only to Cook but all of his determined mates. The lineman were the real stand outs as they rushed the Cobb passers under pressure all night. Hickey played his finest game at defensive tackle. Jeffie Hughes patrolled his flank with great enthusiasm. McKinney backed the line superbly. Freeing up linebackers Verdell Pearson and Willie Holtzclaw made a fine interception. In the huddle, I heard the boys say all for Wilson. I am sure they meant the fine Indian guard that was injured in the Westside of Talladega game. They were not about to lose this one sike.

Indian Flashbacks 1953

September 24

Coach Haywood Scissum won 7 games and lost 2 in his first year as the Indians head coach in Sylacauga.

The Indians stomped Lineville 53 to 13 last night scoring more than a point per minute 53 points in 48 minutes to be exact. The East Highland High School Indians tomahawked Clay County Training of Lineville to the tune of 51 to 13, Monday night in Legion Stadium. Coach Scissum and Coach Mungin freshly graduated from Tuskegee had the boys keyed up for this game that served as a warm up for the big game next week against 4A Carver of Gadsden at Legion Stadium. The Indians back ran wild as they raced up and down the field from one end to the other. Racking up touchdowns and extra points. Andy red Foster playing his first game as the T quarterback tossed to Hollis for the first Indian td. The second td was chalked up by the same and P combination Hollis on an end around play. In the 3rd quarter the Indians really begin to roll. Fleet footed Billy the Jet Harrison turned on the jets and scored on a 25 yard run. Before the crowd could settle in good in their seats, Big Train Holtzclaw running like a diesel locomotive stormed across the goal line with another touchdown. A new star was born when the fleet footed Paul Hubbard playing his first year of varsity football ran 80 yards and electrified the home crowd with a touch down on one of the most beautiful plays of the game. Ditto can be said about the end around play that executed by Hugh Harrison carrying it in for another 6 points. The other touchdowns were made by Billy the Jet Harrison and Hollis who incidentally is the captain of the team. There were many outstanding lineman who made those runs possible. Big Charles Davis of Sylacauga news fame. Davis led this group in both offense and defense. He was able assisted by James Lee who were to numerous to mention all but we can not help but mention the stellar play of the knight boys and Alfred Oden, Sexton and Smith, Grover Miles and old Sam Breedlove the big tough guard.

October 29
East Highland Plays Cobb of Anniston Monday Night

The East Highland High School Indians will play Cobb Avenue of Anniston on Monday night November 2, at Legion Stadium in Sylacauga. Cobb High is undefeated in 7 games this year and the Indians hope to bring this string to an end. The Indians annihilated Jenifer High School 58 to 0 last week. They scored in the 1st quarter in five minutes of the game and continued to do so throughout the game. Coaches Scissum and Mungin had the opportunity to see what their second string could do as they were given the opportunity to play. Bobby Pearson was injured but he is doing quite well. All of the students wish for his speedy recovery. The crack 60 piece band of Cobb High will perform at halftime. Come see them battle the great East Highland band, the best little band in the land. Game time, 7:30 p.m. Monday night.

East Highland Defeats Cobb

The East Highland High School Indians drew the curtain on their home schedule Monday night by defeating tough Cobb of Anniston 19 to 7 in a brutally hard hitting affair. This victory was significant because Cobb had not lost a game until Monday night. The Indians struck early in the 1st quarter as fleet footed Paul Hubbard sliced off right tackle for the score. Within 2 minutes, James Lee connected with Hugh Harrison on a 60 yard pass play that set up the second score. Then Derry Big Train Holtzclaw bulled his way running over two would be tacklers for the score. Making the score at halftime Indians 13 to Cobb 0. In the early stages of the 3rd quarter Cobb recovered a Indian fumble on the Indians 20 yard line. Two plays later the Panthers from Calhoun County scored making it 13 to 7 East Highland. The Indians received the kickoff and promptly drove 70 yard for their 3rd and final touchdown and the scoring was completed for the night. Quarterback Andy Red Foster intercepted 4 Cobb passes and made long returns on two of them. Much credit should be given to the following boys: Big Charles, Sylacauga news Davis James Lee, The Jet Harrison, Paul Hubbard and the Wright brothers, C. Hollis and Sam Breedlove, the Carpenter brothers, French and James and foots Miles.

Closing the Show

County Colored Champs Meet Carver High of Gadsden Tuesday, November 19, 1957

The East Highland High School Indians will draw the curtain on their 1957 season when they play the carver High School of Gadsden Tuesday night November 19 at Legion Stadium. The Indians tied a strong Ullman High of Birmingham team in Legion Stadium recently. On the basis of this feat they feel that they can upset the Gadsden School. The Carver High Wildcats are undefeated in the conference and will be champions if they can defeat East Highland. The Gadsden team has several very fast backs and a tall 6.8 string bean of an end that usually catches 10 passes a game. The Indians will be out to stop the passes and set the top team in the district up for an upset. The 80 member Carver High School band will play during halftime. They will challenge the 53 member crack band of East Highland that always put on a good show. The Indians swamped Carver 26 to 0 in Gadsden last year. And the Wildcats are seeking revenge for that bitter defeat. This game should be tops for the year. See the game and the battle of the bands game time 7:30 p.m., be there.

1967 East Highland High School Football Preview

The East Highland Indians are preparing for another grueling football season. The Indians are working at an accelerated pace to get ready for the powerful Norris of Attala High School. Norris is always a potent threat to opponents and a power in the NEIAA football. Gone from the Indians team that lost 2 games last year are Captain Frank Williamson, All District guard Odessa Hunter, All District halfback Lee the Bull Buford, incomparable fullback and all everything for Coach Scissum for 3 seasons. He will be sorely missed. James Hollinquest, Lamar Walker, Gleamon Oden, Bubba Averette, Dugger Cook, Lionel Player, Hal McLemore and Felton Hicks. Also lost for other reasons are John T. Buford and Charles Curry. This group and several others expected to return this year to make a total of 16 lettermen lost off the Indians squad. To fill in the running guard position, Robert Gunn has been shifted from end to guard. Roland Slick Morris moved from center to tackle and is having a fine fall. Mike Bledsoe is doing well at the other tackle. Johnny Grimmett and Sammy Johnson return at quarterbacks and are waging a strong battle for the starting quarterback position. Others who have looked good are Larry Tootsie Thomas Lightning Threatt, Robert Hollingquest, Robert Williams, Tip Averette and rough and ready Calvin the Russian McKinney.

1967 Indians Schedule

4A	September 7 Norris of Attala	Home	Won 32 to 0
3A	September 14 Calhoun Co Oxford	Away	Won 30 to 0
4A	September 21 Carver of Gadsden	Home	Won 37 to 0
3A	September 30 Laurel of Alex City	Away	Won 52 to 0

Closing the Show

3A	October 12 Westside of Talladega	Home	Won 40 to 6
4A	October 19 Cobb of Avenue	Home	Lost 14 to 18
4A	October 27 Riverside of Tuscaloosa	Away	Won 46 to 0
2A	November 2 Phylliss Wheatley of Childersburg		Won 37 to 0
2A	November 9 Chilton Co of Clanton		Won 39 to 0
3A	November 16 St. Clair County of Pell City		Won 52 to 0

Indian finished 67 season as district champs with one loss to rival Cobb breaking up undefeated season bid. 9 and 1 record.

Thunder and Lightning Strike Riverside 46 to 0

The unstoppable cousin duo of Threatt and Thomas took on another name last night as the game announcer in Tuscaloosa hung the thunder coin on Larry Tootsie Thomas with Lightning's name and legend already established in the Tuscaloosa's school fans memory it was like a homecoming for him. After seeing Thomas break loose repeatedly, they hung thunder on him. This combo of little Indians broke loose for one long run after another to knock Riverside from the unbeaten ranks. For Sylacauga fans memories, this was the same team that spoiled the Indians homecoming in Sylacauga last year. It ended in a 12 to 12 tie with the Indians scoring with 38 seconds left in the game to starve off defeat. The extra point attempt failed that could have given the Indians a great comeback victory. After the Indians defense forced a fumble it was recovered by end Homer Pearson. Johnny Grimmett then mixed his plays well, sending Sammy Louis Johnson , Lightning and Tootsie Thomas into the line. Then Thomas capped the drive with one of the most determined runs I have ever seen. He broke tackle after tackle as he drove goal ward to score. The extra point failed and the Indians led 6 to 0. On the next Indian drive Sammy Johnson scored the second Indian touchdown on a six yard burst up the middle to make the score 12 to 0. Johnny Grimmett passed to Thomas for the extra point to make the score 13 to 0. The second quarter saw Lightning Threatt break loose for a 21 yard score that came forth down and six yards to go. Tip Averette kicked the pat from placement and the score at halftime was East Highland 20 Riverside 0. The second half found the Tigers unable to move the chains after the kickoff and on fourth down they attempted to punt. This proved to be costly for them because Anthony Cooney Russell broke through up the middle and not

Closing the Show

only blocked it but picked it up and raced into the end zone. The extra point attempt failed and the score was now Indian 26 Tigers 0. Larry Thunder Thomas did it again in the third quarter as he took a handoff and behind a wall of pulling Indian blockers, raced 13 yards to score. The next Indians score came as Lightning scored from 31 yards out on a beautiful screen pass. Tip Averette's conversion was true to make it 40 to 0. Billy Robuck Smith scored the last td on a two yard plunge. The final score East Highland 46 Riverside 0. Thirty six Indians dressed and made the trip to Tuscaloosa and 34 played. It was a big win for Coach Scissum since it was on this field two years ago that the Indians gave him his 100th win. Outstanding backs in the game were quarterback Johnny Grimmett and backs Lightning Threatt, Larry Tootsie Thomas and Sammy Louis Johnson. Other backs who played well were Terry Bledsoe, Bill Robuck Smith and Clarence Kidd. Outstanding lineman ere Roland Slick Morris who was all over the field. Robert Sleepy Hollanquest, Mike Homer Bledsoe and Robert Gunn. Other lineman who stood out were Wally Gator Fulks James Thomas, Donnell Prater and PA Young. The Indians journey to Childersburg tonight to play the undefeated Panthers of Phylliss Wheatley. This game has grown in stature steadily since it was scheduled with Childersburg Wheatley having come through the season with an unblemished record of 7 wins and no loss so far. The Panthers are a high scoring bunch with the team scoring many victories over 50 points. The least that they have scored in a game has been 21. The Indians will be sorely tested and hard pressed to beat the Panthers because they have momentum and the home field advantage. This will be the first meeting ever between the two schools in football. They have competed against each other in basketball. Let's go to Childersburg.

Phylliss Wheatley Glides Past Randolph County

Phylliss Wheatley kept its undefeated season intact with a easy 52 to 0 victory over Randolph County in Childersburg Friday night. The Panthers kept another slate clean by not allowing the Bulldogs to score. The Panthers are averaging 35 points per game. In the 1st quarter they scored 32 points last night. The 1st score came on a beautiful 45 yard run off tackle by halfback Ezell Grayson. After receiving the kickoff, the Bulldogs were unable to move the ball against the tremendous Panther defense. The likes of Walter Sims, Larry Embry, Robert Peterson, Larry McKenzie, James Vincent and Richard Jackson contained the Bulldogs all night. On Wheatley first offensive play after holding the dog's halfback Billy Borden swept around right end for a 20 yard touchdown. Following this, all world split end Larry McKenzie entered the picture. He had touch downs runs of 58 yards 54 and 17 yards to go

Michael Catfish Smith

along with a touch down catch of 32 yards. The big play maker had a total of 4 touch downs on the night good for 24 points for the county's leading scorer. Quarterback Frank Black threw his 2nd td of the season. Eddie the Bruiser Cook also scored a td. The defense was tremendous as usual led by co captain Larry Embry, Walter Sims, Robert Peterson and Richard Jackson. They allowed only 3 first downs.

THE EAST HIGHLAND PHYLLISS WHEATLEY GAME FIRST MEETING 1967

In 1966, Phylliss Wheatley had called the East Highland Indians of Sylacauga out and they meant it. Unfortunately the two schools couldn't make the match up happen because of scheduling. The Indians were going to replace the Darden of Opelika game on their schedule which was cancelled because of bad weather with a first ever match up with Wheatley. But the two sides couldn't make it happen. Phylliss Wheatley loaded down with Sylacauga area players to go along with the good players they had from Childersburg like Ezell Grayson, Cecil Hall, William Jackson and Pearlie and Earlie Battle to name a few were ready and willing to take on the powerhouse school from Sylacauga. To add to the intrigue of the game for both sets of fans was the fact that Phyllis Wheatley the new kids was undefeated in 7 games while averaging 33 points a game while giving up only 6 for Coach Clarence Marble. The Indians on the other hand, the established powerhouse under Coach Scissum had lost a heart breaker at home to powerful Cobb Avenue who once again spoiled a undefeated season for Coach Scissum and the Indians. I don't know if Phylliss Wheatley detected a chink in the armor of the mighty Indians or what. But I know that they were confident that they could have given the Indians their second loss of the season. The build up to the game for the first meeting ever in football between the schools was almost unbearable leading up to the weeks before the game. Fans anticipating the colossus showdown had been talking about it for weeks. People that worked and went to church together were choosing sides loyal to their individual schools. I often wonder what the Indians players were thinking on the bus ride over to Childersburg. I don't know for certain because I never asked Lightning, Foots or Danny Morris. But I know in my heart that they were confident of victory as they always were under Coach Scissum despite their lone set back to Cobb. Even though the Panthers were undefeated the Indians knew what they were bringing to the table. The crowd was wildly excited as the Indian buses rolled in to the stadium in Childersburg. The fans were about to witness the Indians playing their first and only game ever in Childersburg. Imagine that a school with the Indians rep having been all over the state and never playing 10 miles from home in neighboring Childersburg. The fans the Indians brought to the game from Sylacauga overflowed the visitor's bleachers in the stadium. They weren't at home but it seemed like home. Let's play the game!

1967
EAST HIGHLAND BLAST STUBBORN CHILDERSBURG 37 TO 0

With its devastating ground game the East Highland Indians knocked Phylliss Wheatley from the ranks of the unbeaten last night. Though the Indians had virtually sewn up the AA championship when they downed Westside of Talladega this win assured it. Powerful Cobb seems destined for the AAA State Championship as they roll on undefeated and untied. If they continue what will East Highland be number two? As the game started the Indians were hard pressed at times to punch in touchdowns against the stubborn Panthers of Wheatley who were showing people that them being undefeated was no fluke. But, the Indians found out that they could run the ball and Wheatley found out that they could not turn the tide of the quick pony backs of East Highland. Lightning Threatt who gained 126 yards rushing scored the first Indian touchdown on a 4 yard run over right tackle. It may be added here that Phylliss Wheatley did not kick the ball off deep all night. The reason was to prevent Lightning from breaking a long run on them for a touchdown as he has done in 5 previous games this year. The extra point failed and the Indians led 6 to 0 early in the game. I don't even know if Phylliss Wheatley is good at coming back from behind or not. I don't even know if they have trailed all year in a game during their 7 game undefeated streak. But, I do know that they better get used to it in this game because the mighty Indians offense seemed like a pack of sharks in a blood feeding frenzy when they smelled blood. Early in the second quarter Johnny Grimmett scored on a naked bootleg play that fooled the poor Panthers so badly he was untouched as he walked into the end zone. Tip Averette kicked the pat and the Indians now led the Panthers 13 to 0. The Panthers playing from behind for the first time this season received the ensuring kickoff and soon found out what other teams have found all year that it's almost impossible to move the ball against the Indians defense. After a Panther punt Johnny Grimmett drove the Indians deep into Panther territory before he fumbled on the Panthers 6 yard line. On the very next play a host of Indians penetrated the Panthers offensive line and trapped Willie Lee McElrath in the end zone for a safety. The score was now Indians 15 Panthers 0. And for all practical purposes this first ever meeting between the two schools was probably over. Because the mighty Indians defense like their offense when they smelled blood they went for the kill. They prided themselves in shutting out opponents. Down and out but the Indians weren't through scoring in this game just yet. The Panthers kick was received and on the first Indian offensive play. Sophomore PA Young made a fantastic catch of the football after slipping behind Panther Larry McKenzie for a touchdown. Lightning Threatt threw the block that took out the final Panther defender on the play. The pass and run covered 60 yards and the score was now Indians 21 and Panthers 0. I was now getting the feeling that the Panthers who had seemed so confident before the game started was now not so confident. The home town Wheatley fans were not so loud anymore either. They were finding the years and that these were not your ordinary band of Indians. Halftime saw the score, Indians 21 Panthers 0. As the band, the best little band in the land or the baddest little band in the land as Indian fans called them performed under the direction of Mr. Larkins with their smooth Motown sound. I wondered what Coach Marble of Phylliss Wheatley was telling his troops in the locker room? The Indians had shell shocked them and took their fans right out of the game seeing them trail at halftime for the fist time this year, the only people happy right now was the ones on the visitor's side from down the road. I wondered what the Wheatley fans were thinking in their minds because they had not seen their team lose a game all year let alone be down by 3 touchdowns at halftime? But if they didn't already know they were about to find out a Haywood Scissum team when they get you down they going to kill you. But one half does not make a football game so let's go on to the second half. The Indians and the choice to start the second half and elected to receive. Quarterback Johnny Grimmett then directed his men on a drive to the Panthers 41. From here he rolled out left and behind running guards Calvin the Russian McKinney and Robert Poor Rob Gunn he broke for the end zone flags. But the score was nullified because of a penalty. Shortly after that, the proud Phyllis Wheatley defense fighting hard to keep the Indian from embarrassing them bowed up and held the Indians on downs a rare stop tonight against the Indians offensive juggernaut forcing them to punt. After the punt the Panthers offense could not gain any real estate against the Indians so on 4th down and 12 they attempted to punt. But Big Wally Gator Fulks mean and nasty playing inspired ball broke through the line and blocked it. On the Indians first offensive play Larry Thunder Tomas, Lightning's cousin, scooted into the end zone. Tip Averette conversion was good and the Indians now led comfortably 28 to 0 over the undefeated Panthers. After kicking off to the Panthers, the Indians held them on downs again and again. The Panthers punted, the Indians received the ball and found out that Phylliss Wheatley still had some fight in them. For their proud defense held the Indians on downs and forced Highland to punt. The Indians punt drove the Panthers deep to their 3 yard line. Then an ill fated call by them that saw all world Wheatley player Larry McKenzie get trapped in the end zone on a reverse play that was blown up by Robert Poor Rob Gunn. The score after the play was now Indians 30 and Wheatley 0. The soon to be defeated Panthers were now getting a taste of Indian football that they had craved last year. Phylliss Wheatley blowing out so many opponents this year, while going undefeated certainly couldn't have liked the taste of what the Indians were dishing out tonight. In a game only one team can experience the thrill of victory someone has to taste the agony of defeat. The next kickoff following the safety, saw the Indians behind fullback Billy Robuck Smith and Little Terry Cat Quick Bledsoe and Lightning. All sophomores push one in for the Indians as Threatt carried it the final 25 yards to pay dirt. Averette's pat was good and the score was Indians 37 Panthers 0. The Childersburg foe was a good match up for the Indians. And should provide good competition for at least another year. Backs that caught my eye were Johnny Grimmett, Terry Bledsoe, Billy Smith and the incomparable cousin duo of Larry Thomas and Lightning Threatt or thunder and lightning, if you prefer. Sammy Johnson quarterback, didn't play because they didn't need him on this night. Lineman that graded well were McKinney, Morris Fulks, Homer Pearson, JD Thomas, Sleepy Hollinquest and Robert Gunn, who seemingly found himself again. Anthony Cooney Russell, sophomore and Travis Oden, senior along with Donell Prater, junior should be singled out. Also Big Robert Williams, sophomore defensive tackle should be singled out. It should be noted that Phylliss Wheatley came into this game undefeated with a 7 and 0 record after calling out the Indians last year. They had the county's top defense and they are to be commended for their record considering that they were a young program. But it was the Indians defense that stole the show.

Note- It seemed like Coach Scissum was just getting the Indians program crunk up and going into over drive when the end came in 1970. Cobb stopped Coach Scissum from having 6 undefeated teams out of 10 years in the 60's by handing the 67 and 68 teams their only defeats in very close losses.

From October 3, 1968 the Sylacauga News
Panthers Slay the Dragons

Phylliss Wheatley rolled to its 3rd consecutive victory of the season Thursday night September 26, 1968. They over whelmed Prentice High School of Montevallo 54 to 0. The Panthers displayed an awesome ground game along with timely passing. Ezell Grayson was tremendous with runs from scrimmage of 58 yards and 25 yards for touchdowns. Eddie Cook had his usual good game with a total of 77 yards and 1 touchdown. Coach Clarence Marble's biggest thrill came in the discovery of a new star. This was in the person of James Vincent who had a catch of 40 yards for a touchdown. The Panther defense which has not allowed a core all season was superb. They allowed the dragons only 3 first downs for the game. The Panthers intercepted two passes. One by Larry McKenzie who returned it 50 yards for a touchdown. Norman Toney recovered a Dragon fumble and rambled 7 yards for another score. Overall, the Panthers are a much stronger team offensively and defensively than they were last season when they lost to East Highland 37 to 0, after starting off 7 and 0. That lone defeat last year came at home in Childersburg to Scissum and his Indians. To date, the Panthers have no serious injuries. The next game for the undefeated unscored on Panthers is October 4, in Childersburg. Come and see a real powerhouse team in action.

Closing the Show

CATCH ME IF YOU CAN — Indian end Donnie Prater (87) scampers into end zone with second East Highland touchdown in second quarter of Highland's 34-6 rout of Phyllis Wheatley Thursday night. Prater was running fast because it seemed as if the whole Panther team was behind him. Hot on his heels are Ezelle Grayson (21), David Adair (61), Larry Garrett (63) and Billy Bordon (20).

Indians Trick the Panthers 34 to 6
October 31, 1968

The Phylliss Wheatley High School Panthers of Childersburg came to Sylacauga for the first time to play the Indians in football game. It would be their only visit ever. The Panthers an upstart program with many talented players came into the game riding high with only one blemish on their record in 6 games. They loss a close one to Westside of Talladega. This game would be the last chance for Wheatley to ever gain a victor over the mighty Indians in football. Or ride off into history knowing that they never defeated East Highland in football leading up to the Halloween night contest the game had been billed as the irresistible force meeting the immoveable object. Phylliss Wheatley in it five victories in 6 games had averaged a county leading 33 points a game on offense. Their defense had been almost perfect giving up only 12 points all season. All in one game in a 12 to 6 lost to Westside. Their average per game 2.0. The Indians statistics were almost as good as they were averaging 31.2 points per game while allowing only 5.2 per game. Coach Clarence Marble of Wheatley said in the loss last week to Westside that we had numerous opportunities to score and win the game but just didn't take advantage of them. But I think the loss will help us against East Highland boy's Thursday. The boy's know they should have won and will be out to redeem themselves Thursday. We night have been a little over confident he said, but not now. They know they can be beaten and will give that little extra this week. We'll play a lot better ball this week and I'll guarantee you we will be out for East Highland's scalp. The county scoring leader Larry McKenzie

Michael Catfish Smith

will be full speed this week said Marble. He was hampered by a minor leg injury last week against Westside. East Highland on the other hand has 9 boys hobbling with ankle injuries and others to boot. They will play but you know it won't be the same as if they were healthy Scissum said, Wednesday. See, we aren't planning anything special for this game nothing different he said. I know it's a big game with big game build up for the fans of both schools. And I know Phylliss Wheatley will get after us. I just hope our boys realize it. Richard Lightning Threatt, the Indians top threat on offense and captain and defensive tackle Roland Slick Morris and co-captain guard Manuel Big Joe Pope are three of the walking wounded Scissum mentioned. Wheatley has a fine football team I know it Scissum said. I just hope my boys can get some of that Indian spirit back that was missing last week. Threatt vs. McKenzie explosive offense vs. stingy defense. Anyway you look at it, it's going to be quite a ball game. The day before the big game with Wheatley some players from the school rode past the Indian practice field while Coach Scisssum was conducting practice with last minute preparations and yelled out of a car window ya'll better practice cause ya'll going to need it tomorrow night. If the Indians needed anymore motivation than they already had, this was it. They knew that 7 players on the Wheatley's team were from Sylacauga among them star player Larry McKenzie a former Indian. They knew that McKenzie and his mates would love nothing more than to have bragging rights till eternity in this last meeting ever with the Indians. The Threatt vs. McKenzie rivalry had its roots all the way back in elementary school in Walco. The match up for supremacy as the best in the county between the two was very intriguing. So, as an 8 year old sitting in Legion Stadium, I watched the Indians line up in the tunnel entrance leading to the field. I could hear the whooping and hollowing among the pads slapping as the Indians were getting fired up and ready to go out onto the field and scalp another opponent. This time another brand of animal, a Panther. As I looked, I saw the Phylliss Wheatley Panthers coming onto the field on the opposite side of the stadium from the direction that the Sylacauga Aggies used as a home team. They were wearing maroon and gold with white jerseys. The Indians meanwhile were entering the stadium from the dressing room that was located next to the one the BB Comer Tigers used. I peered over the railing in the stadium not realizing what I was about to witness. I have to thank my Aunt Bessie and Uncle Henry for letting me tag along to this game. Monkey Wrench Corbin was leading the Indian football team onto the field beating the drums. As usual, the supreme Indian drummer was throwing down beats! Rata ta tat rata tat tat boom! As the Indians cheerleaders were already getting off firing up the home side of the crowd shouting stop! Look! and listen! here comes the mighty Indians! and as the Indians took the field and headed to the sidelines for the beginning of the game. The cheerleaders broke into another classic! We took the little red rooster! Yeah man, the crowd shouted back and we put him on the fence! Yea man! He was hollering for the Panthers! Yeah man! He didn't have good sense! Yeah man! We took another red rooster! Yeah man! And we put him on the fence, yeah man! He was hollowing for the Indians! Yeah man! Cause he had good sense! Yeah man! As the game started it would soon become a double treat for Coach Scissum because winning a game is a treat in itself but, the victory over Wheatley was double delicious as the County Independent Championship was on the line. Line the colored version of the County Championship. The game itself was a tough defensive battle for three quarters as advertised. Then the mighty Indians offense would come to life like a boxer pecking his jab at an opponent feeling him out and then taking him into deep water with nothing to hold onto and drowning him. The Indians offense exploded for 21 points all of the scoring done in the 2nd and 4th quarters. The first half of this hard hitting affair was stunning. The Indians defense refused to give anything and vice versa, the Panthers defense. As I watched, they were going at it like two heavyweight championship boxers. But, I really didn't realize being 8 that Phylliss Wheatley was a good team. For to me the Indians were doing them just like they did everybody else I saw them play in legion. The half ended with the Indians leading 13 to 6. And I must say that I believed the crowd on the other side of the field must have been feeling pretty good about their team chances in this game being down by just 7 points to the Indians. Much different than last year's first meeting where they were out of it at half time. The third quarter ended the same way halftime had with the Indians clinging to a 13 to 6 lead in the defensive head hunting contest. Both defenses were playing like they wanted bragging rights in town church, the barbershop, the grocery store, where ever. Wheatley's defense came into the game as the county's best. But, it's the Indians defense that would steal the show. Phylliss Wheatley gained only 34 yards of total offense for the game. They only crossed the mid field stripe twice. And if it weren't for penalties, the Panthers would not have gotten outside of their own 30 but once. The Panthers picked up 11 first downs but 7 came on penalties as the Indians amassed 135 yards in penalties. An unusually high number for a Haywood Scissum coached team. But, I am sure emotions on both side were running high by these players who knew each other. The top ground gainer for the Indian was Lightning Threatt who picked his way to 59 tough yards in 12 carries against the hard hitting Panther defense led by Walter Sims, Robert Peterson, Ezell Grayson, Larry Embery, Larry McKenzie and James Vincent. The usually grind em up Indians running game was forced to go to the air route and pass for 121 yards one of the highest totals of the year for the

Indians. Wheatley sold out to stop the powerful Indian running game and forced quarterback Jay Grimmett to beat them throwing, he did. Grimmett hit on 5 of 7 passes as the junior signal caller and Indian leader threw for two touchdowns. End Sylvester Beattie McKinney passed once for a 39 yard touchdown. Wheatley's Larry McKenzie, the county scoring leader and former Indians home boy was held to minus 4 yards in 5 carries in the game. His injured leg did not heal in this hard hitting game. Wheatley's Ezell Grayson was healthy but fared no better picking up 32 yards against the tough Indian defense. The hard hitting Sylacugans in blue and white allowed this in 16 frugal attempts for Grayson. He found out what many teams already knew about the Indians. You don't run on a Haywood Scissum coached defense. Ask Cobb. East Highland broke open a scoreless game in the second quarter when junior fullback Billy Robuck Smith burst off tackle for 4 yards to cap a short 20 drive. He drug the final would be tackler into the end zone. The touchdown was set up by Donnell Prater's who partially blocked Larry McKenzies punt from the 15. Five minutes later, the Indians added their second touchdown under almost identical conditions except a little in with longer drive. Slick Morris almost blocked McKenzie's punt from his 40 forcing him to kick the ball high and to the side to avoid the block. Morris broke through enemy lines from his tackle position. The ball carried five yard to the 45. From there it took just 7 plays a complete number for quarterback Jay Grimmett passing 26 yards to end Donnell Prater who out ran the Panther defense in a catch me if you can footrace. Then Ezell Grayson gave our neighbors and friends from Childersburg their only highlight of the night as he electrified the visitors when he took the ensuing kickoff and went straight up the middle of the Indians kickoff team found a wedge and took it home running towards Sycamore as both sides of the stadium stood up 98 yards for the Panther touchdown. I think the Sylacauga crowd was stunned that the Indians gave up the touchdown while the Wheatley crowd was proud to avoid the shutout for the second year in a row. The 3rd quarter was scoreless with the Panthers stout defense stopping the Indians twice inside of the ten yard line to avoid scores. But in the 4th quarter the Panthers seemed to run out of gas and tired. You can't fight a 15 round war with 10 round condition the Indians went on the war path sensing the kill. With 10:43 left in the game, Grimmett scored on a razzle dazzle play that saw him hand off to Threatt who handed the ball to Terry Cat Quick Bledsoe who ran left around end and then just as the defense hit him, he lateral back to Grimmett who was trailing the play and walked in the end zone. The Indians execution was perfect as Grimmett ran 12 yards for the score untouched. Such trickery was not unusual for the Indians especially with a Grimmett quarterbacking. East Highland added two more touchdowns in the 4th quarters last 4 minutes on

Closing the Show

long passes. Somebody must have scouted the Indians wrong thinking the way to beat them was to stop the run and make them pass. Grimmett passed to Terry Bledsoe hitting him with a screen pass on the 25 with 4:02 left and the junior halfback scurried into the end zone quickly for the six. Minutes later, Beattie McKinney hit the other end PA Young for a 39 yard bomb for six and the Indians fans went home happy from Legion Stadium once again with a 34 to 6 win against their neighbors from Childersburg the Phyllis Wheatley Panthers. It would be the last meeting ever between the two schools as Wheatley would not field a team in 69 getting ready to merge with the Childersburg Tigers. In two meetings with the Panthers the Indians outscored their rivals 71 to 6.

East Highland Indians Score 166 points in 5 games

Wednesday, October 16, 1968
By Dan Rutledge

For a word with only two letters, it can be a big word. East Highland High School has a pretty good football team. They have one of the most potent offenses in the county. And one of the stingiest defenses. The Indians have scored 166 points in five ball games and allowed only 31 against them. They have won four and lost only one. And the one loss came to Cobb Avenue of Anniston which is presently undefeated and untied and ranked 11th in the state in class 4A. The Indians are a 2A school. But Coach Scissum says he could have had a much better team and an undefeated record this year if it weren't for a couple of wrong moves. Now these moves weren't made by Scissum or his opposing coaches. They were made by the parents of two boys whom calls two of the finest athletes I have ever coached. Larry McKenzie now a senior at Phylliss Wheatley high School in Childersburg. And Martin Wilson a senior quarterback at Wenonah High School in Birmingham. Both attended East Highland in the 9th and 10th grades. And both were starters for the Indians as sophomores, both families moved away from Sylacauga in the summer of their junior years. McKenzie is currently the Talladega County scoring leader with 73 points to his nearest oppositions 54. As an end for Wheatley McKenzie has scored 9 touchdowns and 1 extra point. Coach Clarence Marble of Wheatley calls him the backbone of the team. Coach Scissum said that Larry is just a tremendous athlete. He played a football, basketball and baseball and started in all of them in the 10th grade here. He is one of the best third basemen you'll ever want to see. Wilson quarterbacks the Wenonah Tigers of Bessemer. Wenonah is currently the number 5 team in the state in class 4A with a 6 and 0 slate. Wilson has scored 3 touchdowns running this season and passed for 2 more. He has completed 51 percent of his throws. He is a good student too on the B honor roll, each 6 weeks according to his principal. But the Wenonah coach says that Wilson's biggest assets are his field leadership his confidence and the confidence he gives the team. I discovered him in a physical education class last year midway through the season. We had lost 6 straight games. After he started as quarterback we won 4 in a row and haven't lost this year. I don't know what I would do without him. East Highland Indians score 166 points continued without him. He is what makes our offense go. Coach Scissum spends a good deal of time thinking about the Cobb defeat. About McKenzie and Wilson. And only if I had been able to keep those two in Sylacauga nobody in the state would have been able to touch us.

East Highland vs Westside 1968

The last time the Indian ventured into their so called death Valley Westside Stadium they were ambushed 13 to 7 in 1966. In that game Westside made only one first down against the Indians defense. It was Lightning and his classmates of 1970 first game against the Panthers. Threatt playing in his first varsity season as a freshman had seen Griffin Holtzclaw and Hickey run off 3 straight on Westside and they soon got a taste of the rivalry that was East Highland vs Westside. Let's see what happened on the Indians return visit to Talladega 2 years later.

A rowdy crowd greeted the Indians of East Highland as they rolled into Talladega's Westside High School Stadium. Perhaps the home town fans still remember what happened the last time the Indians visited and were expecting more of the same. To top this off the Panthers were undefeated. But the Indians were poised to rebound after suffering another tough close loss to powerhouse Cobb Avenue of Anniston. They would tonight take the measure of 3A and previously undefeated Westside of Talladega. Westside was riding a 4 game unbeaten string when the Indians rode into town. The game played in Death Valley Westside's infamous field was packed to the max with excited fans on both sides of the stadium. Many good teams have ventured here and left humiliated. The big blue was not to be denied tonight however. It seemed as though the Indians were still suffering from after effects from the Cobb game as they started. It took awhile for them to realize that they were not facing Cobb's Panthers but Westside's Panthers for some reason it seemed like everybody that the Indians played in those days wanted to be called Panthers. Just like today most high schools call themselves Tigers. Back to the game. The opening game performance of the Indians was sub-par for them under Coach Scissum. The famed Indian spirit was missing and it must be told that junior quarterback, Jay Grimmett starting in his first season after brother Johnny Grimmett how a freshman at Tuskegee graduated was thorn in the Panthers side all night. Now he had his work cut out for him mightily to salvage this one. Jay of A&P fame had help from classmate Threatt who displaying the complete running back talent that he has ran for 142 yards in 20 carries while catching 2 passes for 58 more yards. This gave the brilliant Indians back 20 yards for the night to start the game the Indians won the coin toss and elected to receive. From the 40 Jay Grimmett directed Billy Robuck Smith, Terry Cat Quick Bledsoe and lightning steadily toward Westside's end zone. Lightning got the final 5 yards for the score on a sweep. Davis Cook kicked the pat and the Indians took a early lead 7 to 0. On Westside's first possession the Indians defense stymied the Panther offense and forced them to punt. The Indians then got the ball on their own 24 and started a goal ward drive. Hopes of another touchdown however, were spoiled when Lightning fumbled at the Indians 10 yard line. Westside, enjoying their best field position of the young night threatened for the first time. Their quarterback Curry on first down threw to flanker Fast Eddy Nolen at the Indians 5. Then the proud Indian defense staple since Coach Scissum arrived in 1952 penetrated and pushed them back to the 9 yard line. Four tries and Westside couldn't dent the Indians end zone despite the excellent field position. The Indians offense took over but the 1st quarter ended with the Indians leading Westside 7 to 0. To start the second quarter Indian Lightning Threatt who seemed to be derter mined to erase all memories of what happened in his freshman year in 1966 on this field was running with fire and desire as he sprinted 44 yards to set up the second Indians score. Two play later Jay Grimmett, Indian trick artist fooled everybody in the stadium including the poor Panther defense as he ran untouched on a 4 yard run around right end. Shades of brother Johnny, who used to fool defenses with the same play. The pat failed and the Indians now led Westside 13 to 0. On the ensuing kickoff Westside would get their lone opportunity for their fans to cheer as Fast Eddy Nolen electrified the home crowd as he received the Indian kickoff on his 7 yard line reversed field twice and sped untouched down the sideline 93 yards behind a wall of Panther blockers for a touchdown. The pat failed but there was still hope for Westside in this game. The score was now 13 to 6 Indians. Westside seemed to be playing with new vigor as the next Indian series they stopped us cold and force a punt. Westside got the ball on their 25 after the Indians punted. Then the Indians defense showed Westside and its fans that the touchdown run back by Nolen only gave them false hope. Big Wally Gator Fulks broke past the Panther offensive line and hit Panther quarterback Curry with a vicious lick that forced him to fumble. An alert Panther however, fell on it at the Panther's 1 yard line. This preventing what might have been another Indian score. Westside Panther punter Nolen then boomed a long 53 yard punt to the Indians 46. The clock then ran out in the first half with the

Michael Catfish Smith

Indians leading the undefeated home standing Panthers 13 to 6. One had to wonder at halftime if Westside's fans thought that now that they were only 7 points down to the Indians that they were going to come back in the second half and win. Judging by some of the trash talking going on by their fans on the Indians side of the stadium, this definitely was a game that neither side wanted to lose. Westside chose to receive to start the second half of play. But the Panthers drive was stopped when Lightning Threatt intercepted a pass and returned it 7 yards to the Indians 39. Then the Indians again unleashed their awesome array of offensive strength when Grimmett passed to Threatt for 39 yards. But Westside was determined not to go easy and rose up on defense and held the Indians at their 24 yard line. The Panthers then took over on offense and 3 plays saw them lose 4 yards against the hard hitting Sylacaugans in blue and white. Eddy Nolen then attempted to punt out of trouble and the play that probably changed the game and broke Westside back and spirit was about to happen. The 10 man Indian rush with no return set up commonly now called the jail break was too much for Westside to handle as Boot Pratt, a mean nasty tackle broke through and blocked it. The ball bounced into the end zone and Indian James Blood Pope fell on it. Touchdown! No touchback. The officials said that it had gone out of bounds along the way. No matter the second play from scrimmage Indian quarterback Jay Grimmett saw Prince Albert Young streaking down the sideline and hit him with a beautiful spiral for a touchdown. Little Terry Bledsoe skirted around end real quickly for the pat and the Indians led 20 to 6 going into the 4th quarter. At this juncture this game was probably over except the fat lady singing. Westside's offense hadn't been able to do anything against the mighty Indian defense all night and very few teams were ever able to amount a come back on the Indian under Scissum. The 4th quarter saw the panthers behind Fast Eddy Nolen and all district player Ronnie Mabra try desperate were they tried to pass deep in their own territory on the 20 yard line. Donnell Prater defensive end intercepted it for the Indians and carried it to the Panther 5 yard line. On 3rd down Jay Grimmett lofted his second touchdown pass of the night to Cat Quick Terry Bledsoe the kick was good to Cat Quick Terry Bledsoe. The kick by David Cook failed and the Indians had gained revenge over Westside on this field by defeating them 26 to 6. The loss knocked Westside from the ranks of the unbeaten. Talking to Coach Scissum after the game he said the boys were not as sharp offensively or defensively but it was a very fine win. Outstanding backs were Lightning Threatt, Jay Grimmett, Terry Bledsoe and Billy Robuck Smith. The defense was led by Anthony Cooney Russell and Donnell Prater at the flanks. Roland Slick Morris and Anthony Boot Pratt mean nasty defensive tackles. On the offensive line Manuel Big Joe Pope and James Blood Pope at the guards.

Indians Compete Season in 1963 with Win
By Lawrence Hale

The East Highland Indians completed their 1963 season by crushing the Chambers County Tiger 75 to 7. Coach Scissum let everyone on his team play during the last half. In the 1st quarter of play the Indians consumed two of their touchdowns. One was a 6 yard plunge by fullback Ralph Cook. Jerry Hale added the pat. Then JD Hughes picked up a fumble and ran 21 yards for the other score. Within a few minutes a fumble occurred in the Indians back field and a Tiger carried it 57 yards for the only td the Tigers would score. The pat was good and that provided their 7 points. As the quarters changed, Cecil Son Leonard secured his td for the night on a 1 yard quarterback sneak. Hale again added the pat. Later Leonard connected with Billy brown for a 25 yard td. He also passed to Sylvester Wilson for the extra point. After the Indians filled the scoreboard with points kicker Ralph Cook added another touchdown by twisting and turning for 7 yards. The pat was no good. To end the scoring for the 1st half, the Indians led the home standing Tigers 41 to 7. Throughout the 3rd quarter it was Lee the Bull Buford al the way as he sprinted 50 and 18 yards. For two other td's for the Indians. Terry Player ran for one of the pats but the other one was missed. 3rd quarter score 55 to 7. During the final quarter of play for the Indians this season Terry Player ran 7 yards for a td. Also later in the 4th quarter Calvin Hart scrambled 8 yards with a fumble for a td. With less than 3 minutes left in the game, Alvin Griffin sprinted 43 yards for the final score to complete the season. The Indians have 7 seniors that played in their last game in Legion Stadium. They are Big Melvin Bardwell, left tackle; Cecil Son Leonard, quarterback; Ralph Cook, Fullback; Sylvester Wilson, left guard; Kenneth Dunklin, right guard;

Michael Catfish Smith

Herman McKinney, center; and of course the mightiest linebacker of them all Verdell Pearson. These persons are often known throughout the school as the magnificent 7. The Indians completed the 1963 season with a 8-1-1 record and a district championship.

A General Comparison between the Two Dominate Schools in Talladega County in Football in the 1960s

East Highland Indians
Facts
- The Indians finished the 1969 season winning 9 games and outscoring opponents 498 to 6.
- In the 60's the Indians played 97 games.
- The Indians closed the show on their football program on a 17 game win streak.
- From 1963-69 the Indians lost only 5 games

Record

	Wins	Loss	Tied
1960-1969	84	11	3

Sylacauga Aggies
Facts
- The Aggies finished the 1969 season winning 11 and 1, with a state championship.
- In the 60's the Aggies played 102 games.
- 1969 the Aggies played 3 more games than the Indians but still scored 118 points less.
- From 1963-69 the Aggies lost 18 games, which is more than the Indians lost in the whole decade.

Michael Catfish Smith

Record

	Wins	Loss	Tied
1960-1969	75	25	2
• 1960	7	2	1
• 1961	9	1	
• 1962	6	4	
• 1963	6	3	1
• 1964	8	2	
• 1965	8	2	
• 1966	7	3	
• 1967	7	3	
• 1968	6	4	
• 1969	11	1	

INDIANS VS. AGGIES

It is rare that a city the size of Sylacauga will have two high schools the caliber of East Highland and Sylacauga High especially during the racially charged era of social change 1960's. This was the decade that saw the United States and the world witness the murder of President John Kennedy in 1963; Malcolm X in 1965; and Senator and Presidential hopeful Robert Kennedy along with Dr. Martin Luther King in 1968. It was the era of protest against an unpopular war Vietnam and white students were gunned down on the campus of Kent State University in Ohio at the close of the decade in 1970. Social injustices against blacks were being protested with lunch counter sit-ins through out the south. In Birmingham, Alabama, Public Safety Commissioner Eugene Bull Conner, was turning dogs and fire hoses on black citizens in the streets of Birmingham. It was an era of slow social change in the south. In fact, some white men were so against change that in 1957, the Sylacauga News printed an article where they went into the streets of Talladega and asked some white men would they fight in a war against the United States if it was waged today. Their answer was over whelming. 10 out of 11 said they would. So many were hell bent on holding onto a way of life that they felt was right. A life that did not include equal rights for the south's black citizens. In this era we also witness the birth of braggadocious Muhammed Ali's voice and career crying out in the segregated wilderness like John the Baptist. Black Panthers led by Huey Newton and Eldridge Cleaver in Oakland and the Seales brothers in Chicago were protesting police brutality against black citizens in the streets of Oakland, California and Chicago respectively. Marches were frequent and reported on the news. It was a time when the sweet sounds of Motown music took over and dominated the airwaves of radio. At the close of this tumultuous time in our nations history a time when marijuana became a common item for young people to be rebellious against authority. sexual freedom was born amid the discovery of the birth control pill. Many teens celebrated and indulged themselves into it. A mother putting her daughter on them might as well have been an invitation to go and have sex. It was during these times that the East Highland High School Indians were getting ready to close out one of the greatest decades of high school football that the state of Alabama had ever seen. The Supreme Court with the passage of the Brown vs. Board decision in 1954 championed by NAACP lawyer Thurgood Marshall had outlawed segregation in the nation's public school systems. This decision had virtually sealed East Highlands' and other black schools fates in the south. But strangely it would take Sylacauga and other white schools in Alabama almost 16 years to bring this law into effect after the decision had been rendered. Well, lucky for the East Highland community in Sylacauga that it did take so long for it was during these 16 years plus two that Haywood Scissum would put East Highland football on the map in the state of Alabama. The Indians would write a chapter in Sylacauga's sports history that is still unequaled today. During this time from 1952 the year he arrived until 1970 the year he left, Coach Scissum's teams would write an chapter in Alabama prep sports history that would be for the ages. During the 60's decade his teams turned out 3 undefeated seasons in 1964 1965 and 1969. Three other teams missed going undefeated by one game. They were the 1963 1967 and 1968 teams. In 68, the Indians would finish ranked number 10 in the states final poll of rankings. From 1963 to 1965 Scissum's teams would win 34 straight games. An undefeated season in 1969 which saw them destroy 9 opponents along with the state runner-up in 2A football in 1968 and ranked number 2 at the time the Indians played them, the St. Jude Pirates of Montgomery, Alabama, 70 to 0. the Indians would end their glorious history and reign in 1969 on a 17 game winning streak. After the school was finally shut down in 1970. There would be numerous all-star players during these years, among them Richard Oden who played for the Los Angeles Rams; Joe Nathan Hickey and Cecil Leonard who was drafted and played for the New York Jets; Alvin Griffin who was drafted by the Atlanta Falcons and Bernard Gunn who was drafted by the Kansas City Chiefs. Derry Lee Holtzclaw who played for the Indians in the mid fifties was a hoss who played college ball for the Tuskegee Institute Golden Tigers. He certainly would have been the Indians first pro football player had he not been killed in a car accident coming home from college. So popular was Holtzclaw in Sylacauga, they held his funeral in the high school gym at East Highland. Richard Lightning Threatt the final Indian great back was all-state all-district and honorable mention high school All-American, Sonny Oden a teammate of Richard. Oden was also a out-standing player for Coach Scissum. As a fan, you knew that with the Indians team speed would be awesome. The opponents knew this also. Think of Florida State and the Miami Hurricanes teams from the late 80's and 90's. So as my mind pondered what an Indians vs. Aggies match up would be like in my heart I knew that it would never happen. Sylacauga which proclaimed themselves as the best in the city and many times dominated cross-town rival B.B. Comer in the 60's in football winning 8 out of 10 against them also claimed to be the best in the county. Meanwhile the Indians playing in the county's independent championship series the black version of the Sylacauga claims also laid claim as the best in the city and the county. so the Indians naturally would have liked to put to the test of the theory that the Aggies were the best. Surely the Aggies benefitted from not having to put their reputation on the line in a three school series that would have pitted East Highland, BB Comer and Sylacauga against one another. Segregation laws prevented such an arrangement. These two white schools couldn't face the Indians in anything until the late 60s in fact 69 and 70 when they faced the fleet-footed Indians in track and field. In the late 60's I believe that both schools along with the rest of the white schools in the county that had started to integrate just decided to avoid the high scoring touchdown denying Indians until they just went away in 1970. In fact the only sport the Aggies faced the Indians in was track and field in the 69 and 70 county track meets where the Indians literally ran away with the county title while setting numerous records that weren't recognized against the likes of Childersburg, Munford, Lincoln and Talladega. It was almost as if some people were in a hurry to see the Indians go away. An Indians vs. Aggies match-up in football would have been like the great players from the negro leagues in baseball playing against the great white players from the major leagues. so as I along with my cousins and a few friends stood on the fence surrounding legion stadium in Sylacauga on this Friday night in 1969 trying to watch the Aggies facing one of their opponents we were in the scrutinizing mode. I am not sure who the Aggies were facing this night but I do know that they were winning and dominating as the scoreboard indicated. In fact, the Aggies won often in 1969 their state championship year in football losing only to county rival 21 to 0, the Childersburg Tigers. In this very stadium, it would be the last time the Aggies had won a state championship in football and that was 40 years ago. As we watched the game, the Aggies outstanding running back Randy Billingsley, a junior who wore number 25 on his back had just scored. With me sizing up the competition, I couldn't help but compare him to our own star runner Richard Lightning Threatt. I couldn't help but think about what a match-up the Indians and the Aggies would be. They both were the best in the city and the county in 69, with Sylacauga dominating all the white schools except C'burg and the Indians virtually stomping all the black competition. Competition that included 4A

Michael Catfish Smith

and 3A schools that was larger or equal to the Aggies in size. So what a collossus match-up it would be to have the Aggies prove to us with-out a doubt that they were in deed the finest in Sylacauga or not? But, as I watched the Aggies march up and down the field with ease against another out-manned opponent I wondered if they could drive and score against the Indians unpenetrable defense that didn't allow anyone to score, the Indians team speed against the Aggies power running. Both teams played with heart and the Indian vaulted 52 defense was designed to stop the run. In fact no one rushed for 100 yards against the Indians defense anyone including powerful Cobb Avenue who had to beat the Indians passing the football. But, in 1969 nobody had been able to run or pass with success against the Indians defensive 11. Would the Indians be able to put the brakes on Billingsley the way the Childersburg Tigers had done early in the season? Would the Aggies have to result to passing the football if the Indians stopped their running game? Could Sylacauga stop Lightning and Robuck along with Terry Bledsoe, PA Young and Beattie all among the scoring leaders in the county or the end reverse pass play ran by the Indians dynamic duo Young and McKinney? the Indians ran the play with great success against everybody they played even though they knew it was coming. The Indians offense would be faster and more athletic than any the Aggies had faced in 1969. Would the Aggies kick the ball to Lightning? We all know that the Aggies only loss had come at the hands of the Childersburg Tigers 21 to 0, but nobody held the Indians scoreless and I mean nobody not ever especially in 69 where they averaged 55 points per game. But the Indians routinely hung goose eggs on all but one opponent in 69 who knows the answers to these questions for sure. I do know that many people in Sylacauga black and white had their own opinions on what the out-come in this epic battle would have been. Usually divided along racial lines for your favorite team. But if a scientist could invent a time travel machine in my life-time I would give my right arm for a chance to see history altered with a Indians vs Aggies match-up in 1969. But back to the game at-hand. it was half-time and the Aggies half-million dollar band was performing. I would learn later that they called it that because of the price of the instruments and the band participants involved. The University of Alabama is called the million dollar band so I guess the Aggies were a junior version of them. as they were entertaining in front of the home crowd as we listen to them they were playing a number called Ole Man River and they finished with Hail to the Varsity, their school fight song. The music sure did sound strange to our ears. It made us think we were at the Grand Ole Opry in Nashville or something. We were used to the Indians smooth mo-town sound led by band director Mr. J.M. Larkins.

Closing the Show

I guess it was just cultural to us. But the Aggies cheerleaders and majorettes seemed to be having a good time. I had no idea at the time that in the future the Aggies Ole Man River and Hail to the Varsity would become as natural to my ears as amazing grace is to a Christian. But never the less, it was still those of us in the Indians community that craved a Indians vs. Aggies match-up in football. We wanted to see who truly had the baddest football team in the city and county in 1969. Even more so after the state left us out in the cold by denying us the opportunity to compete in spite of our amazing credentials, after destroying St. Jude 70 to 0, we were certain that we would leap into the top 4 teams in the state class 2A. But that was not the case. After all you don't beat the number 2 team in the state, a team that you invited to the 2A playoffs in 1968 that finished as state-runner-up and not take their place do you? B Well they got the Indians up to number 5 just out of reach of the playoffs. I often wondered how many state championships Coach Scissum would have won if they had let the Indians compete with some of his most powerful teams, or how many they would have won if the school had never been shut down. What if the school had never been integrated like Talladega County Central of Howell Cove wasn't? All we needed was 10 more years. Late in the 69 season the parallels between the two city powerhouse East Highland and Sylacauga one black and one white was starting to take shape. After 8 games, Sylacauga the 3A school record stood at 7 and 1 and they were ranked 7th in the state. East Highland's record was 8 and 0 and they were ranked 5th in the state in class 2 A. The Aggies had 2 games left which they won and catapulted to the top 4 teams in the state, good enough to put them in the playoffs. Meanwhile, the Indians after having two of their games cancelled by the courts because of the closing of longtime 4A rival Riverside of Tuscaloosa and Chilton County Training School of Clanton along with 4A power Cobb Avenue of Anniston dropping the Indians on their own was left with a 9 game schedule. Coach Scissum asked everybody with a football team in the county and through-out the 7 county area to play, but found no takers for his Indians. So after destroying 3A school Calhoun County of Oxford 82 to 0, in their final game in Sylacauga the Indians were left hanging. This powerful display of offense and defense we thought would surely sway the state to put the Indians into the top 4 teams in the state and the playoffs. It didn't! what gives here? It was widely rumored in the community that Coach Scissum had asked Coach Tom Calvin of Sylacauga to scrimmage his Indians with the 3A state champion Aggies, in a game where no score had to be kept but Calvin turned him down. Too bad! because the fans got cheated out of what would have been a titan battle between the two city powerhouses. Two teams with totally different styles going at it. In boxing it is said that styles make fights and the Indians speed and power versus the Aggies power game, two gladiators! But, we knew that it would not happen though the thought of it excited the Indian faithful. For one thing the Aggies had everything to lose and nothing to gain by playing the high scoring Indians of East Highland which would soon serve as their junior high extension. Can you imagine the egg on Calvin's and Sylacauga's face if they were to lose to the Indians and Coach Scissum's East Highland was riding off into the sunset forever? But what if the shoe had been on the other foot so to speak and it had been Sylacauga high shutting down forever instead of East Highland? What if the Indians as impressive as they were with a 9 an 0 record had been treated fairly by the state and allowed to play T.R. Miller of Brewton in a first round playoff matchup? Down there in Brewton since they finished ranked in the top 3 in the state. Miller incidentally crushed the number one ranked team in the state in class 2A Abbeville 41 to 14, in the first round, which probably proves that Abbeville was overrated in the first place. I sure would like to know who Abbeville played on their schedule in 69 that was more impressive than the teams the Indians faced on theirs. maybe someday somebody will fax this information to me. Abbeville ended up being a sacrificial lamb for T.R. Miller who won their first state championship after having to fight their way into the top 4 teams in the state. Miller would win many more championships in football in the future. That championship in 69 helped establish them as a small school powerhouse in the state. We could have met them in the crampton bowl in Montgomery, it didn't matter to us. All we wanted was a chance to compete. In my heart I feel like the stat took the high road on this one choosing Sylacauga the white school instead of having both city schools one black and one white competing for state championships. Having East Highland and Sylacauga in the playoffs in 69 coming from such a small town would have been unheard of in those days. East Highlands' band and fans were ready and willing to travel anywhere the state would have sent us. But this was just a fantasy of my mind to think that the state was going to let the negro school that was about to become extinct ride of into the sunset of history in such a blazing fashion of a state playoff bid with the opportunity to win the 1st state championship in football for the school in its last year of existence. Never the less, the Aggies received the glory and got the chance that had been pre-destined for the Indians in 69. They got it and played Russellville and Robertsdale and won the 3A football title. It's the only state championship in football that the Aggies have won on the field. I think the school lays claim to a mythical state title in 1954 or something voted on by the state and newspaper reporters in a non-playoff situation. But them winning the state title in 69 was by no way an easy task for them because the Aggies, I must admit had to face 3 time defending state champions, the Russellville Golden Tigers that had a rich tradition. But, I think Russellville must have left the game cursed after their defeat by the Aggies in 69 because their last state championship came in 68 a year before they lost to the Aggies and that was 41 years ago. but still a championship is a championship and is respected as such and the Aggies won it in 69. But in the words of legendary Florida State Coach Bobby Bowden dagunitt! We Indian fans wished our Indians could have gotten a shot at the 2A state playoffs and a chance at the 3A champion Aggies in a scrimmage. Sylacauga playing East Highland would have allowed us to see two hall of fame coaches matching wits against one another. But somehow I felt that the Aggies knew that the Indians were still seethingly mad about being left out and denied a chance the powers that be. Coach Calvin probably knew this better than anyone else because having seen the Indians play along with the rest of his staff his luck had been like the man in the casino who came along and hit the jackpot on a machine that some one else had been feeding all night but got up to go to the bathroom or something came back and saw another man feed his machine one time and hit the jackpot. That's what Calvin and his Aggies did in 1969 hit the jackpot. That's what it boils down to when you consider that Sylacauga who was 6 and 4 in 1968 and far from thinking state championship in 69 after losing to Childersburg 21 to 0 at home in the second game of the season. While the Indians on the other hand had finished ranked number 10 in the state in 68 after going 9 and 1 and was loaded down in 69 with a team 25 seniors strong. 17 starters returned and the Indians were a preseason pick to win it all. They were definitely thinking state title in 69 but for some unknown reason the state started the Indians off ranked off the radar at number 28 to start the season, perhaps to make it more difficult for them to fight their way into the top 4 teams in the state. We knew the superintendent of Sylacauga city schools, Mr. Rueben Porch, wouldn't have allowed an Indians vs. Aggies match-up anyway. With East Highland all-black and Sylacauga all white except for one player the school had a few black students that had volunteered to be part of the early transition program. But, the high school would welcome a mass of black students to its campus the next year in 1970. The rumor was that there would be fights and racial tension if one school defeated the other. But, long-time Indian rival Cobb of Anniston did play all-white Oxford High School in Calhoun County that year in the first and only meeting between the two powerhouse schools. In a capacity filled Lamar field in Oxford, the Yellow Jackets pulled out a close victory over Cobb 23 to 20 in a game that featured future Auburn University running back Terry Henley of Oxford. They beat Cobb on the strength of a late field goal. Ironically because of declining white enrollment in the Anniston school system after integration in 1970 Anniston High School almost became Cobb number two with almost no white students on the team or in the school. They won a couple of 6a state championships in the late 80's and early 90's. If one wanted to get a glimpse of what a Indians vs. Aggies match-up might have looked like in terms of styles look no further than Sylacauga's 1989 match-up against Anniston. In that game Sylacauga came into the match with a 5 and 0 record ranked number 2 in the state in class 5A. Anniston was ranked number 2 in 6A at the time. they had some of the fastest team speed I had seen this side of East Highland. Anniston ended up winning the game 39 to 0 over the Aggies. Certainly this game brought back memories of East Highland's dominance to my mind with the team speed that Anniston exuberated. But in 1969, the city of Sylacauga enjoyed and saw possibly the greatest exhibition of high school football in Sylacauga history. Both coaches Haywood Scissum and Tom Calvin along with coach John Cox of Childersburg would eventually enter the state high school hall of fame together. It was a very telling fact about the quality of the coaching and football that was played and enjoyed in those days by the fans that were truly blessed to be able to witness it.

East Highlands 1960s decade under Coach Scissum

84 wins

11 losses

3 ties

Season by season in the 60s record and schedule

1960-m 8 wins 2 losses

Key players-captain gene brut gamble dewey munn johnny sonny cook john gilliam love quarterback clark cook donald Harrison preston leonard frankie hart harry hughes richard corbin harold richards jimmy burns.

Hi light from the booker t. washington game- captain gene brut gamble was outstanding at defensive tackle. his stellar play was responsible for the montgomery powerhouse minus yardage in the rushing department for the night. dewey munn johnny sonny cook jimmy burns and john gilliam were also outstsnding. preston leonard had a interception return for 60 yards.

Ehhs 1960 schedule-
9-6 booker t. washington here lost 0 to 7
9-15 talladega county here won n/a
9-20 calhoun county here won n/a
9-27 carver of gadsden away won 13 to 7
10-4 laurel of alex city here won 33 to 0
10-11 westside away won 31 to 7
10-20 cobb away lost n/a
11- 25 lee county training here won 35 to 6

Michael Catfish Smith

11-1 darden of opelika here won 41 to 13
11-10 moten of leeds away won 18 to 7

1960 record 8 wins 2 losses 223 points scored 55 points allowed

1961 8 wins 2 losses

Ehhs schedule 1961-
1. booker t washington there lost 6 to 24
2. norriss of attala here won 19 to 0
3. calhoun county there lost 7 to 12
4. carver of gadsden here won 13 to 7
5. laurel of alex city there won 25 to 12
6. cobb of anniston here won 12 to 10
7. westside of talladega here won 32 to 7
8. hayes of birmingham here won 18 to 7
9. drake of auburn there won 21 to 6
10. moton of leeds there won 27 to 0

1962 Ehhs schedule-
1. norriss of attala here won 21 to 0
2. calhoun county here won 13 to 6
3. carver of gadsden away won 20 to 18
4. lAUREL OF ALEX CITY HERE won 6 to 0
5. westside of talladega there tie
6. cobb of anniston there lost n/a
7. talladega county here won 28 to 6
8. hayes of birmingham there won 32 to 0
9. chambers county of layfayette here won 27 to2
10. booker t. washington here lost 7 to 14

1962 record 7 wins 2 losses 1 tie

1963 schedule Ehhs-
key players cecil leonard alvin griffin joe hickey willie holtzclaw david grimmett melvin bardwell

schedule-
1. hudson of selma there won 13 to 12

2. norriss of attala here won 31 to 6
3. calhoun county here tie 0-0
4. carver of gadsden there lost 7 to 18
5. westside of talladega here won 12 to 7
6. laurel of alex city there won 14 to 7
7. cobb of anniston here won 19 to 6
8. talladega county here won 37 to 0
9. hayes of birmingham here won 45 to 6
10. chambers county there won 75 to 7

record- 8-1-1 points 253 allowed 59 points   district champions

1964 schedule- key player- coach scissum claims this as a rebuilding year as he has lost quite a few top boys over the last 2 seasons. He indicated that this year only 35 boys reported for fall practice. The main weakness of this year's team is that there is no real leadership. The offense is weak and there is much inexperience at the tackles guards and center position. However, all is not lost as Coach Scissum is returning at tackle Big Joe Nathan Hickey and at guards Williamson and Robert Gunn and backs Jimmy Walker, Jerry Hale, Lee Buford and lastly, the quarterback spot will have to be shouldered by rising star Alvin Chock Griffin who should come around alright. Coach is depending heavily on David Grimmett and Willie Holtzclaw at the ends.

Ehhs schedule for 1964-
Sept 3 hudson of Selma here won 43 to 0

ehhs schedule for 1964 continued
sept 17 calhoun county there won 33 to 13
sept 12 norris of attala there won 41 to 7
sept 24 carver of gadsden here won 24 to 0
oct 1 laurel of alex city here won 42 to 13
oct 15 cobb of anniston there won 13 to 6
oct 22 talladega county here won 69 to 0
oct 29 hayes of birmingham here won 53 to 0
nov 6 westside of talladega there won 21 to 6
nov 12 darden of opelika here won 56 to 6

1964 district champions record 10wins 0 losses 403 points scored 51 points allowed note- many points on this team was scored on the Indians second and 3rd teams after the games got out of hand

1965 schedule key players- alvin griffin willie holtzclaw joe hickey lee buford robert gunn mike bledsoe robert sleepy hollanquest roland slick morris john buford

1965 schedule-
1. norriss of attala here won 33 to 0
2. calhoun county there won 39 to 0
3. carver of gadsden there won 39 to 0
4. laurel of alex city there won 57 to 7
5. cobb of anniston here won 33 to 0
6. westside of talladega here won 25 to 0
7. st. clair county training here won 54 to 0
8. riverside of tuscaloosa there won 33 to 0
9. darden of opelika there won 41 to 7
10. hudson of selma there won 41 to 6.

1965 district champions record 10 and 0 403 points scored 19 allowed

1966 schedule- the East Highland High School Indians are preparing for the upcoming season without Hickey Holtzclaw and Griffin for the 1st time in 3 years. The invincibles owners of 34 straight wins and 3 straight victories over big rival Cobb will be sorely missed. The Indians lost 16 players off its great 1965 team. The 1966 edition will be larger but slower. Practice periods have proved very little as the Indians seek to replace the fab 3. The bright spots reported by Coach Scissum are Robert Gunn Frank Williamson Johnny Grimmett and Tip Averett.

note- this is Lightning's debut year as a varsity player on the Indians as a 15 year old freshman.

The East Highland High School Indians will open the season in 1966 tonight Thursday night sept 8 when they tackle the strong Norriss of Attala High School. The Indians who have won 34 straight games hope to continue their unblemished streak. With the loss of such great stars as Hickey Hughes Griffin and Holtzclaw, Coach Scissum has his work cut out for him. If his unbeaten streak is to continue in the realms of the undefeated some body new will have to step up. The Indians will field a flashy array of backs and quick lineman.

The 1966 Indians football schedule
sept 8 norriss here won 34 to 0
sept 15 calhoun county here won n/a
sept 22 carver of gadsden there won 20 to 6
sept 29 laurel of alex city here won 52 to 12
oct 6 cobb of anniston there lost 7 to 26 Indians 1st loss in 3 seasons
oct 14 westside of talladega there lost 7 to 13 rare and last los to them.
oct 22 pell city there won 48 to 14
oct 27 riverside homecoming tied 12 to 12
nov 10 darden of opelika here cancelled bad weather
nov 17 hudson of selma here won n/a

Finished with 6 wins 2 losses and 1 tie a disappointing season for the Indians under scissum.

1966 would be Coach Scissums worst season of the decade. What a lot of schools would have been pleased with was sub-par for the Indians under Coach Scissum. Rivals Cobb of Anniston and Westside of Talladega finally beat the Indians after 3 years of humiliation the rebuilding year that coach scissum predicted in 1964 for his team actually came in 1966 having to replace Hickey Holtzclaw and Griffin. Not bad for a rebuilding year. In most teams rebuilding years they lose 5 or 6 games. Some even go 0 and 10. Something the Indians never experienced. Darden of Opelika cancelled what was a home game for the Indians against them. If not, the Indians might have won 7 games this year. Not a bad choice for Opelika considering they have never beaten the Indians in football. There was talk of a replacement game against Phylliss Wheatley of Childersburg, a new program. But, the game fell through. It would be 1967 before the Indians faced the new kids on the block the Phylliss Wheatley Panthers

1967 schedule Ehhs
key players- robert gunn mike bledsoe calvin mckinny roland slick morris Johnny grimmett sammy louis johnson robert hollanquest wally gator fulks larry tootsie thomas anthony boot pratt houston averette cooney russel and new stars richard lightning threatt P.A.young and billy robuck smith who were about to have break out years and become stars for the indians.

1967 schedule-
sept 7 norriss of attala home won 32 to 0
sept 14 calhoun county away won 36 to 0

sept 21 carver of gadsden home won 37 to 0
sept 30 laurel of alex city away won 52 to 0
oct 12 westside of talladega home won 40 to 6
oct19 cobb of anniston home lost 14 to 18 in last minute
oct27 riverside of tuscaloosa there won 46 to 0
nov 2 phylliss wheatley of childersburg there won 37 to 0
nov 9 chilton county training home won 39 to 0
nov 16 st. clair county of pell city home won 52 to 0
district champions 9 win 1 loss 358 points scored 24 allowed

1968 schedule- Ehhs key- note- in 1968 the indians were hit hard by graduation. gone were robert poor rob gunn mike homer bledsoe calvin the russian mckinny Johnny grimmett sammy louis johnson houston tip averette james J.D. thomas homer pearson larry tootsie thomas travis olden and clarence kidd.

key players returning- donnell prater and P.A. young at ends cooney russel at tackle big robert williams at tackle manuel big joe pope wally gator fulks roland slick morris anthony boot pratt lightning threatt billy smith and Jay grimmett in the backfield.

1968 schedule-
1. sept 6 norriss of attala away won 42 to 0
2. sept12 calhoun county home won 38 to 6
3. laurel of alex city here won 38 to 6
4. cobb of anniston away lost 13 to 19 in last minute
5. westside of talladega there won 26 to 6
6. riverside of tuscaloosa here won 22 to 0
7. phylliss wheatley of childersburg home won 34 to 6
8. hudson of Selma there won 14 to 0
9. prentice of montevallo here won 54 to 0
10. ST. clair county of pell city there won 54 to 0

289 points scored and 43 allowed

1969 schedule ehhs
key players- the 1969 team would be the highest scoring team in school history and also the stingiest on defense allowing no points scored on them. The offense would give up 6 for the only points scored on them. The stars were plentiful with Lightning, Robuck, P.A. Beattie, Cooney, Big Robert Williams, Aaron Moon, Lyn Foster, Jerry Chic Holtzclaw and Sylvester Bliss

Shealey among the 24 seniors that anchored the team. James Fatso Odum and Gary Oden were the two newcomers that stood out. Underclassmen stars were Danny Ace Morris, Anthony Sayers, Walton Neil Hart, Greg Foots Holtzclaw, Wayne Cow head Harris, Gill Weechie McKinney, Nathaniel Williams and Donell Williams. This touchdown denying defensive team also was the highest scoring in the state that set records in Talladega County that still stand today for a 9 game season.

Ehhs 1969 schedule-
1. Hudson of Selma won 50 to0
2. Oliver of Fairfield won 40 to0
3. O.S. Hill of Munford won 36 to 0
4. Laurel of Alex City won 68 to 6
5. TCTE of Howell Cove won 52 to 0
6. Darden of Opelika won 54 to 0
7. Westside of Talladega won 46 to 0
8. St. Jude of Montgomery won 70 to 0
9. Calhoun County won 82 to 0

record 9 wins 0 loses   498 points scored   6 allowed this 1969 team was by far Coach Scissums highest scoring and stingiest on defense. This denied bunch will always be remembered for excellence on the field but denied the opportunity to compete in the state playoffs in spite of receiving the maximum 80 points in the system.

Merger May Mean Sports Dynasty For Sylacauga

By Larry Canterbury
The Montgomery Advertiser

Montgomery- East Highland Indians the reigning class 2A basketball and track state champions while also perfect on the football field will merge with the class 3A state football champions the Sylacauga Aggies next year. The Indians Football team went 9-0-0 last year scoring a whopping 498 points to the oppositions 6. These impressive statistics were left hanging however, as East Highland was denied the chance to compete in the 4 team state tourney. Football Head Coach Haywood Scissum was naturally straight with the outcome. We ended up ranked fifth 2 ½ points behind Abbeville High School, he said. We should have had the chance to play but we didn't, we felt we were the finest. Scissum who has achieved a won loss record of 135 wins 27 losses and 11 ties in 18 years at East Highland will move to Sylacauga as an assistant to Tom Calvin. Coach Scissum has won 85% of his games as the head man at East Highland. John Carter, Line Coach at Sylacauga for the past 3 years will join Scissum in an assistant's role. I think they, the Board of Education feel they are treating me fair said Scissum and I suppose they are. One fact that Scissum noted was that other schools were combining also producing unclear situations and solutions. A lot of long time men will be out of head jobs said Scissum. Which makes it a bad thing. I don't know how they'll solve it but I guess they'll try to be fair about it. One man who is currently in a state of uncertainty is basketball Head Coach Dwight Duke. Duke's Indians capped off this past season Saturday in Tuscaloosa. Labeled underdogs, East Highland whipped pre-tourney favorite US Jones of Demopolis to take the state title. Dwight Duke doesn't know right now what he'll do or where he'll be said Scissum. I guess he'll hear something soon. Scissum will also control the Sylacauga baseball team. The decision to merge will definitely affect the overall picture in all high school athletic Scissum said. The combining of two schools will make teams tougher he said. But everyone else is combining too. This will make all teams better and harder to beat. As an example, Scissum noted that Westside would emerge with Talladega. Anytime you give a coach 25 boys, it has to help him and the team said Scissum. Track is the thing right now at East Highland. The Indians capped the basketball season off with a 2A title and also won the 2A state title in track last year. Coach Scissum says his team has a desire to repeat. We won the title last year and lost only one boy he said. We are out to win it again this season and I think we can. East Highland athletic will soon be known as Aggies instead of Indians. Scissum summed it up saying everybody associated with the school is mighty sad right now However, we hope we can combine with Sylacauga and repeat as champions in all sports in future years to come.

THE AFTERMATH

Things changed dramatically for black kids many years after East Highland High School shut down. Black participation on the Sylacauga football team dwindled down to as little as 2 or 3 players as late as 1975. Most of your best black athletes that would have played for Coach Scissum chose to play basketball or run track with many others choosing to just walk the halls for 4 years and graduate. Even some of the kids that had played in the East Highland's best little band in the land chose not to become a part of the Sylacauga's half million dollar band. The sad part, the band director didn't really care. Though a few Indian football stand outs from the 1969 team like Danny Morris, Greg Foots Holtzclaw, Anthony Sayers, Walton Neil Hart and Wayne Cow Head Harris and Lamar Prater did play for the Aggies many other Indian Underclassmen chose not to play at all. A number of things could have contributed to this situation. One of them could have been the new grading system implemented by the board of Education which was one of the toughest in the State of Alabama. The Sylacauga High School grading systems was as follows.

60 to 69 F
70 to 76 D
77 to 85 C
86 to 93 B
94 to 100 A

Under the grading system, a student at Sylacauga had to maintain a C average in all his core subjects to be declared academically eligible to participated in sports. Sylacauga had this in place long before the state mandated 2.0 rule went into effect in the early 80's. But I doubt that this was the reason for the black participation drop off at Sylacauga. The black kids that would have went to East Highland from the Walco Thomas Hill Overbrook and Quarry areas of the city went to Sylacauga rival and county school BB Comer and prospered under Coach Bobby Overton. But the black kids from East Highland under this grading system not only met this challenge of tough academic standards but many also graduated. The real reason for this early black desertion probably lied in the fact that most of these kids were born and bred on Indian football and had East Highland history in their blood. Loved and respected Coach Scissum and his program this they refused to play on a team where they felt like they would have to either share or play behind some kid that they felt they were better than. Sylacauga High School had a powerful quarterback club ran by former athletes and teachers of the school. Many who played in the late 50's and 60's for Coach Tom Calvin. Some of these former players even coached with Calvin in the 70's. They knew the kids that were playing now fathers and mothers many of which were their former classmates. Without saying that some of them was showed favoritism you could clearly say that they had an inside track to playing time. I think some the Aggie coaches had tasted success as an all white school and felt like on a whole they could win without much black participation. This mainly on the strength of their 1969 state 3A football championship where they won with only one black player on their roster. So when black participation dwindle down to a little bit of nothing the coaches and white parents of Aggie players didn't ask why and they didn't seem to care as long as their kids got to play and make high school memories. As a result the juggernaut that most people predicted and thought would happen when East Highland and Sylacauga combined two premier programs never materialized. But just down the road a few miles in Alexander City, Alabama, it did. When Laurel High, all black and Benjamin Russell all white combined, they became a powerhouse in football. Much of what was expected when the Indians combined with the Aggies. Benjamin Russell whom the Aggies had broke even with in the 60's became superior to the Aggies on the gridiron. For Sylacauga their have been some decent years since integration in 1970. A lot of playoff years but the Aggies haven't been able to duplicate the success that they had in 1969 and win another state championship in football. They manage to get back to the state championship in 1970 a year after they won their only state football title on the field. But, they failed to defend their title losing to Valley of Fairfax 23 to 16. In an odd twist the Alabama High School Athletic Association which had denied Coach Scissum and the Indians a chance to play for a championship in 69 by 2 ½ points choosing to take who they deemed as the top 4 teams in the state in their 4 team playoff format completely changed the format in 1970 to an 8 team playoff. A grain of salt that I am sure the Indians fans took as rubbing salt into the wound. So, naturally Indian fans a lot of them cheered for Valley of Fairfax in the State Championship game where they handed the Aggies a close defeat. This was in spite of the fact that the Aggies had former Indians, Danny Morris Wayne Harris, Neil Hart, Greg Foots Holtzclaw and Anthony Sayers Walton on their roster. I guess with East Highland freshly shut down bitter feelings still existed among some Indians fans for the school after the Indians were slighted in 69. While the Aggies celebrated, maybe they didn't have the foresight to see that East Highland was gone and never coming back. This school was now their children and grand children and unborn generations school. Initially during integration there was some fights and skirmishes as the racial mix up of white kids and black kids adjusted to one another. Some name calling prevailed and in the lunchroom the kids segregated themselves with the white kids on one side and the black kids on the other side. This was a situation that existed all through the transition period in the 70's and even into the 80's. There was even a racial standoff in the integration period of the 70's that caused the principal to lock rooms. But cooler heads prevailed when Assistant Principal Jesse Cleveland got on the intercom and pleaded with the former black students of East Highland to calm down. Like some kind of experiment like Jackie Robinson went through to integrate major league baseball in 1947 was taking place. In retrospect maybe it was. For surely there were those who hoping that the two races couldn't coexist in the high school. Ultimately they did and many black students have since graduated from the walls of Sylacauga High School. One thing the merger of the two schools did produce was dominance in track and field where Sylacauga virtually owned the county while winning a few state titles. Basketball saw the Aggies boys and girls win state titles with kids that certainly would have shined for the Indians.

Indian Summarize the 1969 Football Season

The most stinging defeat the Indians suffered in 1969 and the only defeat came not by an opponent on the field where the Indians dominated all competition but was delivered by the state in a crushing blow that stunned the highland supporters and ended the teams dream of a state championship in football in 1969. The news was delivered to the Indians and their faithful as 2 ½ points short of being ranked 4th in the final season poll of regular season play. Two and a half points denied the Indians the right to participate on the highest level in the state 2A football playoffs. 2 ½, 3 ½ points less that the Indians gave up all year. 2 ½ points 52 ½ points less than the Indians offense averaged all season. All this and having to watch teams play for the title that surely they thought they could compete with and defeat. The crowning glory denied to the Indians by the state was ironically passed on and handed to Sylacauga High, the Indians sister school in the small town. The Aggies 3A and having gone 6 and 4 in 1968 and a team with less experience and seniors than East Highland had to be pleasantly surprised to get a bid for post season play after being handed a 21 to 0 defeat by rival Childersburg at home in their home opener. Childersburg on the other hand would have received a 3A bid I the playoffs with a 8-1-1 record had they defeated cross county rival Talladega late in the season. People were even talking about a rematch in the playoffs between Sylacauga and Childersburg in 3A football when the right thing for the state to do would have been to have East Highland and Sylacauga in the playoffs. But, the Indians were totally overlooked for their accomplishments on the field by the state after destroying Calhoun County 82 to 0 in the last game of their season. The Aggies thoughts had to be far from the state playoffs after game two of their season. Yet on the strength of an 8 and 1 win streak they were allowed to steadily climb their way up in the polls from number 32 taking significant leaps in the polls all the way to the top four. In two totally twist of fates the Aggies won from 6 and 4 in 68 to 9 and 1 in 69 and stole the glory that had been predestined for the Indians by experts in 1969. The Indians on the other hand went from 9 and 1 in 68 with a top ten ranking to end the season to 9 and 0 in 69 and after starting the season strangely ranked number 28 rose to number 5 to finish the season just short of the playoffs. This in spite of having 24 seniors and 17 starters returning. They were denied a bid and stayed home, grounded for eternity by the powers that be no matter how excellent on the field. So while the Aggies and their student body celebrated their accomplishment, the Indians and their students and fans were left despondent after being left out in the cold. In their last season ever they witnessed Sylacauga play for a 3A state championship both games in their hometown. When the scribes of history write, let it be said that the East Highland High School Indians undefeated in 9 games, are the true uncrowned 2A football state champions in 1969. The name of East Highland will always represent a winner. Strangely after that 1969 season when the Indians were left out by 2 ½ points the very next year in 1970 the state changed to a 8 team format from their original 4 team format. A decision that came inconveniently to late for Coach Scissum and his Indians.

Basketball Season

Closing the Show

The excitement of East Highland High School basketball was second in excitement in the hearts of Indians fans to football which was king. The Indians over the years have always produced very good basketball teams. In fact they never had a losing season in basketball in the history of the school. From the early fifties with stars like Derry Lee Holtzclaw leading them till closing time in 1970 with PA Young, Beattie McKinney and Danny Morris the Indians were tough on the hardwood. Throw in the fact that basketball was a sport that was played year round in Sylacauga in the spring and summer on the out door courts in the recreation center. And if you think making Couch Scissum's football 38 was tough, then you should have tried making the Indians varsity squad of 12. Competition was stiff for the 12 uniforms representing the best that the school had to offer. And what a deep talent field it was. With many a boy left hart broken over the fact that after the final cut his name was not on the list, posted by the coach on the next day in the gym on the wall. If you were an underclassmen you might find yourself playing B Team for a year hoping that graduation would land you a chance for varsity next year. Though the Indians usually fielded a heavy upperclassmen laden team there was some exceptions to make varsity as youngsters. Larry McKenzie and Prince Albert Young were two of them. McKenzie made it as a freshman and Young played and starred as a sophomore. Coach Dwight Duke the original white shadow, a white coach coaching basketball at an all black school was getting ready to lead the final edition of Indian basketball in 1969-1970. If timing is everything in life then fate couldn't have smiled on young Coach Duke's life any better than it did in 1969, the year he arrived in Sylacauga to coach the Indians. In 1969, Coach Duke and East Highland were getting ready to close the show on the Indians basketball program. A program that over the years had been very strong competing against 4A schools like Cobb of Anniston and Carver of Gadsden along with 3A schools Westside of Talladega and Laurel of Alex City. Coach Duke arrived at East Highland two years ago and inherited a program that had won district champs in 1965, going 27 and 3 with player like Marion Harrison possible the purest left handed shooter Indian fans ever saw at the school and possible in the county. Other players on that team were David Grimmett, Willie Holtzclaw, Willie Isome, Alvin Griffin, Joe Hickey, Terry Vincent, James Hollanquest, Billy Brown and Larry McKenzie. Six of these kids were football players. An unusually high number for Indians basketball. But, these guys were athletes outstanding in both sports. The Indians winning attitude carried over from football to basketball where they didn't miss a beat and showed that they were not some one dimensional schools that was only good in football. That Indian spirit ran deep and there was no drop off in winning for the Indians basketball team. The basketball team in 1969-1970 took the baton from the undefeated football team and ran with it. Applying the same winning formula and attitude East Highland's little gym would be rocking with over flow standing room only on the walls crowds dinging nah nah nah nah nah nah nah nah hey hey hey good bye! To another vanquished opponent. Truly passion ran deep for East Highland basketball second only to football in Indian fans hearts because of the enormous success of Coach Haywood Scissum. But basketball at East Highland was not just some sport that the football player played in the off season to stay in shape. Only Danny Morris a rising junior along the PA Young and Beattie McKinney both exceptional athletes and seniors made the Indians12 in 1969-1970. These 3 players formed the nucleus of the Indians rugged rebounding machine. Sylvester Beattie McKinney, the Captain and leading rebounder could jump out the gym. Danny Morriss the tenacious rebounder with the soft one-handed jump shot and PA Young could shoot the ball from 25 feet accurately. He also could rebound with the best of them Young a defensive mismatch for teams could play small forward and the two guard, Beattie was very physical and the Indians trouble shooter and power center. Danny Morris was the first of the athletic Morris clan to make his mark in basketball in Sylacauga. Lets examine for a minute East Highland basketball talent and how it came to be. Most of the Indians basketball talent was developed and rooted in the projects. Frankie Hart, a star in the early 60's was an exception. He came out of the Thomas Hill Walco are of Sylacauga. But, most got their schooling in the projects. These guys in the projects took their basketball seriously. Even in the pickup games. I remember once as a 14 year old waiting on the side line for my down, I witnessed Jake Oden, the local play ground intimidator grab a guy by the throat and choke him on the fence over a disputed call on the court. It was very intimidating in the mind of a 14 year old rookie to witness such passion over street basketball. But in the project was where you found out what kind of game you had if any. Many a fight would break out sometimes in these games. Basketball in the projects was very physical. Dave Baker, a multi talented 6 foot five forward who didn't play high school basketball but graduated from Sylacauga High School in 1974, and was discovered playing rec ball out scoring Talladega colleges best athletes was offered a scholarship on the spot. He had the best bank shot that I ever saw on a player. In fact, everything Baker shot was a bank which he did consistently. He told me that the older East Highland football players and basketball players would be playing pick up games for money that they weren't informed of as teammates. These guys were already physical in nature from Indian football and legends like Cecil Leonard, Joe Nathan, Hickey Anthony, Cooney Russell and Robert Gunn. They didn't want to lose their money and they weren't accustomed to losing any way at nothing so games would be very physical with elbows and sometimes fist flying. Such was the nature of pick up games when you dared venture on the courts against these guys. But if you could hang in there and hold you own. Nobody could intimidate you in a high school game. Back in those days basketball was played all the time. Everyday the rec would open from 1 to 3 and again from 6 to 9 and in between you played on the courts right above the rec center. When you played ball in the projects you cut your teeth against older guys and grown men who had been good in high school but didn't go on to the next level and play college ball. In fact once your turned 18 or graduated you played men's league ball. It was like playing against guys who were pro age 21 to 35 who were physically stronger than you but you couldn't back down. These guys wouldn't give up cheap lay ups and if you had a hot hand they would play mind games to take you out of you rhythm such a well placed elbow in your rib cage or something. These guys didn't take it easy on a 15 year old high school kid either. They roughed you up and if your were use to playing intimidation you were in for a rude awakening. Competition was stiff every day in the rec and nobody wanted to lose and have to wait for another down. Of course the very best would have a spot waiting for them by the guy who chose the next five. Many a fist fight would break out but nobody killed anyone. It was unusually left on the court and forgotten by the next day. Because of the rough treatment administered by the likes of Joe Hickey and Cecil Leonard on the Younger guys the future Indians were already battle tested. Troy Morris, nephew of Indian great Danny Morris was the best I ever say in Sylacauga very physical and strong unmovable under the goal he too was a product of the physical nature of projects basketball. Once these younger guys got to high school they were ready for varsity basketball. Coach Duke came to East Highland and inherited a winning tradition. That's not to say that Coach Duke didn't earn his stare championship because he certainly did. The man could coach and we all know how important that is a coach has to know how to make second half adjustment in games where you play teams with a chalkboard and yes's and no's. Duke whom I mentioned I dubbed the original white shadow was embraced the Indian team the students the whole East Highland community. In those racially charged times the only color that mattered to Indian fans was blue and white and red of East Highland. Coach Duke loved and helped coach the Indian football team as an assistant along with Coach Showers. Memories that I am sure he still treasures with him today amid all those wonderful victories that Coach Scissum and his football team brought to East Highland fans. In fact Coach Duke only saw the Indians lose one football game in his two year stint with the Indians and that was to Cobb in 68. I really don't know if Coach Duke knew when he arrived in Sylacauga that the Indians were a small school powerhouse in three sports on the brink of writing history in football basketball and track. But he certainly didn't seem to be uncomfortable with the fact that he was a white coach at a black high school. Coach Duke was respected by his players and students and not thought of as nothing more than a East Highland Indian. He knew what he was doing coaching young men and proved it by winning the state title in 1970. The last year before integration. Coach Duke was not retained by the Sylacauga City School System after the 1969-1970 school year. But he was probably better than the one Sylacauga already had in place. But one door closed and God opened another for him as he went on to become a successful lawyer in North Alabama. The bond that he and his former players formed still exist today where all the players still alive meet up with the coach for a reunion every few years. On with the second show the basketball season!

2nd Show
Basketball

The 1969–1970 East Highland High School Basketball Team the Starters and Sixth Man

Point Guard- Charles Charlie Boy McGowan, The Indians floor leader point guard McGowan was a 5ft 7 tenacious defender. A mentally tough player and competitor. Probably got that way by playing against older guys in the projects and Indian football players who cut you no slack because of your youth.

Off Guard- Donnel Bear Corbin, Smooth shooting guard known to talk trash on the playground court. When I was a 15 year old youngster he took me to school on the playground. Telling me what he was going to do, then doing it.

PA Young- Prince Albert was a freak of nature to pattern and guard. Could play the two guard small forward or center. A multi talented player in 3 sports football, baseball and basketball for the Indians he starred in all 3. A right handed assassin who led the Indians in scoring while shooting from 25 feet accurately. Young was way ahead of his time and would have killed from 3 point range. A big time pressure player Young was Mr. Consistent.

Center - Sylvester Beatttie McKinney, the most physical Indian player and captain Beattie averaged 20 rebounds a game as the teams leading rebounder. He also was a 3 sport star for the Indians in football basketball and track. Could jump out the gym and always produced

Power Forward - Danny Ace Morris, Ace as he was called was also a 3 sport star underclassmen for the Indians the only junior in the starting lineup . Had a soft one handed jump shot to along with his tenacious rebounding. Teamed with Beattie McKinney to form an awesome one-two punch rebounding tandem for the Indians. First of the athletic Morris clan in Sylacauga to make his mark in basketball. There would be others in the future.

Sixth Man- Jerry Doc Houser, Doc as he was called was a good athlete as good a swimmer as he was a basketball player. Intelligent player who knew his role. Got the name Doc from the Indians football players who he taped and bandaged up as head manager.

Other contributors- Roland Tweet Tinsley, six man number two Tweet was instant offense coming in off the bench. The brother of former Indian Ronald Tinsley he hit 15 points in the state championship game against favored U.S. Jones of Demopolis to help the Indians win the state title. In the championship game Coach Duke told him to shoot the open shot. He did.

Forward Robert Kirkland- Kirk had a good mid range jumper. Was a good defensive player who hustled.

Guard- James Drake was a very likeable player who contributed to the Indians success

Forward Jerome Oneal, should have called him Doc because he became one. The class valedictorian in 1970. Jerome was a smart player lanky and long who could rebound. Also the Indians football beat writer for 3 years. The first of the Oneal clan of outstanding athletes to make his mark in Sylacauga. He wouldn't be the last.

1969 Basketball Season

Indians Young Leading Scoring Parade
By Dan Rutledge

East Highland's Lightning Threatt won the 1969 football scoring race for the Talladega County area. And another Indian PA Young is out front in the daily homes first weekly basketball scoring I list the Indians have played but two games but Young has already fired in 66 points through the hoop. His big game was the 118 to 70 shellacking the Indians put on TCTS Tuesday night. In that one the senior guard scored 44 points 36 of them in the first half. The performance was the second best individual showing of the season. Two weeks ago Millerville's Larry Simmons topped it by Fayetteville. Simmons also a senior guard started the cage season early. As a result Simmons has already played in 9 games and scored 212 points for an average of 23.5 points a game. Steve Mitchell of TCTS holds down 3rd place with a matching 23.5 average Mitchell has scored 47 points in two games both losses. His best showing was 29 points in the loss to East Highland. Mitchell is a 6.0 junior forward. Millerville also got the 4th place spot as not unusual considering the Bulldogs are averaging 97 points a game. The player Richard Gortney center. Gortney is a 6.5 sophomore and still growing. He average 23 points a game as a freshman here are the early scoring leaders in the area.

1. Young, East Highland 2 games 66 points ave 33.0
2. L. Simmons, Millerville 9 games 212 points ave 23.5
3. Mitchell TCTC 2 games 47 points ave 23.5
4. Gortney Millerville 9 games points 207 ave 23.0
5. Little Lincoln 4 games 87 points ave 21.8
6. Embry Lincoln 4 games 87 points ave 21.8

7. Usrey Fayetteville 8 games 171 points ave 21.0
8. Geralds Ashland 2 games 42 points ave 21.0
9. Elliott Childersburg 4 games 80 points ave 20.0
10. Hartsfield Sylacauga 2 games 36 points ave 18.0
11. Wilson Westside 1 game 17 points ave 17.0
12. Williams TCTS 2 games 32 points ave 16.0
13. Bardwell BB Comer 5 games 78 points ave 15.6
14. Nelson Millerville 9 games 139 points ave 15.4
15. Hodges Odenville 4 games 61 points ave 15.2
16. Odum ASD 5 games 71 points ave 14.5
17. McGowan East Highland 2 games 29 points ave 14.5
18. McLain Sylacauga 2 games 29 points ave 14.5
19. Tanner Westside 1 game 14 points ave 14.0nt

January 1969
East Highland High School Basketball

The Indian Invitational

The Teams
East Highland
Phyllis Wheatley

Closing the Show

R.R. Moton
Shelby County Training
J.D. Thompson
Drew Pell City

    The East Highland Indians won their 17th annual invitational tournament in a rather easy fashion over the weekend. The Indians never had any real challenges from it opponents. They beat opponents by the margins of 62, 37 and 24 points in their 3 victories in the tournament. The Indians were led by junior assassin PA Young who has averaged 22 points a game this season. He hit 19, 21 and 29 points against Moton of Sycamore Shelby County Training of Columbiana and J.D. Thompson of Cottage Grove. He also grabbed 37 rebounds in three contest. Sylvester Beattie McKinney named the tournament M.V.P. led the Indians in rebounding with 47. Other contributors were Tyrone Stone, Ronald Tinsley and Lawrence Ervin. The Indians and Moton tipped off the tournament Friday night. Moton offered the Indians little resistance as the little school from neighboring Sycamore just 7 miles up the road off highway 21 was overmatched and lost to the Indians by the score of 112 to 40 as the Indians cracked the century mark and clocked the scoreboard. The next game on Friday night was the Panthers of Phylliss Wheatley taking on Drew High of Pell City. The Panthers defeated Drew by the score of 89 to 72. On Saturday in the two o'clock game the Indians turned back Shelby County Training 88 to 52. JD. Thompson defeated Wheatley of Childersburg 65 to 60 in the closest and most thrilling game in the tournament so far. In the consolation game Phyllis Wheatley squeezed by Shelby County 67 to 66 to capture 3rd place. In the championship game the Indians stunned J.D. Thompson 81 to 57. Thompson trailed 20 to 16 after the first period of play. But the Indians behind their crowd soon pulled away and were never challenged again. Tuesday night the Indians defeated Calhoun County of Hobson City 92 to 67. Tyrone Stone led the Indians in scoring with 26 points followed by Ronald Tinsley with 25. Beattie McKinney had 18 rebounds. This win boosted the Indians record this season to 11 to 1. The B Team defeated Calhoun County 70 to 50. Danny Morris led them in scoring with 14 points. Aaron Moon hit for 12.

    The Varsity Indians must have the most powerful offensive team in the area. They have scored over 100, 3 times this year and hit in the 90's 3 times. Several teams have frozen the ball against them to hold back Indian scoring but the hustle on defense won't let them hold the score down. Desire hustle and team work are the keys to Indian basketball success. Both teams varsity and B Team take on powerful Cobb of Anniston tonight.

East Highland Bombs Drew High in Thursday Night Cage Action
February 8, 1969

Sylacauga- The East Highland Indians bombed Drew High School of Lincoln 93 to 60 here Thursday night. The win placed Coach Dwight Duke's Chargers at 19 and 3 on the season. Other results in the county had Westside of Talladega easing by Calhoun County 87 to 83. Talladega finally getting one on Walter Wellborn 77 to 64. And Munford felt the wrath of high flying White plains 78 to 63. Coach Duke said of his Indians after the game we played a real good steady ball game tonight. We played real good together. Duke had praise for a number of players as four of the starting five ended the night's effort in double figures. Leading the way for the Indians was PA Young with 26 and Tyrone Stone with 18. Other double digit scorers for the Indians were McKinney with 13 and Aaron Moon with 12. Drew's Little, led their scoring parade with 22 and Embry had 16 and Nixon 11. The hot shooting Indians who are averaging over 86 points per outing jumped off to a quick 26 to 20 lead but made it 47 to 32 at the half. Putting it literally out of reach for the Drew team. East Highland 63 rebounds during the contest with Beattie McKinney cleaning the boards for 19. The Indians play Laurel of Alex City next in a road game.

Indians on Warpath Toward State Berth
1969

West Blocton- It all went according to form in the opening round of the region 4 area 7 tournament at West Blocton. As all 4 seeded teams advanced to the semifinals. Sylacauga's East highland High School the only Talladega County team alive in the playoffs after two weeks took another step close to the 2A state tournament at Tuscaloosa next Thursday by out scoring Tipton High of Selma 100 to 93 Wednesday night. It was a close game but the Indians of Coach Dwight Duke in his first year as Indians coach were I command most of the way. The 1st period ended in a 20 to 20 tie. But East Highland out scored Tipton 27 to 20 in the 2nd period and never looked back. The teams each scored 53 points in the second half. The Indians shot a fantastic 67 percent from the floor to take the victory. They hit 70 percent in the second half. It was a case of have to as Tipton was on fire and swishing the nets also. Ronald Tinsley was high point man for East Highland with 25 points. All five Indian starters were in double figures. Daniel Wilson netted 19, Tyrone Stone hit for 17, Sylvester Beattie McKinney was good for 16 and PA Young, Mr. Steady hit for 14. Jerome Walker of Tipton put on a scoring display to no avail. The little guard sizzled the nets for 49 points in a losing cause and lit up the Indians defense like a 4th of July fireworks display. In Thursday night action the Indians will take on Vincent at 7 p.m. followed by Davidson with their high scoring sophomore guard Charles Cleveland taking on Jemison.

INDIANS ELIMINATED BY VINCENT
FEBRUARY 1969

TYRONE STONE   ALBERT YOUNG

West Blocton- I don't mind getting beat by 20 or even 50 points if the other team is better than us said Coach Dwight Duke of East Highland High School. But I don't like to have a game taken from me he said. An angry Coach Duke after his team had been eliminated from the 2A region 7 area

4 basketball tournament in Vincent. Coach Duke in his 1st year as the helm of the Indians was visibly upset as the top seeded Indians fell by a 59 to 55 tally their lowest out put of the year. I don't think it was fair for us to lose that way and I don't think it was fair for them to win with the help of an outside agency that neither team could control and I mean the officials he said. When you have a bad game you usually shoot the ball bad and pass bad but we did neither last night. For example he said we threw only 5 bad passes all night. But we had 36 turnovers violations that were called against us for traveling stepping into the lane on free throws stepping out of bounds 3 second violations etc. East Highland athletic director Haywood Scissum said they would file an official protest to the states Alabama High School Athletic Association on the game. But Coach Duke knew that there was little that could be done now about this game that he felt was taken away from his top seeded all black Indian squad. Seldom does an appeal overturn what officials have sealed in a game. The refereeing was one sided I don't have to tell you everyone present saw it. It's true we did play bad enough to lose but they helped us play that way a great deal he said meaning the officials who set the tone for the game. The officials who called the game were Fred Salter and SR Allen both of the Bessemer Association. East Highland never led in the contest. It was Vincent by 5, 26 to 21 at halftime and Vincent by nine 39 to 30 at the 3rd quarter mark. In the final period with only one starter remaining in the lineup the Indians made a valiant try for a comeback. 3 times in the last 3 minutes they came to within 2 points in the action packed standing room only crowd in the little West Blocton gym. 49 to47 , 55 to 53 and 57 to 55. At these points the Indians felt like they had a real shot to come back and win. Twice they had the ball but each time they missed a shot. Once a 1-1 situation from the free throw line. Vincent substitute Roger Duke iced the game for his side when he made his only 2 points of the night 2 free throws with 13 seconds left in the game and Vincent leading 57 to 55. To make matters worse with the officiating in all six Indian players fouled out of the game including starters Tyrone Stone, PA Young, Roland Tinsley, Dan Wilson, Ron Tinsley and Lawrence Ervin. East Highland had 33 fouls called against them while Vincent had only 16 called against them. In the second game Jemison went to the free throw line 36 times they hit 25 of them to down second seeded and all black school like East Highland, WD Davidson of Centreville 71-66. If I had known something like this would have happened, I would have not brought my boys down Coach Duke said. It makes you want to get out of coaching. A coach tries to teach boys to help them grow into young men with the correct attitude. You want to teach them sportsmanship. But what can you say to them after something like tonight happens? He asked sadly. Surely Coach Duke was feeling badly for

his senior players. The boys he knew had put on the Indians basketball jersey for the last time last night. Coach Duke came into this tournament knowing that he had a very good basketball team seeded number one and very capable of winning it and advancing to the state tournament in Tuscaloosa. East Highland scoring went like this Roland Tinsley 10, Ron Tinsley 17, Sylvester McKinney 7, Wilson 6, Ervin 4, PA Young finished with 11. Tyrone Stone playing in his last game as an Indian never got untracked and into a groove because of foul trouble. The high scoring senior forward will be sorely missed by the Indians next year. Vincent scoring went like this, Eddie Baker 15, Freddie Carter 14, Ricky Sanders 10, Harold Garrett 9, Phil Weldon 8 and Duke 2. In the second game Jemison knocked off second seeded Davidson of Centreville spoiling the highly anticipated match up between top seeds East Highland and Davidson that would have matched up the Indians Prince Albert Young against Davidson super sophomore guard Charles Cleveland. Jemison scoring Mike Burnett 24, Charles Hubbard 22, Mike Parker 13, Joey Jackson 10, Davidson scoring, Charles Cleveland 26, Leon Hester 19, Charles James 11, Olie Wesley 4, Clemmie Russell 2, Kagil Stoudemire 2, Jack Fisher 2. East Highland met Davidson at 7 p.m. Friday night for third place the championship contest was at 8 o'clock between the two low seeds Jemison and Vincent.

Indians Lose to 4A Gadsden Carver Rams in Squeaker
January 1970

CLOSE CALL — East Highland's P. A. Young (11) gets shot off here during loss Tuesday night to Carver of Gadsden. Defending are Marlow Phillips (25) and Victor Moore (23).

Indians- Sylvester McKinney and PA Young, East Highlands two brightest stars each had a chance to turn defeat into victory in the fading seconds of the jam packed Tuesday night game. But both failed as Gadsden Carvers 4A

Michael Catfish Smith

Rams out pressed East Highlands 2A Indians coming from behind in the last period to nip the home standing Indians of Coach Duke 69 to 688. The game had the feel of a thrill a minute for the fans in attendance. McKinney had a one situation with 14 seconds left and everybody in the bleachers standing up with people also on the walls of the Indian gym. The free throws came with the Indians trailing Carver 67 to 65. McKinney calmly sank the 1st shot through hitting only the nets and the Indians trailed by one 67 to66. Then he missed the second but it was rebounded by PA Young who turned dribbled for the corner probably to shoot a jump shot from there was his favorite spot on the court. But he lost the ball out of bounds. The last exciting seconds was typical of the whole ball game which was tied 10 times and saw the lead change hands 6 times. In the last minute and a half the score was tied 3 times and the lead changed hands twice as both teams blew chances to win easily. The largest Carver lead was 6 points at the half with them leading 37 to 31. East Highland was up by 8 early in the final quarter 54 to 46. Carver fought back and tied the game 64 to 64. A basket by Carver's Victor Moore put the visiting Rams out front again by a 66 to 65 score. Carver upped their margin with what proved to be the winning point a free throw by Steven Scott with 43 seconds left. It was a one and one situation and he could have put the game on ice by making the second. But he missed the Indians rebounded and then the Indians Danny Morris was fouled and had a chance to tie the game with a one and one. But he missed Carver rebounded and the Rams Marlow Phillips was fouled bringing it down the floor. He missed the 1st free throw attempt and Highland's McKinney was fouled on the rebound. With the crowd tense and loud, I always heard that pressure would bust a pipe as each team was missing out on golden opportunities to win the game from the charity stripe. As McKinney went to the line with a chance for two points then came the fateful miss with the score 67 to 65 that finally spelled defeat for the Indians. After taking the ball out with 13 seconds left Carver scored on two free throws by Moore, a final two pointer by Morris for the Indians at the buzzer made the final score 69 to 68. There would be no victory sung for the Indians tonight singing na na na na na na na hey hey hey good bye on this night as the Indians lost a heartbreaker to the fine basketball squad from Carver of Gadsden, PA Young led all scorers for the night hitting 28 points. Three other Indians were in double figures for the Indians they were Beattie McKinney with 12 Danny Morris with 11 and Charlie boy McGowan with 11. Carver had 4 players in double figures, Phillips with 17, Roy Avery 15, Big Center Howard Hatcher11, and Moore 16. Hatcher dominated the board as he pulled down 22 rebounds and blocked several shots. We could have won it several times probably should have but we just couldn't put everything together said an obviously dejected Coach Dwight Duke after the game. They out rebounded us even though McKinney tried. He only got 12 rebounds, good for most people but 9 rebounds below his average per game and free throws killed us. Morris had a chance to tie it and McKinney could have won it. The loss left the Indians with a 14 and 6 mark for the year.

Note- This lost to 4A power Carver of Gadsden would be the last one for the Indians in this final season of basketball for East Highland. They would go on a 12 game winning streak to finish the season.

From the Talladega Daily Home Friday January 16, 1970
By Dan Rutledge

To Cheer or not to Cheer. Lincoln Cheerleader Question Sportsmanship and School Spirit is for Everyone

Sportsmanship is an important part of sports; all sports and all facets of the game. It is not only important to the players and coaches but to the score keepers referees cheerleaders etc. Now any good athlete knows what sportsmanship is on the field. They have learned it the hard way. It is saying nice move to the fellow who just drove around you for the winning basket or mumbling good tackle to the 225 pound giant lying on top of you. It is going to play the team that whipped you by 50 points early in the season and hustling all the way. Or it is a coach who has seen his team outplayed the opposition only to have the breaks go the other way. Walking across the field to congratulate his counterpart. Bad sports do not make good athletes. Coaches spot them quickly and they don't stay long. But bad sportsmanship does not have to come from the players or coaches as said earlier Tuesday night evidence of bad sportsmanship was witnessed at Lincoln. But it was not by the players, coaches or even score keepers officials or cheerleaders, but by adults. Parents of the Lincoln cheerleaders were conspicuous in their absence from the Lincoln East Highland game. When asked where they were, Miss Virginia Benefield, Cheerleader Sponsor answered that they had all quit. But don't blame the girls she said quickly. They wanted to cheer, they all said their parents wouldn't let them. I had one girl crying in my office all day today. The heart of the problem is of course the fact that Lincoln a predominantly white school was playing East Highland a predominantly negro school from Sylacauga. It is thought here that Lincoln Coach Tommy Garrett and Principle SL Waldrop were looking ahead in scheduling the match. Someone had to break the ice. The Lincoln East Highland game was a first for Talladega County. But games between the white and negro schools are now old hat in Calhoun and Jefferson and most other counties by now. The old myth of trouble occurring at such games has been completely dispelled. In the past two years there have been well over 100 games in football and basketball with not one recorded disturbance. A column in the Birmingham Post Herald by Sports Editor, Bill Lumpkin started off talking about Kansas City Chiefs Head Coach Hank Stram It said Stram is a non prejudiced fellow. He will play anyone. Regardless of size, shape, color, creed, or nationality if he can get the job done. Coach Garrett is the same type. A coach has to play his best 5 boys or best 11 boys or best 9 boys. If he doesn't, he is not being honest with himself while being dishonest to the school and most of all the team. Lincoln's varsity is all Negro. There were 3 white boys on the squad at the beginning of the season but all quit because they felt they did not get enough playing time. (Note from the author there lies the real reason those cheerleader quit) This plus the fact that Lincoln was scheduled to play East Highland led to the cheerleader departure. Several girls according to Miss Benefield had earlier said that they would not be able to cheer at the East Highland games. But since Christmas the Bears have played 5 games, and no cheerleaders have shown up. Actually we have one of the 7 left Ginger Astine a junior, Miss Benefield said. The others haven't come and told me they have quit.(note from the author, Duh! who is in charge!) But that's what I heard through the grapevine. (Note from the author those must be some sour grapes!) They haven't been to the games. It is sad indeed when something like this happens. It is a bad example for the kids to see the parents react this way. It hurts school spirit immeasurably. Miss Benefield was right when she said it isn't the kids, don't blame the girls. The kids are fine. Prejudices are not inherited it is taught. Although Miss Benefield says those are our boys out there regardless. They go to our school are playing for our school and they deserve our support. Maybe all parents in Lincoln don't feel the same way, If 6 girls can't be found that are willing and able to lead cheers for the Lincoln Golden Bears then maybe the Pell City fans know what they were yelling about at a game earlier in the season at Lincoln which they used repeatedly. It went something like this you can take Lincoln out of the country but you can't take the country out of Lincoln!

From the Daily Home
Thursday January 15, 1970
By Dan Rutledge

STRONG MAN ACT? — Is it Charles Atlas or maybe Hercules? No, its only Lincoln's ... McGowan is coming down on top of Jordan head after releasing the ball on a high flying layup shot. Looking at the action is the

Michael Catfish Smith

In County's First
East Highland Rips Golden Bears

Lincoln- It is history now. The first basketball game between predominantly white and predominantly Negro schools in Talladega county was played here Tuesday night. And despite some muttered protests and predictions of trouble the only trouble for Lincoln was on the basketball court where the Golden Bears saw an early lead slip away to defeat. Lincoln led early by as much as 5 points. Holding a 12 to 7 lead with 5 minutes left in the opening period. But couldn't hold on. East Highland came back to lead 21 to 26 at the end of the period and finally triumphed 82 to 65. It was a full court press employed by Lincoln that gave them the early lead. But when the bears came out of the press the Indians rallied swiftly. Lincoln Coach Tommy Garrett said he had to pull out of the press because 3 of his boys were half sick with colds and just couldn't physically stand it. (Note from the author don't feel bad Coach Garrett the Indians had that effect on many teams sick or well) The Bears had one starter Albert Jordan out of the game with a virus. East Highland let 47 to 29 at halftime. The Bears came back outscoring the Indians 16 to 12 in the 3rd period. But East Highland poured in 23 points in the final frame to win easily. Rebounding was the key in the final analysis. East Highland won the battle of the boards with a 49 to 22 advantage. Danny Morris took top rebounding honors with 15 bodies or boards if you speak proper. Sylvester McKinney added 11. Morris was also the top scorer for the Indians with 24 points. He hit on eight field goals and was 8 or 9 from the free throw line. Two other Indians were also in double figures, PA Young and Robert Charlie Boy McGowan each had 14 points. The game left the two Talladega County teams with almost opposite records. East Highland is now 9 and 3. While Lincoln record to 3 and 8.

Basketball Season 1970
The Laurel Game

The Surprise of Surprises

We were on our way to the basketball game between the Indians and Laurel High of Alex City. We came up the hill on the backside of the school facing the housing authority. The four of us me my two cousins and a friend. The oldest of the group 12 and the youngest being 8. We were trusted to walk to the games alone because the Indians gym was maybe a thousand feet from my Aunt Mary's apartment located on the front row of the projects next to the housing authority building. As we approached the top of the hill we could hear the crowd in the gym as the buzzer sounded signaling the beginning of the 4th period of the B Team game. We really didn't want to see the junior varsity game so we were deliberately late for this game but early enough for the main game, the varsity one to get good seats. It was dark as we came up the hill on the backside with only one street light shining close to St. Paul Church parking lot. As we topped the hill we heard some low moaning going on slightly not loud but clear enough for us to make out as that of the female persuasion, we stopped and listened for a second as my cousin, the 12 year old and the oldest in the bunch said to us ya'll hear that? And we said what, he said shh! Listen, and we did and there it was the clearly audible voice of a female moaning. We began to snicker but curiosity led us in the direction of the noise. It was coming from the steps down where the Indians football team dressed out for practice. As the moaning became more intense being young kids and curious, we knew something was going on down there that should not have been going on. As we grew closer to the action we could barely make out the figures of two people in the shadows. One was a guy with what looked like an Indian football jacket on the other was what looked like a cheerleader who we could not identify because she was bent over at the waist . This unidentified person the male I assumed was probably a football player because of the jacket and he and the girl was clearly engaging in a sex act in what was a case of teenage lust going on. We started laughing being juvenile kids and the guy heard us as we startled them. He hollered ya'll lil niggers! Get out of here what ya'll looking at! We took off running because we didn't want to suffer a beat down for a teenage boy especially a football player but it was clear to us that he intended to finish what he had started. To this day I don't know who that guy and girl was though I assumed she was probably a varsity cheerleader with a little free time before her game probably dropped off by a parent earlier and because she thought she was in love was trying to please her boyfriend possibly under peer pressure from him. One of the oldest tactics that a popular boy used on girls was that old line if don't have sex with me I am going to break up with you. Or if you love me you will have sex with me. And the girl usually emotionally involved over her head will give in to the teenage lust demand. That kind of thing was common in those days and not just to East Highland. Just like today all teenagers are told not to have sex until marriage but usually out of pressure and lust seize on any opportunity that presents itself to engage in sex with the person they think they are in love with. Obviously there were some teenage pregnancies at East Highland along the way as well as other schools. And East Highland was no different than any other high school when hormones started acting up in kids too young to be adult and too old to play with dolls and BB guns. But I guess it was all part of the growing up process in going from boys to men and from girls to women. On to the Laurel game.

In Only Area Game

East Highland Rips Laurel 102 - 74

Sylacauga- Due to cold weather and snow only one of four scheduled basketball games was played last night in the area. East Highland scalped Laurel of Alex City in the single encounter. The Indian picked up win number 12 against only 3 defeats as they beat Laurel 102 to 74 with PA Young leading a host of Indian scorers with 26. Big center Sylvester McKinney and powerful forward Danny Morris each added 20 points a piece to the East Highland total. Point guard Robert Charlie Boy McGowan and Roland Tweet Tinsley were also had no trouble at all in downing the visitors from Alex City for the second time this season. East Highland roared out to a red hot 31 to 17 first period lead. They had upped the margin to 56 to 38 at halftime. Robert

Gamble was the high man for Laurel and the only Laurel player to hit in double figures with 23 points. East Highland goes to Gadsden Friday night to take on powerful 4A rival Carver for the last time ever in Gadsden.

MCKINNEY HITS TWO—Rebound king Sylvester McKinney (35) of East Highland here shows he is just as much adept to scoring as he lays in two in the Thursday night win over Drew of Lincoln. McKinney finished the night third in scoring with 13 points. The big ace is averaging 22 rebounds per game. In the picture are East Highland's Tinsley (33) and Drew's Jordon (25).

East Highland Dismantles Rival Westside of Talladega 107 to 82

Sylacauga - For Westside Coach Charles Pinkston it was deja vu all over again as Westside lost to rival East Highland in a 25 point blowout last night 107 to 82. Westside was also blown out by 4A Oliver of Fairfield Wednesday night losing that Westside yielded 100 or more points to an opponent. With East Highland and Westside bring such powerful adversaries over the years and both shutting down after this season you knew the Indian gym was going to be packed and it was. The East Highland Westside game was close for a half with the home standing Indians leading by 4 41 to 37 at the half. With the comradery between the two inter county schools for bragging rights between the old rivals you knew this game was going to be an intense battle early on. As both teams traded shots and baskets in the first half. But after the half the Indians seemed to turn it up a notch as good teams do and Westside seemed to wilt in the dessert heat of the Indians onslaught. It was Indians all the way in the 3rd and 4th periods to the delight of the Indian fans. We were just unbelievable hot in the second half Coach Dwight Duke said. We hit 78 percent of our shots and only missed 9 shots hitting 28 of 37 in the second half. Hot was an understatement by the Indians mentor. More like sizzling would have been a better choice of words. A team shooting 78 percent from the field especially a home standing team will beat you 100 percent of the time. When you are hot and that hot you can beat anyone. And on one was hotter than Indians Guard forward PA Young who seemed to feed against the Talladega county rivals. The 3A Westside team didn't have an answer for Young no matter who the Panthers tried guarding the 6 ft. 2. Young lit them up like a Christmas tree as the areas leading scorers averaging 23.4 points per game elevated his game a little scoring about 14 points over his average. The all state Young as steady as his game bred and nurtured on the playgrounds of the Drew Court Housing Projects could always be counted on in pressure time to produce points for the Indians. Darnell Corbin a 5.8 senior guard that has won a starting position in the past two weeks was the second highest scorer for the Indians with 15 points. Also in double figures was junior forward Danny Morris 13 points. Westside's senior center Charlie Barclay had his second good night in a row in a losing cause. Barclay led the Westside attack with 23 points. He had 25 against Oliver of Fairfield. East Highland is now 15 and 6 on the year and seems to be peaking after losing a close heart breaker to 4A Carver of Gadsden 69 to 68 a couple of days ago. The Indians 6 losses this year have come at the hands of 2A power St. Jude twice 91 to 74 in Sylacauga and 86 to 85 in Montgomery as the Pirates barely escaped. I'm sure the Pirates fans enjoyed both victories over their Sylacauga rivals considering what the Indians did to their state runner up football team. Other Indian losses this year were to 4A power Gadsden Carver once in Gadsden; one to 4A power Cobb of Anniston who they avenged and to a strong 3A Pell City team the 3A finalist in 1970. Coach Duke upped his schedule against the strongest competition he could find in this final year of Indians Basketball hoping it will pay off in the playoffs we will see.

East Highland Upsets Cobb

Sylacauga- For the first time in five years the East Highland Indians whipped the Cobb Avenue Panthers of Anniston on the basketball court. The Indian gym was packed to capacity with a standing room only crowd wall to wall. The game had the big game feel that only a rivalry like East Highland

and Cobb could bring out. The East Highland Cheerleaders were getting down in front of the crowd leading the Indian students and fans in a spirited cheer! While on the court the Indians basketball team of Coach Dwight Duke was turning the trick against Cobb here Thursday night winning 90 to 87 in a nail biter. The Indians was able to do this behind the deadly duo of PA Young and Sylvester Beattie McKinney. For East Highland it was do or die time. The very last chance. The last time for this soon to be graduating class of 1970 the last class that would ever graduate from among these walls to beat Cobb in anything. Both East Highland and Cobb due to federal court decrees are to be phased out next year. Turned into junior highs for Sylacauga and Anniston. So the Thursday night meeting was the last ever between the two power house 2A and 4A rivals. You don't know what it means to the school much like Alabama and Auburn. In football basketball anything. Since I have been here (2 years) they have beaten us in everything. I'm just glad we could have the last laugh. Young scored 33 points and had a game high 7 assists in the win. To say that Prince Albert was fired up and ready is probably a under statement. His shooting Thursday night was hotter than a Motown hit record. McKinney did an magnificent job on the boards hauling down 20 rebounds and also scoring 21 points. Robert Charlie Boy McGowan and Danny Ace Morris were also in double figures for the Indians with 18 and 10 points respectively. Roy White and Tony Glover were highpoint men for Cobb with 28 and 19. The Indians closed their rivalry with Cobb sending the 4A Panthers up highway 21 north for the last bus ride with a loss. In this class of 1970 only Anthony Cooney Russell had tasted victory over Cobb in the big two sports football and basketball. Russell's football victory against Cobb came when he was an 8th grader in 1965 playing with Hickey Holtzclaw and Griffin. As the final seconds ticked of the clock in the high scoring action packed game the Indians fans rushed the court savoring the big victory over the Indians biggest rival Cobb.

Michael Catfish Smith

2A All-State Team

The 10-man All-Tournament Team selected by the coaches and sportswriters attending the 2A tournament at Memorial Coliseum in Tuscaloosa are from left, Robert McGowan of East Highland; Albert Lomax, U. S. Jones; Will Moore, U. S. Jones; Danny Morris, East Highland; Joe Powell, St. Jude; P. A. Young, East Highland; Eddie Calloway, St. Jude; Louis Watters, U. S. Jones; and Dale Atkins, Ashville. Not present for the photo was Saul Castrophney of T. R. Miller.

February 1970

Highland Earns State Tournament Berth with Regional Win Over Holy Family

Cold Springs- PA Young sank a basketball with only 3 seconds remaining on the clock here Saturday night to give his East Highland High School Indians an 80 go 78 win over Birmingham's Holy Family to earn the region 4 championship. A automatic berth in the state tournament was at stake and the Indians rose to the occasion. Young's counter was the second of two chance he had giving the Indians the lead for the first time in the entire game. Robert Kirkland had tied the thrill packed game at 78 all by sinking two shots from the free throw line with just 20 seconds left in the game. We were just plain lucky East Highland Coach Dwight Duke said following the contest. But I guess sometimes its good to be lucky and good. We just wanted it a little more than they did. Holy Family, the Birmingham small school powerhouse in basketball had taken a 23 to 18 lead at the end of the initial period and held on to it throughout the contest. The game had been nip and tuck all night with the Indians staying in one and one situation tied it at 78 all but Holy Family still had a wining chance. Holy Family had a man standing directly under the basket on the throw in but the ball was thrown astray it was just destiny for the Indians and we know good teams cash in on their breaks. Bringing the ball down court with 14 seconds left PA shot one for the corner. He missed but grabbed his own rebound and with the Indians history in basketball riding on his shoulders he made the shot from about

5 feet. It was pandemonium for the Indians fans present as the shot went through the net with just 3 seconds remaining on the clock. The game ended with Holy Family tossing up a desperation shot that clanged off of the rim, no good! The shot set off a wild celebration among the Indians throng that was present. The Indians had lived to fight another day. Deepening their quest alive for a state championship in basketball that was denied them in football. After the game Indian's Head Coach Dwight Duke said we didn't do anything good we shot only 36 percent from the floor and missed 11 free throws. The difference in the game was Sylvester McKinney's rebounding. The big senior pulled down 23 rebounds. East Highland watched Holy Family take a 23 to 18 lead at the end of the first period of play. They went in at halftime down to the family 43 to 37. The Indians refused to let them get too far ahead in this single elimination contest. What with the yeomen board work that Indian Captain Beattie McKinney was doing it was eliminating Holy Family's offensive rebounding opportunities. Many times it was on shot and done for the family. In the 3rd period the Indians cut the family lead to 56 to 53 but never got ahead of the Birmingham school until Young's heroic shot. Young once again as the Indians leading scorer this season took high game honors for the Indians as he rose to the occasion again and hit for 24 points. 3 other starters did hit in double figures for the Indians though. Coach Duke cleaned his bench in an effort to get a hot hand other than Young's. Danny Morris had 14 and Beattie McKinney and Donnell Bear Corbin 10 each. Also getting a piece of the action were Robert Kirkland and Jerome Oneal with 2 each. Jerry Doc Houser with 4 and point guard Robert Charlie Boy McGowan and Roland Tweet Tinsley with 6 each. Henry Charles was high point man for the Tolberts 21. G. Feagin had 14 for Holy Family. East Highland advanced to the regional finals by downing Coach Gary Garretts Vincent Yellow Jackets in what I guess you could call a revenge out of the area tournament last year in a game that Coach Duke felt was taken away from them by some shoddy calls on the officials behalf. But the Indians gained revenge a year later by shipping the Indians will now travel to Tuscaloosa to take on the region 8 winners in a Thursday state championship contest. Of getting a shot at the state title Coach Duke commented. We sure are playing the kind of ball we did in the tournaments. But we are going to play some ball when we get there he said. This is our last year here at this school and the boys really wanted it. That could have been the difference in this game tonight. We just wanted it more than they did, he said.

In State Tourney
March 1970

Highland Opens Campaign for State 2A Cage Title
By Dan Rutledge

Tuscaloosa- Talladega county's only representative in the four class state basketball tournament East Highland of Sylacauga begin play here this afternoon, In quest of the 2A crown in the schools last year of existence. The Indians of Coach Dwight Duke compiled a 22 and 6 record against the toughest competition they could find en route to the state playoffs. They lost twice to basketball power St. Jude Montgomery. Twice to 4A power Carver of Gadsden, once to strong 4A school Cobb their rival and once to a strong 3A Pell City team the 3A state semifinalist. We didn't come over here to lose Duke said. We want to close out or program and last season with a bang he said.. East Highland is to be absorbed by 3A Sylacauga High School next fall. The Indians compiled a 9-0-0 mark in football a few months ago while finishing ranked fifth just barely out of reach 2 and a half points from the football 2A playoffs. We would dearly love to win the 2A basketball crown. We and St. Jude are in different brackets and I hope we can meet them for a 3rd time in the finals he said. They are touch and will be hard to beat but we would like another chance and are not afraid of them. St. Jude defeated the Indians 91 to 74 in Sylacauga, but barely escaped in Montgomery winning a cliff hanger 86 to 85 over the Indians. In the return match Druid High of Tuscaloosa with a 25-2 record is the 4A favorite. But defending champion Parker High of Birmingham cannot be ignored. The thundering herd pulled amid upset by downing Ullman High of Birmingham to get here. With Allen

Closing the Show

Murphy one of the Parker heroes of the 69 tournament who sat out most of the early season with a injury, will be back in from Parker will be hard to beat.

The schedule for today:

10:30 a.m.	Parker vs Foley 4A
1:00 p.m.	East Highland vs Collinsville @a
2:30 p.m.	Vigor vs Druid 4A'4:00 p.m. TR Miller vs US Jones 2A
6:00 p.m.	Decatur vs Gadsden 4A
7:30 p.m.	St. Jude vs Priceville 2A
9:00 p.m.	Phillips vs Dothan 4A

EAST HIGHLAND INDIANS ARE NUMBER ONE!

New 2A Champions

It's great to be champions, say the smiles of the East Highland basketball team as they all give the No. 1 sign after winning the 2A state championship at Tuscaloosa Saturday. Team members are, from left, Coach Dwight Duke, Sylvester McKinney, P. A. Young, Jerry Houser, Jerome O'Neal, Robert McGowan, Robert Kirkland, Darnell Corbin, James Drake, Danny Morris and Ron Tinsley.

State 2A Cage Kings
By Dan Rutledge

Tuscaloosa- I can't believe it! I just can't believe it! We are state champions! The number one team out of over 100 2A schools! Was the reaction of coach Dwight Duke Saturday after his East Highland Indians came from behind in the 3rd period to win the 2A state crown over us. Jones of Demopolis 82 to 72. People have asked me several times this year if this team is better than last years (when the Indians lost by two points in the region finals). I really don't know talent wise but I'll tell you one thing they have what last years team doesn't Duke said. They don't know when to give up. They will keep fighting whether they are 2 points down or 10. Duke said that if any one factor was most important it might have been the fact that East Highland is playing in its last. Combining with Sylacauga High next year. We've talked about it for sure many times. We the whole schools the team wanted to go out with a winning year. Plus after the tournaments begin the boys knew if they lost it would be their last game as Indians. It just gave us extra incentive. The victory for the Indians was a milestone upset with US Jones and St. Jude of Montgomery being the pre tournament favorites. Jones jumped off to a 24 to 18 first period lead on the hot shooting of guard Will Moore. Who received the most valuable player trophy for the tournament and led from 5 to 7 points throughout most of the 2nd period. But with the Indians down by 7 sixth man Roland Tweet Tinsley came off of the bench. The 6 ft. one senior immediately began to change the games complexion. He hit 3 quick baskets his last bringing the Indians to within 1 point 37 to 36 at halftime. In the 3rd period center and team Captain Sylvester Beattie McKinney began doing his specialty hauling down rebounds. Hitting little point guard Robert Charlie Boy McGowan on two consecutive fast breaks that kept the Indians close. Then with 2:17 left in the 3rd period, PA Young hit a jumper from the corner that tied the score 51 to 51. Seconds later the Indians took the lead for the first time in the game and for good on 2 free throws from Tweet Tinsley. The Indians now led 59 to 55 at the end of three. In the 4th and final period Young got hotter as he finished off the 3rd with a 3 two pointer at the buzzer. The 4th period saw US Jones get frantic as the Indians begin to pull away. There was much argument on press row immediately after the game when Moore's selection as MVP was announced. Many people figure that Young should have been the one so honored. Young broke the 2A tournament record for most points in a tourney. Scoring 84 points 23 against Collinsville, 34 against Ashville and 27 against US Jones. Beside young Tinsley, Morris and McGowan were all in double figures in the final East Highland basketball game. 16, 15 and 12 were scored respectively as in the semifinal win over Ashville, McKinney was the leading rebounder with 11. In the consolation game, Ashville was downed by St. Jude 76 to 53. Joining Moore and Young on the all tournament 2A team were Danny Morris and Robert McGowan from East Highland Louis Watters and Albert Lomax of US Jones. Eddie Calloway and Joe Powell of St. Jude and Saul Castrophney of TR Miller.

From The Talladega Daily Home Thursday, July 16, 1970 By Dan Rutledge

Indians PA Young named to AAA Stars

Montgomery- Coach Dwight of East Highland will be at the reigns of the south 1A-2A basketball squad when it take the floor for the annual all start game at Alabama's Memorial Coliseum August 6. Along with Duke will be the Indians top scorer in the county and the state championship game last season Price Albert Young. Young finished the season last year as valuable player on the Alabama High School Athletic State Basketball Representatives for Talladega County. The players will report for practice July 31st.

Final Act
Track and Field

Track and Field

The East Highland High School track men were a sight to behold. We all know that nobody is going to give you a footrace. You have to earn it. For a school known for its speed the Indians had to earn the title of fastest in the county and state against many challengers. Coach Scissum the mastermind of the Indians football program also oversaw the Indian track program. He motivated many young men to bring out the best in them to excel in track and field. Track being one of the sports that he starred in at Tuskegee, Scissum's midas touch transcended into track where he already had a mother lode of talented kids. People came out to watch the Indians run against who ever. The stars were plentiful with Michael Roy Williams, Danny Morris, Anthony Cooney, Russel Lawrence, Smokey Williams, Anthony Jack Boy Jackson, Sylvester Beattie McKinney, Bruce Burney and of course, track captain Richard Lightning Threatt , the star attraction. Often times the entire Indian squad of 19 men would qualify Indian sprinters milers would be running against the clock because the trackmen would often win their individual heats in meets and end up first, second and third in most meets.

Michael Catfish Smith

The same Indian pride that drove the trackmen. Some of the schools that the Indians dominated in football thought that they had a chance against the Indians in track because they had some fast guys that they thought could take Lightning and the gang. A lot of betting unbeknown to Coach Scissum took place in the stands between Indian fans and other schools when the sprints took place. Those in the county who thought they could take the Indians were dead wrong. The Indians dominated the county like Muhammed Ali dominated boxing in the 60's. East Highland always seemed to possess a lot of speed. Even in the early years of Scissum's reign. In the 50's guys like Billy the Jet Harrison, Paul Hubbard, Sonny Oden, and Red Foster but they were not allowed to run against the white schools like Talladega, Childersburg, Sylacauga, Lincoln, and Munford. So thus being shut out of county competition the Indians competed against one another for the fastest man title. Coach Scissum showed the kids love on the track team and they competed and ran hard for him. The East Highland track men possessed the same drive inside of them to excel that propelled Jackie Robinson, Willie Mays, Muhammed Ali, Jim Brown and others in that era that drive that black Olympians had when they competed against the world. The drive to overcome personal difficulties and obstacles put in their way by society in the 60's. Two miler, Bruce Burney displayed that Indian spirit and inner strength in his famous two mile dual against then Birmingham Mayor Siebels' son who was the best in Birmingham and the state in class 4A the states largest in a large invitational meet at Hewitt Trussville when he came back from 70 yards down against the 4A state champion hawked him down with a tremendous sprint and kick to win his two mile dual, 2A state champion vs. 4A state champion to see who was the best. Burney had to clearly be feeling the burn of lactoid acid build up in his legs and chest with what track people call the bear on your back when he made his kick. Yet like the champion that he was he didn't let his teammates down as he rose to the occasion. I don't think the Indian fans really realized what they were watching with the Indians. Michael Roy Williams the Indians fine quarter miler taking the baton in a meet on the mile relay team anchoring the squad but 40 yards behind the leader when he received it. Then with the crowd chanting run fool run! Run fool run! Hawking down the leader running like a negro running for his freedom Billy Boy as he was called overcame the stunned leader who couldn't believe a man could maintain that kind of speed for 440 yards as he beat the guy to the tape to take the field for the excited Indian fans. You see Indian fans expected the track team to dominate just like football and basketball did. Otherwise, the Indians speed would have just been a myth right? Early on East Highland didn't have a pole vaulter on the team. Never did nor did they have any hurdlers, didn't need them. But powerful Birmingham University School commonly called B.U.S. did and won a few meets against the Indians because they garnered enough points in these events to off set Indian dominance in the sprints. Since B.U.S. was the state champions and standing in the way of Indian dominance Scissum knew that he had to find events to offset points in those events. He needed points in the triple jump and the broad jump. He found both in Cooney Russel and Danny Morris. Both Indian athletes set state records in each event. In fact many of the records that the Indians set in 2A still remain today because the state went from yards to the metric system of measurement. Often times before meets Coach Scissum would be tallying up points that he expected to get in each event. It didn't matter about who they were running against 1A, 2A, 3A, 4A, it didn't matter, and the Indians didn't care about class ranking. Coach Scissum tallied up firsts and seconds and some thirds in running events and field events knowing that his kids would come through. Track and field if you look in the newspaper today at the results you'll see that the larger schools usually dominate and have the fastest times. That wasn't the case with East Highland. In the big Hewitt Trussville meet in Birmingham competing against 39 other schools 1A through 4A, the Indians dominated and won the meet that include the 4A state champion Hewitt Trussville team. They didn't care about class ranking to the Indians it was just bring it on. In 1968, Lightning's big rival was Cecil King fullback from Cobb Avenue in the 100 yard dash. With King a fullback in football running the 100 yard you should get a feeling about what kind of speed Cobb Avenue had and with Cooney Russel playing tackle and end for the Indians and running the 100 and 200 for the Indians you get a feel for what kind of speed East Highland had. But in the 100 King barely edged out Lightning in the meet. But in the 200, Threatt gained a measure of revenge and ate him up. Another Cobb, and East Highland rivalry of course both schools represented the best. By the way the Indians won 10 out of 11 meets in 1970 losing only the indoor invitational in January when key members of the track team were playing basketball. In that meet however, Lightning did set a state record in the 60 yard dash in 2A running a 6.3. Because there has not been another track team in the county that has even come close to the accomplishments that the Indians achieved in 1969 and 1970, the memories live on. In the times we live in now the 2000's, the track program at Sylacauga has virtually died, replaced by people who care more about baseball, softball and soccer than the sport. Hard to believe that East Highland and Sylacauga High once dominated the county and were among the best in the state. The milestones the Indians set in track and filed will probably stand the test of time. But as I watched Bruce Burney dominate the two mile run in 1970, I really didn't understand or fully appreciate the beauty of what he was dong. I like so many others was captivated by speed and what the sprinters were doing. I didn't realize the strength speed and stamina that such a grueling race took to excel in. A person had to truly be special athlete to do this. Imagine running an 880 and how tough it is. Now imagine running 8.888 with speed. This is what Bruce did and was the best in the state period. I used to see Bruce running in the summer heat up and down hills in the projects talking to me while he was running in the streets. So, one day I asked him what he was doing. He said he was training for the two mile. I couldn't understand back then why any negro would be running in the hot Alabama sun talking about training for the two mile. But, such dedication paid off for Bruce as well as for his outstanding teammates. Carlton Cunningham an underclassman usually finished second behind Bruce in most meets and never placed lower than third. But back to Bruce he was not only a great athlete but he also was a scholar. He won the states science fair in Auburn on the same day he dominated the two mile and the Indians won the sectional meet sending all 19 team members to the state. I knew in track that the sprints were always the black athlete's strength and the distance runs were dominated by outstanding white athletes. Note the cross country events. But, that mold Kenyans and Ethiopians who now dominate the distance runs didn't have anything on Bruce. I'll never forget you Bruce.

On with the final act of the Indians closing the show in Sylacauga, the track season.

East Highland Indians Track Team,

The Standouts 1968-1970

Michael Roy Williams – Billy Boy as he was called had a high knee kick to his running style which made him look like a Tennessee walking horse when he ran. The fastest quarter miler the Indians had for 3 seasons. Billy Boy ran like a negro running for his freedom. Indian crowds used to holler, " Run Fool Fun! Run Fool Run!," when Michael Roy ran his leg of the mile relay.

Bruce Burney – Scholar athlete Bruce was the best high school two miler I've ever seen. He dominated the event like the Ethiopians and Kenyans did in the Olympics. The son of a preacher, Bruce did everything with style and grace.

Anthony Cooney Russel – What more can I say about Cooney Russel except he was a winner in everything. Cooney had exceptional speed anchoring the 440 relay team and running and placing the 100 and 200 yard dashes. He won the state in the high jump and the triple jump.

Danny Ace Morris – Another Indian football and basketball player who also dominated in track and field. Set the state record in the strength and speed combined 880 yard dash race that stood 12 years until his nephew, Troy Morris broke it in 1981.

Anthony Jack Boy Jackson – Fine Indian quarter miler who always won the event in 1969 and 1970. Ran third leg on the Indians state champion 440 relay team.

Lawrence Smokey Williams – The youngster on the Indian sprints medley. Smokey once outran Lightning in a heat. But often finished behind the Indian's great team captain.

Sylvester Bliss Shealey – Fine quarter miler who always placed for the Indians and garnered points for Coach Scissum.

Donnell Bear Corbin – Fine Indian miler who was very close to setting state records in the events. Always placed for the Indian team and was a state champion on the Indians basketball team as a guard.

Sylvester Beattie McKinney – Three sport star for the Indians. Beattie threw the discus farther than any 2A high school athlete ever. Won the state in the shot put and the discus.

Other Contributors – Carlton Cunningham – Underclassman that usually finished second behind dominant Bruce Burney in the two mile.

Gill Weechi McKinney – Underclassman brother of Sylvester Beattie McKinney. Weechie finished 3rd in the discus event in the state meet in 1970.

Kerry Clisby – underclassman who excelled in the 40 yard dash. Kerry was a future state champion in the event for Sylacauga.

Larry Stone – Strong 440 yard dash man who excelled on the Indians mile relay team.

Ricky Player – Rickey's accomplishments were overshadowed by the great athletes that he competed with on the Indians. Excellent student who became a doctor.

Alphonso Oden – Youngster who contributed to the Indian team.

Richard Lightning Threatt – The MVP of the Indians track juggernaut. Many people, Indian fans and foes alike came to see the incomparable soft spoken star run. Threatt was a 2 sport star for Scissum who could have been a 3 sport star. When Lightning ran the 100 and 220 yard dashes, the crowd in the stands would stand up.

Robert Kirkland – Kirk was a strong 880 yard dash man placing for Scissum in the event.

Track and Field 1968

East Highland State Runner Up In 2A Track

The East Highland High School Indians participating in the state track and field competition for the first time in school history in the Alabama High School Athletic Association sanctioned meet. The Indians captured second place honors at the meet in Montgomery. For winning this honor, a beautiful trophy is on display at the school. Individual medals were given to 15 boys on the Indian squad. To get to the state the Indians were first thrust into competition with 18 other schools at the sectional meet held at Hewitt Trussville High School. The meet won by powerful B.U.S., saw all 19 Indians qualify for the state meet in Montgomery. The powerhouse of the state B.U.S. took the measure of the Indians by a score of 57 ½ to 41 ½. Part of this total had to come from the fact that the Indians did not have any entries in the high Hurdles, low hurdles, pole vault, or triple jump. The now defunct AIAA did not use these events or the two mile run. This advantage gave B.U.S. the edge over the Indians that they held in two other meetings with the Sylacauga team. In a meet in Birmingham known as a small school meet sponsored by the state association, the Indians were again second to B.U.S. This time ten teams participated but the local entry picked up a trophy and 20 individual medals at this meet. Anthony Cooney Russel set a new school record in the broad jump with a leap of 21.1. Richard Lightning Threatt was second with a leap of 20.10. Both of these sophomores will be hunting in the state meet next year. In the state meet, Coach Scissum expressed hope that some hurdlers, pole vaulters, triple jumpers and two mile runners would be able to cut into the points of the B.U.S. team, this did not happen. With the 45 other schools that made it, none could do anything with the powerful knights of B.U.S. The points mounted and were virtually a run away but entries from East Highland qualified and placed in every event they entered.

Michael Catfish Smith

In our favor also is that Coach Scissum has a sophomore studded team that will be heard from in the future. While the knights were reported to be losing to graduation nine gold medals or nine first place events. This Birmingham school is the finest group of high school trackmen these eyes have ever seen. They broke records in 7 out of the 15 events on program. Our 440 relay team of Jack Boy, Clarence, Cooney Russel and Lightning won the gold medal and missed the state record by .5 of a second. Three of them will run 2 more years. The Indians placed in the state with Lightning and Cooney Russel in the broad jump; Michael Roy Williams in the 440 yard dash; Rickey Player in the mile run; Don Buford in the 880; and Lightning in the 220 yard dash. The mile relay team of James Thomas, Anthony Jackson , Don Buford and Michael Roy Williams finished 3rd. We at East Highland are proud that we could be number two in the whole state of Alabama the very first time that we were allowed to participate. We would like to add that we will be heard from in the future and be a force to be reckoned with. This sophomore heavy team will set a few records of their own before they graduate.

1968 Track and Field

The powerful Birmingham University School had been taking the measure of the young Indians last year and in a meet early in this season. B.U.S., the old school equivalent to the modern day Briarwood Christian School in Birmingham was about to find out along with the rest of the state that the Indians were the best in Sylacauga and Talladega County and a sleeping giant had awaken with the Indians and the prediction of Jerome O'Neal, Indian Beat Writer predicted for them last year in their first AHSAA competition was about to happen as they became a force in the state.

East Highland Blast B.U.S.

By Jerome O'Neal

The East Highland Indians track team traveled to Birmingham on Saturday and deposed of powerful B.U.S. on their home track. The Birmingham University School that has dominated track and field in the state in 2A was about to relinquish their crown. But they did not fall easily because the stiff competition pushed the Indians to 3 record breaking performances. All total 5 records were broken on Saturday, the perennial powers of the Alabama High School Athletic Association. B.U.S. held thirteen records in the small school meet. They now hold 9 after yielding 4 of them to the Indians. Sophomore Danny Morris broke the triple jump record of 42.5 by jumping 42.11 and a half for the Indians. This is amazing in itself because this is Danny's first year in the event. Incidentally this was his only jump in the competition. He was taken out by Coach Scissum because the pit was short. Morris has a 43.3 and 3 fourths leap set at the sectional meet in Auburn. This sophomore should shatter all the state records before he is through. Michael Roy Williams our fine quarter miler sped the 440 on the 220 track at bus faster than anyone has ever done. He shattered the record of Milton Bresler by speeding to a 50.8 time in the event. Bresler now at Auburn University could only do a 51.5 Billy Boy has been beaten only once this year in the 440 and has since gained revenge by defeating his rival from Ohatchee. Bruce Burney, the awesome Indian two miler, sped his 8 lap's course in 10.31 minutes. He clipped 22.7 seconds off Palmer's record. His nearest challenge was Palmer of B.U.S. He was badly beaten by Bruce. Bruce will break a state record when he is really challenged. Anthony Cooney Russel broad jump record was able to stand but barely. He was challenged by Indian Springs Bray. Russell's record is 21.1 Lightning Threatt took 100 and 220 yard sprints but broke no records. He also ran the 3rd leg on the winning 440 relay team. He missed a record in the 100 by 4 tenths of a second and the 200 by 1 tenth of a second. Darnell Corbin ran the fastest mile of his career but it was not good enough for a record. He remains unbeaten this year in the event in 7 meets. Danny Morris legged the grueling 88 yard dash in 2.05. He remains unbeaten in this event and the triple jump. He also ran the first leg on our fabulous mile relay team. All total the Indians won 9 first place events; 2 second place events; 1 third place and 1 fourth place. This was good for 58 points. B.U.S. picked up 30 points, Oneonta had 30 points, Indian Springs had 16 points, Marshall had 8, Bullock County had 5, Cleveland High had 3 and other schools did not score.

1968 East Highland Second in Alabama Relays

The young spike man from East Highland captured second place honors in the 2A division of the Alabama relays in Tuscaloosa. The meet got off to a good start for the Indians with Anthony Cooney Russel taking 1st place in the long jump with a leap of 20 feet 4 inches. The weather hampered the meet for many of the events were performed in a down pour of rain. Russel has a record jump of 21.11, at the Birmingham University School. The distance medley relay team saw the Indians an early lead when Michael Roy Williams sped his 440 yards leg in 51 seconds. Danny Morris and Bruce Burney held on to this lead through the next two legs. But the fine miler from B.U.S. overtook our miler on the last leg to capture the race. The two mile relay was taken by the Indians with the fine running of Anthony Jackson, Sylvester Bliss Shealey, Danny Morris and Michael Roy Williams. The crack sprint relay team of Lawrence Smokey Williams, a ninth grader, Anthony Jack Boy Jackson, Lightning Threatt, and Anthony Conney Russel took the 440 relay. These young trackmen expect to crack the 440 and the 880 relay records in the state meet. In the 880 relay, the Indians anchorman dropped the baton with a 25 yard lead. When he finally picked it up school was out. It might be added in passing that the young Indians captured first or second in every event they entered except the shot put and the dropped baton in the 880 relay. B.U.S. starts every meet against the Indians with a potential 20 point advantage. The pole vault high and low hurdles and the triple jump. The meet was much closer than the score indicated.

From the Talladega Daily Home

By Tommy Hornsby, Sports Editor

East Highland Favored to Become the First Negro Team to Win the County Championship

Sylacauga - Without a doubt, Coach Haywood Scissum's East Highland Indians will be favored to become the first negro team to win the Talladega County High School Track Championship as the 7 team meet gets underway here Tuesday afternoon. Scissum's Indians cinder men are the favorites because of two reasons. One, they are fast, very fast and because they have been one of the top contenders on the state level for the past couple of years. The Indians finished second in the state in 1968, their first year competing and took second in the state in the Alabama relays behind B.U.S. a couple of weeks ago. The Indians will perhaps get their stiffest competition from another all negro school, Talladega County Training. County Training hasn't fared as well in competition as the Indians but is expected to field a very fast team. County training perhaps will cut in on our points because they run the same events we do and do not participated in the events that we can't, Scissum said. The Indians do not have a pole vaulter and do not run in the hurdles. While the white schools are racking up points in the field events East Highland and County will be battling it out in the track events. The meet which will get underway at 2:30 p.m., at Sylacauga Legion Stadium will run simultaneously in both junior and senior high divisions. The seven teams in the meet will be besides the Indians and County Training, and Childersburg host Sylacauga, Munford, Phylliss Wheatley of Childersburg and Talladega. Finishing in last years county meet were Munford, Sylacauga, Talladega, Comer and Childersburg. Reigning champ Munford, seems to be in a rebuilding year after losing most of their more competitive tracksters and Lions Coach Clarence Vinson said that we will have almost everyone well and we'll be there and that's about all. Host Coach John Carter of Sylacauga offered this. We're looking forward to a real good meet and one that will be well organized. We have more teams in the championships this year and the events will have time. We'll also be looking for some pretty good times because some of the (translation East Highland). The Aggies themselves could provide some stiff competition as several records in their school were rewritten last weekend at the Selma invitational.

East Highland Runs Away With the County Track Title

April 24, 1969

The junior heavy track team of Coach Haywood Scissum East Highland High School Indians took 8 first place events and easily out ran all the opposition to claim the 1969 Talladega County Track Championship. In taking the senior high title Scissum's spike men became the first all negro high school to win a Talladega County Championship. Unlike a number of winners that accumulate winning points for second, third, and fourth place finishes. East Highland cruised or should I say ran to first place wins in 8 track events and added 3 first place finishes in field events. Behind East Highland's 84 points total in the final counting, came Sylacauga at 46 points; Talladega County Training at 28 points; Munford at 24 ½ points, Talladega 13 ½ points; Phylliss Wheatley of Childersburg who did not place. All of the Indians points came off performances of juniors and sophomores with one senior,. Michael Roy Williams. The Highland tracksters, it is thought rewrote some of the standing county records in existence but they were not available for confirmation, huh? Bruce Burney's 10.443 two mile victory was just short of the state record time recorded last year. East Highland took 2nd placed in the last years 2A state meet their first time competing in the AHSAA. The Indians finished 2nd in this year's Alabama relays and is favored to be a top contender in the district meet this weekend at Saks High in Anniston. Of the win, Coach Scissum said we are real pleased. The school is real pleased and our team is real pleased. We appreciated the invitation to run in the meet and hope we represented ourselves and the school well, he said graciously. The Indians mentor added that he thought the times of the meet were a little faster than those of the quintuple meet at the same track a few weeks back. Host Coach John Carter of Sylacauga offered his opinion of the meet as we think it was a real good meet. The times were good but we had a little trouble with people changing entries, but overall I would say it was a good meet.

Final results of the 1969 County Track Meet

April 24, 1969

Final results and winning times
1. East Highland
2. Sylacauga
3. TCTS
4. Munford
5. Talladega
6. PWHS
7. ASD
8. Childersburg

Mile Relay: 1st EHHS; 2nd-Syl 3rd-TCTS 4th Mun Winning time 3.395

Two Mile Run: 1st Burney-EHHS; 2nd Duepree-Syla; 3rd Bearden

440 relay: 1st East Highland; 2nd TCTS; 3rd Syla; 4th PWHS

Mile run: 1st Corbin-EHHS; 2nd Moore-Syla; 3rd Williams-TCTS

Broad Jump: 1st Russel-EHHS; 2nd Bently-Syla; 3rd Rhoades-PWHS

High Jump: 1st Swinford-Mun; 2nd Bently-Syla; 3rd Threatt-EHHS 4th Garrett-PWHS

440 Yard Dash: 1st Williams-EHHS; 2nd Jackson-EHHS; 3rd Fuqua-Syla; 4th Sprayberry-Syla Winning time 53 flat

Pole Vault: 1ˢᵗ Butterworth-Mun; 2ⁿᵈ Holt-Syla; 3ʳᵈ Ivey-Syla; Winning height 9.6

100 Yard Dash: 1ˢᵗ Fomby-TCTS; 2ⁿᵈ Threatt-EHHS; 3ʳᵈ Williams-PWHS; 4ᵗʰ Williams-EHHS Winning time 9.9

Discus: 1ˢᵗ McKinney-EHHS; 2ⁿᵈ King-TCTS; 3ʳᵈ Smith-Talla; 4ᵗʰ Ackles-EHHS winning toss 130.2

Shot put: 1ˢᵗ Tyler-Syla; 2ⁿᵈ Watts-Mun; 3ʳᵈ King-TCTS; 4ᵗʰ Highfield-Talla Winning throw 44.8

120 HH: 1ˢᵗ Perkins-Talla; 2ⁿᵈ Bently-Syla; 3ʳᵈ Fike-Talla; 4ᵗʰ Butterworth-Mun Winning time61.4

880 Yard Dash: 1ˢᵗ Morris-EHHS; 2ⁿᵈ Moore-Syla; 3ʳᵈ Kirkland-EHHS; 4ᵗʰ Adams ASD Winning jump 39.7

220 Yard Dash: 1ˢᵗ Threatt-EHHS; 2ⁿᵈ Fomby-TCTS; 3ʳᵈ Williams PWHS; 4ᵗʰ Russel-EHHS Winning time 23.0

The Aggies took third place among 14 3A and 4A schools in the meet. Last year the Aggies lost the district meet to Saks High of Anniston, then edged out the same team to win the sectional meet to qualify for state competition. The broken records were by Ted Ham and Keny Bentley. Carter said of this Aggies, "We'll have to say we don't know how we'll do we've fun against some of the teams in the county meet but there are some we haven't run against." (translation: we can't beat East Highland) "We'll just have to wait and see," he said. Reigning champs Coach Vinson added, "I think it will be one of the better meets we have ever had." (translation: We haven't seen a team as fast as the Indians). "The times should be faster thane we've had in the last three or four years. (translation: This is the first meet the Indians have ever run against us in). "It will certainly be a good meet and we'll have a lot of fun he said."

East Highland Track Team Members

Members of the amazing East Highland High School Indians Track Team in 1970 were as follows:

Richard Lightning Threatt

Ricky Player

Larry Stone

Anthony Jack boy Jackson

Lawrence Smokey Williams

Alphonso Oden

Sylvester Bliss Shealey

Donnell Bear Corbin

Robert Kirk Kirkland

Kerry Clisby

Bruce Burney

Gill Weechie McKinney

Sylvester Beattie McKinney

Danny Morris

Anthony Cooney Russel

Carlton Cunningham

Coach Haywood Scissum and Assistant Coach Dwight Duke, all of placed and received individual trophies along with the big blue state 2A championship trophy.

Note- The district meet at Saks High School in Anniston was postponed twice because of bad weather. When they finally ran it, the Indians amassed 116 points to destroy all competition.

On to the state meet.

From the Talladega Daily Home, Saturday April 18, 1970

By Dan Rutledge

> Indians and Aggies to run at Hewitt Trussville today
>
> Lightning (9.7) vs. Carver's Odums (9.8)

Trussville – Three area track teams including two from Talladega County will be among the 38 to take to the cinders today in the sixth annual Hewitt Trussville High School Invitational. Sylacauga High and East Highland also of Sylacauga will represent Talladega County at the meet with Ashville of St. Clair County being the third area team. East Highland is the defending state 2A champion and will be one of two state championship teams entered. 4A state champion and defending Hewitt Trussville invitational champs Birmingham Carver will also be running. Auburn High the defending state 3A champion is running in the Parrish Invitational in Selma today. Some 21 high schools and 17 junior highs have entered. More are expected at the last minute. All senior high teams will run together in spite of class. An exciting dual is expected in the 100 yard dash and the 220 yard dash between Carver's Raymond Odums and East Highland's Lightning Threatt. Odums holds the meet record for both events 9.9 in the hundred and 22.1 in the 220. Threat has clocked a 9.7 in the 100 and a 22.9 in the 220. Other performers to watch for are Gary Collins of Hayes who did a 9.9 in the 100 this year. Host Hewitt Trussville's Jesse Hooks who last week posted a 22.5 in the 220. East Highland's Sylvester McKinney who placed two firsts and a second in field events in the Alabama Relays, including a 143.2 discus throw this year. East Highland has finished second in the Auburn Indoor Meet early this season to Auburn. But in all fairness to Highland, the team was missing some key athletes who were involved in basketball. They came in first in the Alabama relays fully loaded. Sylacauga finished fourth in the Alabama relays and has since posted victories in dual meets over Lincoln and Heflin. Indians Coach Haywood Scissum said that he was hoping for a good showing at the meet. The competition is going to be tough but we are ready, I think, he said. We have no injuries no pulls and we have been running good. But, we aren't as fired up as we were before the Alabama Relays not as sharp. Because of lack of competition, the Indians have been idle since April 4th meet in Tuscaloosa. Hewett Coach Dwight Norris is meet Director Assistant Sec Commissioner; Cliff Harper is the Starter and B.U.S. Coach Phil Mulkey is referee. Scratch preliminaries will start at 9:00 a.m. and finals in all events will start at 1:00 p.m. Senior high teams entered in the events include East Highland, Sylacauga, Ashville, Hewett Trussville, Birmingham Carver, Western Hayes, BUS, Mountain Brook, John Carroll, Erwin, Ensley, Parker, Shades Valley and Gardendale.

The Meet of All Meets

In the big Hewett Trussville meet last week the event was set up to run all schools against each other no matter what class. The Indians with the same swagger that they exhibited in football and basketball strolled into this gigantic meet and stole the show from the likes of defending state 4A champion Carver of Birmingham with their big star runner Raymond Odums of 9.8 100 yard dash speed. It was dubbed Lightning vs. Odums. Also, Gary Collins of Hayes was there with his 9.9 100 speed. Add to this, Hewett Trussville's Jesse Hooks in the 220 with his 22.5 speed and you had a show down of titan's magnitudes. But, if it was a UFC fighting matchup of today, the Indians, a 2A school would have been in a handicap match going up against heavyweights out weighing them by at least 50 pounds. But with all classes competing against each other, 1A through 4A, the Indians met the defending 4a champions Carver of Birmingham and all the Jefferson County schools: Parker, Hayes, Ensley, Mountain Brook among them along with host Hewett and soundly trounced them. Its unheard of today for a small school to beat the times of larger schools in track and field but East Highland was a super team. The meet included Sylacauga High and Ashville as the only other area teams. The Indians won with Lightning winning his duels with Raymond Odums and Jesse Sawyer Hooks. Odums was probably Birmingham's fastest athlete but Threatt beat him in the 100 and 220 along with anchoring the winning 440 relay team. For his efforts Lightning was named as the meets most outstanding athlete. He was selected as most valuable athlete and called Mr. Trackman.

From the Talladega Daily Home Wednesday, April 22, 1970

Indian in a Runaway, no Contest in the County Track Meet

By Dan Rutledge

Sylacauga – As expected, the East Highland High School Indians easily captured their second straight Talladega County track championship Tuesday by winning 12 of the 17 events in the senior division of the annual affair. East Highland further piled on the points by finishing 1-2 in 7 of the 12 and 1-3 in another. The final totals showed East Highland did not compete in the junior high division although none was named mvp. As in Hewett last week, the Indians senior stat Richard Lightning Threatt, the most valuable performer in the meet. Threatt took 2 individual firsts and anchored 2 winning relay teams. His times in the 100 and 220 yard dashes were almost sure to be records although none have been accurately kept for the meet. Threatt won the 220 with a good but not great time in 22.9. He ran a 22.1 in winning the same event at Hewett Trussville last week. But, in all fairness Hewett Trussville track is a faster surface than Sylacauga's whatever this surface is. But, in the 100 Threatt got of to a good start and finished in a blistering 9.9 10 yards ahead of teammate Lawrence Smokey Williams. Junior Danny Morris also was a standout performer for the Indians. Morris won the 88 yard run with a time of 2.09, he also finished first in the triple jump (41.8) and the long jump (20.9). He was the only triple winner of the day. Junior Randy Billlingsley was the top performer of Sylacauga scoring a 1st in the 180 yard low hurdles with a time of 21.8 and a 3rd in the 120 yard high hurdles. John Rhoden of Childersburg was the Tigers tip performer getting their only

Michael Catfish Smith

first with a 5 ft 10 high jump. He also finished 3rd in the long jump contest. Stevie Fike was the Talladega team stand out. Fike captured Talladega's only first with a 17.0 in the 120 yard high hurdles. He also finished 3rd in the 180 lows. Comer and Lincoln did not win any events. Mike Williams of Comer did place twice, getting a 3rd in both the 100 yard dash and the 220. Sylacauga's Mike Fluker and David Whitehead led the junior Aggies to the junior division title. Fluker won the 100 yard dash and the 220 yard hash and anchored the winning 440 relay team..

Indians Capture County Title

The East Highland High School Indians did not walk away with the county track and field title here at the county meet they ran away with it. They almost received double the number of points that second place Sylacauga got in the senior division. This, while smashing many of the existing records in the county. To our understanding the county meet has no established records so we are going to assume that we hold all of them. At least it was no contest as we piled up a whopping 96 and a half points to the second place finishers who had a measly 50 points. Perhaps the record book will be found next year and our times will not be lost. This was the second straight year that the Indians dominated the county. Lightning Threatt was the outstanding performer for the winners. The Sylacauga Aggies won the junior division for the second year with 86 points. The top performer was Randy Billingsley. Following are the complete results and scores of the meet.

Team Scores:

Senior High   East Highland 96 ½

Sylacauga 50

Talladega 20

Childersburg 20

BB Comer 7 ½

Lincoln 4

Junior High   Sylacauga

Michael Catfish Smith

>Childersburg
>
>Lincoln
>
>Talladega

Individual events – Senior High Jump- 1st Rhoden- Cburg; 2nd Russel EHHS; 3rd tie between Blocker-Syla and McKinney-EHHS

Two Mile Run – 1st Burney-EHHS; 2nd Cunningham-EHHS; 3rd Smith-Talla; 4th Webb-Syla

Pole Vault – 1st Adair-Syla; 2nd Ivey-Syla; 3rd Cotney-CBurg 4th tie between Morris-EHHS and Paris –Talla

440 Relay- 1st East Highland –Williams, Jackson, Threatt, Russel; 2nd CBurg Comer

Mile Run- 1st Corbin-EHHS; 2nd Stoney-Talla; 3rd Holt-Syla

Discus- 1st Sylvester McKinney EHHS; 2nd Jenks-Talla; 3rd Gill McKinney-EHHS; 4th Cotney-CBurg

Long Jump- 1st Morris-EHHS; 2nd Russell-EHHS; 3rd Rhoden- CBurg; 4th Freeman-Talla

440 Yard Dash- 1st Jackson-EHHS; 2nd Shealey-EHHS; 3rd Fuqua-Sylac; 4th Ivey-Sylacauga

Shot put- 1st Tyler-Syla; 2nd McKinney- EHHS; 3rd Gill McKinney; 4th Bradford-Linc

100 Yard Dash- 1st Threatt-EHHS; 2nd Williams-EHHS, 3rd tie between Williams-BB Comer and Horn-Syla

Closing the Show

120 High Hurdlers- 1st Fike-Talla; 2nd Smith-CBurg; 3rd Billingsley-Syla; 4th Carghran-Talla

880 Yard Dash- 1st Morris-EHHS; 2nd Kirkland-EHHS; 3rd Dupree-Syla; 4th Holt-Syla

Triple Jump- 1st Morris-EHHS; 2nd Adair-Syla; 3rd Jenks-Talla; 4th Downing-Syla

220 Yard Dash- 1st Threatt-EHHS; 2nd Russel-EHHS; 3rd Williams-Comer; 4th Hagan-Syla

180 Low Hurdlers- 1st Billingsley-Syla; 2nd Smith-CBurg; 3rd Fike-Talla; 4th Williams-Talla

Mile Relay- 1st East Highland(Jackson, Russel, Powell, Williams); 2nd Sylacauga; 3rd Comer; 4th Childersburg; Winning time 1.352

From the Talladega Daily Home Tuesday, April 28, 1970

Written by Dan Rutledge

Indians Again Big Favorites in the Mid State Track Meet

It has been true in other meets this year but today it may be doubly so, unless there is a complete reversal of form by East highland or a thousand percent improvement in one of the other teams the Indians of Coach Scissum will again be running against themselves. In the mid state track meet which gets underway at 2:00 p.m. Thursday. I'll never forget last year said Coach Ralph Bell of Shelby County High School who's Wildcats hosted the 1969 mid state meet. They walked in here knowing they were going to win. Before each event the boy running would ask what the record for the event was and then he would go out and break it. Heck, I think they broke every record in the meet that was established, in each event that they ran in. Actually, the Indians only broke 7 records last year although they won 12 events and finished 47 points ahead of the second place finisher while compiling 87 total points. All but one of the 7 record holders will be back of defend their titles. Lightning Threatt will be trying to better his own mark of 10 flat in the 100 yard dash. Anthony Russel will be trying for a better than 5 feet 10 in the high jump. Sylvester McKinney is the discus record holder with a throw of 143 and three-fourth and Donell Corbin is the mile champion. Records were set by the Indians 440 mile and relay teams and the 440 yard dash. The 440 record holder and also a member of both record holding relay teams is Michael Roy Williams. Williams was the only senior on last year's team. He is currently running for the Jacksonville State Gamecocks on scholarship. As last year, the battle should be for second place. If it was anymore close and exciting than last year that will have to be a three way tie somewhere. Phylliss Wheatley of Childersburg(now phased out) Shelby County and Indian Springs battled right down to the wire in the last event. Wheatley won second with 30 points but by a half point over Indian Springs 29. Indian Springs who won its own invitational meet two weeks ago and who have been running a good deal this spring would be the team to give the Indians the most competition. Add to this the fact that they are the host team and will have the home track advantage, Shelby County Coach Bell says his team is stronger than last year with the East Highland High School Indians rolled into Helena, and won an easy victory in winning their second straight mid state conference track meet here at Indians Springs High School Tuesday. With all but one event finished the Indians held a 106 to 58 point lead over host Indian Springs. As usual, the Indians were lead by team captain Richard Lightning Threatt who posted first place finishes in the 100 and 220 yard dashes. He also anchored the winning mile relay team and 440 relay teams to victory. Sylvester McKinney also a double winner taking first place in the shot put and the discus. Danny Morris also won two events for the Indians. The triple jump and the 880 run. The only event left to be unfinished was the high jump with four participants still in the running for first place, McKinney and Russell of East Highland, John Rhoden of Childersburg and Gary McFarland of Indian Springs. The Indians took 11 first places in the meet and were one-two in five events. The Indians would probably have scored a matching 12 out of 12 first place finishes as they did in the Talladega County meet last week except the coaches agreed not to run the 88 relay. Talladega County's only other entry in the meet the Childersburg Tigers made a good showing finishing fifth. The Tigers were in second place for half of the meet until the relay event which Indian Springs picked up second place points. Rhoden was Childersburg's top performer placing in four events. He finished 3rd in the long jump, 4th in the triple jump, and 4th in the two mile run and was still among the high jumpers. Rhoden won the high jump event at the Talladega County Meet last week. East Highland and Childersburg along with Sylacauga and Talladega were scheduled to participate in the district track meet at Saks High in Anniston Wednesday.

Individual Events Scores

Shot put – McKinney-EHHS 1st place

Discus – McKinney-EHHS 1st place

Long Jump – Russel-EHHS 1st place

Michael Catfish Smith

Triple Jump – Morris-EHHS 1st place

Pole Vault – McFarland- Indian Springs 1st place

120 Yard Hurdle – Yancey-Shelby County 1st place

440 Relay – East Highland 1st Place

Mile Run – Corbin-EHHS 1st place

100 Yard Dash – Threatt-EHHS

220 Yard Dash – Threatt-EHHS

880 Yard Dash – Morris-EHHS

Mile Relay – EHHS 1st Place

Two Mile Run – Burney-EHHS 1st place

The whole team back plus a couple of new boys should really help us. Billy Mitchell should pick up some points for the Wildcats in the hurdles. Mitchell won the event with a 21.8 last year. David Stone in the 220 and Robert Montgomery in the 100 should give East Highland's Lightning something to run against. Stone ran a 22.3 in the 220 last year. Montgomery's one of the promising new members Bell spoke about. He has posted a 10.2 in the 100 this season. Members of the mid state conference all of whom were invited are East Highland, Childersburg, BB Comer, Thompson, Indian Springs, Shelby County, Vincent, Montevallo, Calera, and Pell City.

Indian Record Setter wing 2A Sectional Crown at Auburn

By Jerome O'Neal

The East Highland High School Indians cinder man traveled to Auburn on Saturday and captured the 2A sectional crown. This is a must step to win the state championship. All 13 of the Indian participants qualified for the state meet to be held in Selma on May 8th and 9th. The Indians assaulted the record book 9 times and some marks represent state records. But to be considered state records however, they must be made at the state meet. Sylvester Beattie McKinney had a tremendous heave of the discus when he whirled it 147.4 and thus has thrown the discus farther than any boy in 2A school history in Alabama. He put the shot 54.4 to be a double winner for the day. Both tosses were sectional records. Bruce Burney the scholar athlete was a unique double winner at Auburn. He had a first place winner in the social studies fair at Auburn University on Friday. Then he came to Auburn High and clipped 22 seconds of his existing section record of 10.411 by running a 10.121. Lightning Threatt the captain of the track team was in on four records. He ran a 10.1; Century a 22.5; Furlong ran third leg on the 440 relay team and anchored the mile relay team. The mile relay team cut 6 seconds off the sectional record. East Highland held the 440 relay record time of 44.8 but speeded to a 43.9 to break their own record. Anthony Cooney Russell broke the record in the long jump with a 22.0 leap. Was second to Lightning in the 220; second to Morris in the triple jump and anchored the fabulous 440 relay team. Darnell Corbin broke his mile run record of 4.469 by speeding to a 4.980. He was forced to share with another miler who reached him at the tape. These eyes caught Corbin as the winner they will meet again in Selma and we know who will take it. Corbin was second in the 880. Danny Ace Morris holds the record in the triple jump and the 88 at Auburn. He won both but could not break his record in either. His record in the two is 43.34th he could only do 43.2 and a half. His 880 record of 2.055 was not violated since he could only do 2.07. Danny had dine a 2.021 this year. His other points came on a second place long jump of 20.1 and running on the winning mile relay team. Anthony Jackson had a good day on the strength of his winning the 440 yard dash. He ran a 51.2 second 440 missing the record by two tenths of a second. He ran second leg on the 440 relay team second leg on the winning mile relay team. Others showing well and scoring points were Carlton Cunningham, second in the two mile; Ricky Player, second in the mile; and Sylvester Bliss Shealey, second in the 440. Gill McKinney took third in the discus and the shot put, Kerry Clisby and Robert Kirkland round out the fine Indian team.

Auburn 2A Sectional Records 1970

Pole Vault – B. Powell-Bullock County (1969) - 11.6

High Jump – Hamilton-Girmsley (1969) - 5.9 ¼

Broad Jump – Russell-East Highland (1970) - 22.0

Triple Jump – Morris-East Highland (1969) - 43.3 ¼

Shot Put – Sylvester McKinney-East Highland (1970) - 45.4

Discus – Sylvester McKinney-East Highland (1970) - 147.4

440 Relay – Jackson, Russell, Williams, and Threatt-East Highland (1970) - 43.9

Mile run – Corbin-East Highland (1970) - 4.390

440 Dash – Crawford-Coopinville (1969) - 51.1

100 Yard Dash – Threatt-East Highland (1970) - 10.1

120 Yard High Hurdles – Hogan Stanhope-Elmore (1969) - 17.6

220 Yard Dash – Threatt-East Highland (1970) - 22.5

180 Yard Low Hurdles – Swinford-Munford (1970) - 21.3

2 Mile Run – Burney-East Highland (1970) - 10.123

Mile Relay – East Highland-Threatt, Stone, Morris, Jackson (1970) - 3.288

880 Yard Dash – Morris – East Highland (1969) - 2.055

EAST HIGHLAND HIGH SCHOOL INDIANS IN STATE RELAYS

SYLVESTER McKINNEY ... set a new record for the discus, 150'7" seven feet further than the previous record.

ANTHONY RUSSELL ... triple jump record breaker, 43' 6½".

Stop look and listen! Here come the mighty Indians! The above is one of the most often used cheers by the East Highland cheerleaders. Opponents have probably gotten a little tired of it this year as they have watched the Indians roll over 9 football teams with little effort and then win the state 2A basketball championship. And it isn't over yet. Here come the Indians again. The reigning 2A state track champions, East Highland is favored by most to win it again. Saturday, East Highland will join 60 other schools in the

Michael Catfish Smith

24th running of the annual Alabama High School relays at the University of Alabama. It will be a record number of team entries which are separated into 3 divisions by the Alabama High School Athletic Association. Prepsters will run in 4A, 3A and 2A to 1A classes. The action for what will be the largest track meet with 60 schools competing in history will begin at 9:30 a.m. Last year Birmingham Carver won the 4A State Championship and Auburn was a runaway victor in 3A. East Highland was nosed out by Birmingham University School 64 to 42 in the small school division. But the Indians came back to whip B.U.S. in the state meet later in the year. In their two years of competition in the AHSAA, the Indians have finished 2nd then 1st in track. The only 2A school to ever defeat the Indians is B.U.S., a private school and vice versa they have won the state title for 5 straight years until the Indians came on the scene and beat them last year. East Highland has already gotten in one meet this year participate in the Auburn Indoor Invitational in March. In that one the Indians finished 2nd to the 3A defending champion Auburn as the schools were divided into only two classes 4A and below. The Indians got their 2nd place with 5 3rd place finishes and a record breaking 1st place by Richard Lightning Threatt in the 60 yard dash. Threatt's record was 6.3 bettering the old mark set by Auburn's Richard Cope in 1968 which was a 6.5. East Highland lost only one outstanding athlete to graduation. Michael Roy Williams who is presently running for Jacksonville State University. But the Indians should be as strong or stronger than they was last year. Threatt stars on the 440 relay team and anchors most of the Indian relay teams. The 440 relay team consists of Threatt, Jackson, Russell, and newcomer Smokey Williams. Last year the Indians tied the state record of 44.0 in this event at the start meet but were disqualified because of a bad baton exchange. On the mile relay team is Threatt, Danny Morris, Jackson, and Sylvester Bliss McKinney. Coach Scissum said that new comer and sophomore Kerry Clisby was looking good and could break into the quartet. Running the 880 relay is the same quartet that runs the 440, Threatt, Russell, Jackson, and Williams. This was another event that the Indians last year at the Alabama meet that they should have won. We were leading by 60 yards and Russell dropped the baton. Scissum recalled with a grimace. Threatt, Jackson, Williams along with Ricky Player make up the sprint medley team. In the field events Russell, Morris, and Beattie McKinney do the work. Russell is the jumper both long and high. Morris is the triple jump man and McKinney throws the discus and the shot. Russell's best jump last year in the long jump was 21.1 the state record is 21.9 and his best jump in the high jump was 5.10. McKinney's best performance was a 143.2 throw of the discus last year. The state mark is 143.8 ½.

Closing the Show

The State Meet, Shug Jordan Stadium Selma, Alabama

The sectional meet at Auburn saw the Indians break 9 records and qualify the entire team for the state meet. Some of the records broken by the Indians already belonged to them. The state meet at Selma's Shug Jordan Track attracted a great audience. The field of athletes numbered about 600. This was the first time that all classes have assembled on the same day to have a state meet. It was a thing of beauty to see the field of finely tuned athletes dressed in their gaily uniforms colored like beautiful flowers. Our Indians left their marks in the books that only time will erase. And I do mean time. The Indians were definitely the favorites to repeat as 2A champions any doubt was destroyed after the Indians soundly trounced the defending 4A big school champions, Carver of Birmingham. Who by the way was also here today to defend their big school title. One had to wonder if the state had allowed just one champion to be crowned overall if the Indians would have probably been them too. Lightning Threatt set 3 records while winning 4 events. He set the 2A 100 yard dash record with a time of 10 flat; the 220 with a 22.4 running and ran 3rd leg on the unbeaten 440 relay team who clocked a state record 43.5, the old mark was 44.0. His other win came on his anchor leg of the winning mile relay team. Bruce Burney scholar athlete blistered the two mile course in 10.35 to better his own state record of 10.12. Bruce is also undefeated against all competition no matter what class. An odd twist came with Danny Morris in the triple jump. Cooney Russel set the state record of 43.6 and a half to erase the old record of 42.8. Morris also broke the record at 43.4 and a half jumping 21.7 and three fourths Russell could only do 20.10 this day he has a 22 feet jump at Auburn. The last event saw Sylvester Beattie McKinney spin the discus farther than any Alabama school boy in class 2A ever has with a heave of 150.7. The old record was 143.8 which also was his. His little brother Gill Weechie McKinney took third with a throw of 126.3. Other winners were Morris in the 880 and the mile relay team of Stone, Jackson, Morris and Threatt. Point maker were plentiful for the Indians with Bear Corbin and Ricky Player in the mile. Bliss Shealey and Jack Boy Jackson in the 440. Carlton Cunningham placing in the two mile behind champion Bruce Burney. Out of the field of 26 2A schools, the Indians garnered 90 points to far out distance their old nemesis Birmingham University School, who had 41 points. Others placing were Oneonta with 21, Geneva County with 16, Clark County with 13 brilliant with 10 ad Montevallo with 10. The list grows negligible after this. Thus the curtain falls forever on one of the most fantastic sports years in the history of prep athletics in the state of Alabama. Check it and see if you can find better anywhere for that time period. Indian beat writer Jerome O'Neal.

Michael Catfish Smith

East Highland High School Graduates of 1970

The Final Class
Otis Averette
Myris Averette
Terry Bledsoe
Brenda Sue Brownfield
Teresa A. Buford
Bruce Burney
Darnell Corbin
James W. Drake
Lyn Foster
Roger Foster
Earnestine Goodgame
Edwin J. Grimmett
Lillian Hale
Geraldine Holtzclaw
Jerry Holtzclaw
Jerry Houser

Cynthia Frances Hughes
Anthony Tyrone Jackson
Carol Jemison
Robert Kirkland
Constance Lang
Roderick McElrath
Charles McGowan
Levetta McIntyre
Sylvester McKinney
Roslyn Miles
Shirley Miles
Aaron Moon
Gloria Jean Norris
Gary Oden
Henry Jerome Oneal
Diane Pilate
Rhonda Player
Barbara Ann Pope
Anthony Russell
Deborah Faye Scissum
Barbara Ann Smith
Billy Smith
Louis Stearns
Glenda Jean Stone
Mary Carolyn Teague
Richard Threatt
Joanne Vincent
Gail Jean Williams
Robert L. Williams
Betty Wilson
Shirley Wilson
Albert P. Young

Michael Catfish Smith

Court Approves Alternate School Closing Plan
Thursday, March 13, 1969

Sylacauga- Ruben H. Porch, Superintendent of Eeducation of Sylacauga City Schools announced at a special press conference that the U.S. District Court in Montgomery had approved an alternate school-closing plan submitted by the school system at an informal hearing on March 1. The court had previously ordered the closing this fall, of grades 10 through 12 at East Hihgland High School, thereby, integrating 30 percent of Sylacauga's Negro pupil population. The alternate plan as accepted by U.S. District Judge Frank M. Johnson Jr. includes total integration of Sylacauga High Schools 8th grade which will be accomplished by the closing of that grade at East Highland School. Approximately 300 students, 100 of those Negro, are enrolled in this grade. Also affected by the plan will be the city's first three elementary grades. Approximately 60 Negro students in these grades will be placed at Pinecrest School. Another 40 will attend Main Avenue School. Porch said the formula for placement is as follows- Negro students residing south of Ft. Williams Street and West of Norton Avenue must attend Pinecrest School. Those living south of Ft. Williams Street and east of Norton Avenue will be assigned to Main Avenue School. All other students he said will be assigned according to the current freedom of choice plan. Prior to the acceptance of the new plan the court had ordered last August, the closing of grades 10-12 at East Highland High School. Porch said several physical reqirements must be met so that the schools will not be overcrowded. Among them will be the addition of fournew classrooms at Pinecrest and the rearrangement of auditorium space at Main Avenue. He also stated some elective classes from the high school will be transferred to East Highland but these will be limited to one class a day for individual students. The system already has ample transportation facilities to enable this move. Under this plan it will no longer be necessary for classes to be held at the education building located on Second Street. Sylacauga is one of 16 systems that have been allowed to substitute alternate plans. The court agreed last fall following its August order to close some 150 Negro schools before the beginning of the 1969-70 school year, to hear those alternate proposals so long as they achieve the same objective. The closings were to be a step toward total desegregation of the Alabama School System. The court had said it realized that individual systems might have varied administrative problems connected with the cleanup. The alternate plan was presented by City School Superintendent, Reuben Porch accompanied by Dr. Bill Berryman, Curriculum Coordinator; Mayor Joe P. Dark; City Attorney, C.W. McMann Jr.; and School Board Member Bill

Closing the Show

Edwards installed at a March 3 hearing of the board of education. Other school system integration orders have been extended are: Demopolis, Auburn City, Escambia County, Fayette County, Randolph County, Elba City, Shelby County, Geneva County, Baldwin County, Limestone County, Washington County, Chilton County, Clarke County and Marengo County.

And with this decree a federal court did what no opponent on the field could do and that's stop East Highland.

EHHS Alma Mater

East Highland School beloved alma mater now one and all we sing our praise to thee. Proudly we stand thy valient sons and daughters to pay thee homage for all time to be. O! alma mater our dear alma mater we will never forget, no we will never forget

Down through the years thy guiding hand has led striving to give us aims and ideals true to thee we owe our love and our devotion to thee we give eternal loyalty O! alma mater our dear alma mater we will never forget no, we will never forget.

Words written by the late Annie Grace Lawson

East Highland All-Sport Banquet a Huge Success

By Jerome O'neal

The East Highland Indians really lived it up in the school cafeteria March 26, 1970. The occasion was to pay tribute to the athletes who had led the school to possibly the greatest athletic achievements in the history of the school or any school for that matter. To refresh your memory the Indians started off the year 1970 with a fine win for the state 2A track championship. This had come in only our second year in the Alabama High School Athletic Association. Our very first year in 1969 had seen our school beaten by Birmingham University School who had dominated track in the AAA division every year of its existence. The Indians' fine group of athletes led by the incomparable Lightning Threatt, won 10 of 11 meets in 1969. This set the stage for the champions of the state in track. A few months and many bruises later most of these same boys started a run of the most fantastic football victories these eyes have ever seen. The team was so well disciplined so well coordinated and had so much desire that they ran rough shod over 9 opponents including 2A power St. Jude of Montgomery the number 2 team in the state. The score was a whopping 70 to 0; it could have been worse. This set the state in motion to buzzing that East Highland sports was no fluke. It also prompted the Montgomery Advertiser to say recently that in all probability East Highland would have won the state championship in football had they let them in. Then came basketball, and East Highland lost 6 games and won 25. They lost to 4A Carver of Gadsden twice by one point. They lost to St. Jude twice, once by one point. The only other lost was to 3A Pell City by 5 points in the mid

Closing the Show

state tourney at Childersburg. It is needless to say the kind of team Pell City had in basketball. The team went on to win the regional tournament by beating Montevallo and Vincent at Holt High School. Then came the regional at Cold Springs, a tough Holy Family team that we beat by two at the buzzer. Then on to Tuscaloosa and wins over Collinsville, Ashville, and a fine US Jones team brought state honors to us again this then was the occasion of the all sports banquet at East Highland. The principal speaker was former Indian great Cecil Leonard of the New York Jets. The captains of all sports made short talks of appreciation to their teammates and coaches in rapid order. There were short talks from Mr. W.L. Davis, Coach Duke, Coach Showers and Miss Margaret Newman. Jay Grimmett read a tribute to an Indian and it was a thing of beauty. Superintendent Mr. Rueben Porch sent his condolences to the group of 125 and it was well received. Trophies went to P.A. Young, most valuable player in basketball; Lightning Threatt, MVP in football and track; and Sylvester Beattie McKinney won most valuable lineman on the football team. The awards were presented by Coach Scissum. Guest of honors besides Cecil Leonard were Alvin Griffin of Tuskegee; Houston Averette; and Donell Prater, end at Alabama State. Johnny Grimmett, quarterback, Tuskegee Institute and Calvin McKinney, center, Alabama State University was unable to attend.

From the Talladega Daily Home, Saturday, May 30, 1970

East Highland Awards Day
An End to 20 years of Athletic Excellence
By Dan Rutledge

Sylacauga- In statistics released last year it was revealed that the University of Alabama was the number one football team over the past decade. The stat men also figured that Notre Dame was the top team over the past 50 years. The same thing has been done in basketball and baseball. With the Yankees the all-time baseball champs and the Boston Celtics, king of basketball. If there was to be named an all sports best school for the past 20 years in Talladega County, the winner would have to be the East Highland High School Indians. The Indians record under Coach Haywood Scissum almost defies belief. In the 60's decade the Indians won a staggering 84 games lost 11 and tied 2 from 1960 to 1969. From 1963 to 1969, they won 60 games and lost five times. East Highland closed out its sports history Thursday morning with the final sports awards day, an annual affair when athletes were presented with various trophies and their athletic letters earned during the year. Usually a happy occasion Thursdays was just the opposite. Many males and females were seen with tears in their eyes or rolling down their cheeks. At the close of the program the football players were each given their jerseys from the past year since there will be no one to use them next fall. East Highland's proud sports tradition is now only a memory as the school combines with Sylacauga High next year and East Highland becomes a junior high. But the Indians closed out in style. On the long table at the front of the room, 101 trophies held center stage. Over 20 of them were won this year. The track team was 2A state champions and earned 15 trophies. The basketball team was 2A state champions and won 5 trophies. The football team was 9 and 0 undefeated and untied and almost unscored on, won a trophy as mid state conference champions. The Montgomery Advertiser said in an editorial at the end of the season that East Highland would have been the number one team in the state if they had made it to the playoffs. And there really can't be much argument to that testimony. The week before the statement in the Advertiser, St. Jude of Montgomery had come to Sylacauga. They came once beaten but by on a 15 to 7 score that came at the hands of powerful 4A school Booker T. Washington of Montgomery who were ranked number 4 in the state. St. Jude had been in the state championship game in 2A last year and probably came to Sylacauga as a slight favorite. It is history how East Highland took a 36 to 0 halftime lead and ended up with a 70 to 0 victory, the worse whipping St. Jude had ever taken in any sport. The basketball team was 25 and 6 for the year and really got rolling in the tournaments. They seemed to win when they had to and lost only to 4A Cobb which they avenged at home and Gadsden Carver 4A St Jude which they seemed to win when they had to and lost only to 4A Cobb which they avenged and 3A state runner up Pell City. In track and field the Indians swept every meet they were in except the early indoor meet at Auburn when part of the team was still playing basketball. In the state meet where pints are hard to come by, the Indians rolled up 96 points to runner up BUS 45. Several times during the season in the mid state meet for instance, the Indians scored well over a 100 points. In 1970 the Indians had the individual start also. The county's top scorer in football was Richard Lightning Threatt with 144 points 20 touchdowns and 12, 2 points conversions. Threatt will be a participant in the Alabama High School all-star game and will attend either Pratt Junior College in Kansas or Alabama A & M University in Huntsville on a football scholarship. In basketball, P.A. Young topped the county in scoring averaging 25.0 points a game in 31 contests. He broke the 2A state basketball tournament record with 84 points in 3 games at the tournament in Tuscaloosa. In spite of this he was shunned for the most valuable player by the tournament committee who despite protest gave it to losing team player Will Moore of US Jones. This year was only a fitting end to 2 decades of athletic excellence at East Highland. In 20 years East Highland had had one losing football season, none under Coach Scissum and one losing season in basketball. In the annuals of history, the name East Highland will always be a winner. In the now defunct Negro Athletic Association, the Indians were either district chaps or runner-ups each year but one since 1950. In their 2 years competing in the AHSAA they finished 10th and 5th in the state in football. In basketball they were division champs twice, area champs once and state camps once. They won under 17 games only 3 times in basketball in 20 years. In track since joining the AHSAA, the Indians finished state runner-ups once and then added two straight titles. From mid season, 1961 to midseason 1966, the Indians won 34 straight games in football. A loss to Cobb of Anniston ended the streak in 1966. They have never lost to a 2A football team in football or track. In basketball only St. Jude and Jemison in the area tournament finals in 1969 have beaten the Indians. We never really played many schools our size they just wouldn't schedule us Coach Scissum said. These eyes also noticed that of the many jamborees put on by Talladega County teams, the Indians wee never invited to any, wonder why? Coach Scissum said, we played them all and beat them, the biggest we could find. In fact, though East Highland came up a game short in the Cobb rivalry 8 games to 9, Scissum actually broke even in his personal rivalry with Cobb in a Mexican stand off 8 to 8. It is good that the Indians finished as winners. The great dynasties of the past, the Yankees in baseball, the Celtics in basketball and the Packers in football, all finally crumbled and were forced to eat humble pie. But, the Indians went out flying high. It was a sad and somber Coach Haywood Scissum that directed several students in putting the many trophies back into two huge trophy cases that greeted visitors to the school as they came in the front door. It's just hard to believe that it is all over; he said in a soft voice, it's just hard to believe. But it's been a good 20 years and what a year this last one was, he said with a million dollar smile. Then Coach Scissum lapsed momentarily into silence smiling, probably in his minds eye he saw a team dressed in blue and white sharply break huddle and come up to the line as a large crowd chanted in the back ground stop, look and listen! Here comes the mighty Indians!

Final Analysis

I believe personally that some people went out of their way to keep the East Highland High School Indians out of the playoffs in 1969. I am not expecting anyone to come forth with an apology 40 years later. Now, they know who they are if they are still alive.

If you look back at East Highland's program, they were not just some flash in the pan one good season and done school in 1969. They won 84 games in the 60's decade alone against 11 defeats and I will put that record up against any program competing in high school football in this era. This 84 wins, which many came against much larger in enrollment 4A and 3A schools should have been enough to earn the Indians the respect in the state for a top 4 finish in 1969. Besides that, the Indians never ever lost to a school in its own class which was 2A. I don't know who the 4 schools that they let in front of the Indians played, but I'll bet you my last dollar that they didn't play the larger schools or win as many games as the Indians did in the 60's decade. How the Indians were able to excel in the 50's and 60's under the atmosphere of such racial hatred was remarkable amidst the era of Medgar Evers, Malcolm X, John Kennedy, Robert Kennedy and Dr. Martin Luther King Jr., all martyred leaders in the radical 60's. This little black school powerhouse in Sylacauga, Alabama, marched on to victory year after segregated year. In the class rooms and the athletic venues. Overcoming obstacles and stumbling blocks of hate, they triumphed. The name East Highland was money. It carried weight in academics led by the efforts of principal Lawson and his dedicated staff; and sports led by the dedication and love of Coach Haywood Scissum. The Indians regularly sent players to schools like Alabama State, Alabama A & M, Tuskegee Institute, Florida A & M, Xavier University, and even the University of Missouri. But like a super nova that shinned brightly and beautiful for a short period of time, the Indians left us way too soon.

Closing the Show

East Highland High School gave the people of Sylacauga, Alabama, many glorious years of wonderful sports memories to treasure. It was a school that was established in the 1930's to educate Sylacauga's colored children. But the school touched many lives, black and white. It was permanently shut down as a high school in 1970. But the wonderful history they wrote for us will burn in the memory of everyone privileged to see them play until they die. Their glorious history will live forever through the efforts of this book until the end of time. Ladies and Gentleman, the Indians have left the building. Let the church say amen.